Hector Guimard

Hector

Edited by David A. Hanks

Essays by Barry Bergdoll, Sarah D. Coffin,
Isabelle Gournay, Philippe Thiébaut,
and Georges Vigne

Yale University Press, New Haven and London
in association with
The Richard H. Driehaus Museum

Guimard

Art Nouveau to Modernism

Published on the occasion of the exhibition *Hector Guimard: Art Nouveau to Modernism*, organized by the Richard H. Driehaus Museum and Cooper Hewitt, Smithsonian Design Museum.

The exhibition at the Richard H. Driehaus Museum was made possible in part by the National Endowment for the Arts, Robert and Carolynn Burk, and the Richard H. Driehaus Annual Exhibition Fund. Additional support for the accompanying publication *Hector Guimard: Art Nouveau to Modernism* was provided in part by the Graham Foundation.

The Richard H. Driehaus Museum
40 East Erie Street
Chicago, IL 60611
www.driehausmuseum.org

Smithsonian Design Museum

Cooper Hewitt
Smithsonian Design Museum
2 East 91st Street
New York, NY 10128
www.cooperhewitt.org

Yale

Yale University Press
P.O. Box 209040
302 Temple Street
New Haven, CT 06520-9040
www.yalebooks.com/art

A Note on the Objects
Many of Guimard's decorative objects were designed for particular buildings. However, some of the objects in the exhibition have been collected without knowledge of provenance yet are identical to those identified as belonging to certain commissions.

A Note on Street Names and Addresses
Many streets in Paris were renamed and/or renumbered during or after Guimard's life. For instance, rue la Fontaine, where Castel Béranger is located, is now rue Jean de la Fontaine. Addresses in this catalogue are those from Guimard's time.

Designed by Rita Jules, Miko McGinty Inc.
Set in Freight Sans and Mara des Bois type by Tina Henderson
Printed in Singapore by Pristone Pte. Ltd.

Library of Congress Control Number: 2020933616
ISBN 978-0-300-24836-4

A catalogue record for this book is available from the British Library.

The paper in this book meets the requirements of ANSI/NISO Z39.48-1992 (Permanence of Paper).

10 9 8 7 6 5 4 3 2 1

Cover illustrations: (front) View of Métro Entrance, c. 1900 (p. 178); (back) Bracket for Bench, Model GO, c. 1912 (cat. no. 85). Frontispiece: Hector Guimard's Desk, c. 1899 (cat. no. 29). Pages viii–ix: Jardinière, Model GD, c. 1908 (cat. no. 93).

Contents

Foreword

The extraordinary French architect and designer Hector Guimard was a leader of Art Nouveau, a decorative style that emerged in late nineteenth-century Europe. Equally significant is the contribution of his work to the ethos of the modern age. It is thus with great enthusiasm that the Richard H. Driehaus Museum and Cooper Hewitt, Smithsonian Design Museum, present *Hector Guimard: Art Nouveau to Modernism*, the first exhibition on this French architect in the United States in more than two decades.

The exhibition, co-organized by the two institutions, and accompanying scholarly catalogue, published by Yale University Press, bring to light objects that have never been on public display, among them designs for prefabricated housing from Cooper Hewitt's strong holdings of Guimard drawings. The existence of this collection illuminates the critical role played by his partner in life and in business, Adeline Oppenheim Guimard, an American from New York City, who went to great lengths to preserve his remarkable legacy.

Throughout the co-organization of the project, we have forged new relationships and renewed many old ones. Most happily, *Hector Guimard: Art Nouveau to Modernism* marks the first collaboration between Cooper Hewitt and the Driehaus Museum. These museums have in common the advantages—and the challenges—of presenting exhibitions on architecture and design in Gilded Age historic homes: the Driehaus in the Samuel and Matilda Nickerson House of 1883 and Cooper Hewitt in the Andrew Carnegie Mansion of 1902.

We are indebted to our colleagues in Paris and New York: le Cercle Guimard, the Musée d'Orsay, the Musée des arts décoratifs, the Metropolitan Museum of Art, and the Museum of Modern Art. We thank consulting curator David A. Hanks, who worked tirelessly on behalf of both institutions not only in developing the concept, themes, and exhibition checklist but also to keep the exhibition and catalogue on track.

Finally, we thank those sponsors without whom the exhibition and publication would not have been possible.

Richard H. Driehaus
Founder
The Richard H. Driehaus Museum

John Davis
Interim Director
Cooper Hewitt, Smithsonian Design Museum

Dining room in Hôtel Guimard,
c. 1913. Cooper Hewitt,
Smithsonian Design Museum,
New York, 1956-78-11.

Lenders to the Exhibition

Alain Blondel and Yves Plantin, Garches, France
Cooper Hewitt, Smithsonian Design Museum, New York
Frédéric Descouturelle, Montreuil-sous-Bois, France
The Collection of Richard H. Driehaus, Chicago
Nicolas Horiot, Auberville, France
Christie Mayer Lefkowith Collection, New York
The Menil Collection, Houston
The Metropolitan Museum of Art, New York
Musée d'Orsay, Paris
The Museum of Modern Art, New York
Thomas J. Watson Library, The Metropolitan Museum of Art, New York

Preface

This catalogue and exhibition present the work of Hector Guimard to an American audience and offer fresh interpretations of his work.[1] Included are his visionary architecture; his entrepreneurial approach to practice and self-promotion, which included exhibitions, publications, graphic art, and postcards; his utilization of industrial technology and mass production to achieve economies of scale; his projects for the social good, including affordable housing; and his interest in standardized construction. Evident throughout is Guimard's dedication to the *Gesamtkunstwerk*, or total work of art. By bringing together architecture, furnishings, and decorative arts, the exhibition attempts to re-create this unity, now known only through archival photographs. Guimard was a proponent of modernity throughout his career, according to scholar Georges Vigne, author of a seminal monograph on Guimard's work: "For him classical culture had value only as an educational resource—a foundation for developing artists but not an end in itself. Thus, the word *modernity* is not only omnipresent in his declarations and texts: Guimard went so far as to try and have a street named rue Moderne."[2]

The present catalogue and its associated exhibition are organized according to five themes. The first, M. & Mme Guimard, introduces Hector Guimard and his wife, Adeline, and shows the life they lived in Paris. Both were devoted to the arts, including the design and realization of their dream home, Hôtel Guimard. An essay by Isabelle Gournay illuminates the world within which the couple lived and worked: Auteuil, a suburban neighborhood in the southern part of the 16th arrondissement. The second theme, Visionary Architect, covers two of Guimard's most important projects, Castel Béranger and Castel Henriette, and includes drawings, photographs, architectural fragments, and furnishings. Philippe Thiébaut's text discusses Guimard's training in drawing, the importance of line in his work, and the exquisite detail of his drawn plans. A second essay by Thiébaut explores the surprisingly contemporary ways in which the architect promoted himself and his work: through exhibitions, publications, graphic art, and postcards.

The third theme, Entrepreneur, both illustrates and expands upon Guimard's penchant for self-promotion. An essay by Georges Vigne focuses on Guimard's designs for production. An essential aspect of Guimard's work in Art Nouveau was his use of the technology of the day as a means of creating a new style. Although Guimard's architectural commissions were for specific clients, he also designed for prefabrication and industrial mass production. The fourth theme, Design for Production, presents the designs Guimard developed in partnership with manufacturers like Saint-Dizier Foundries (for works in cast iron) and Langlois (for glass-pendant lamps and light fixtures). Barry Bergdoll's text highlights an overarching theme of the exhibition—signature vs. standardization—and addresses Guimard's concern for the well-being of the people. The fifth theme, Guimard for the People, presents the architect's vision for standardized construction to meet the need for housing following World War I. The final text, by Sarah D. Coffin, discusses Adeline Oppenheim Guimard as a partner to Hector—in both life and work—and also as a determined preserver of his legacy.

David A. Hanks

OPPOSITE: Guimard, Immobilière de la rue Moderne, Front Elevation of Building No. 6, Immeubles Agar, November 20, 1909 (detail of cat. no. 68).

NOTES

1   The exhibition *Hector Guimard* opened March 10, 1970, at the Museum of Modern Art, New York, and traveled to the California Palace of the Legion of Honor, San Francisco, and the Art Gallery of Ontario, Toronto, in 1970, and the Musée des arts décoratifs, Paris, in 1971. See F. Lanier Graham, *Hector Guimard*, exh. cat. (New York: Museum of Modern Art, 1970).

2   Georges Vigne, *Hector Guimard: Architect, Designer, 1867–1942* (New York: Delano Greenidge Editions, 2003), 18.

Société Immobilière de la Rue Moderne

Introduction
Sarah D. Coffin and David A. Hanks

The work of French architect Hector Guimard (1867–1942, fig. 1) has come to define Art Nouveau in the popular imagination. Introduced to an international audience at the 1900 Exposition universelle in Paris, the Art Nouveau style represented a radical break from the classical and revival styles of the nineteenth century in its embrace of naturalistic forms and its unity of architectural, decorative, and fine arts. Perhaps the most famous extant exemplars of Art Nouveau are Guimard's station designs for the Paris subway, or Métropolitain: built between 1900 and 1912, these are considered so emblematic of the style that French Art Nouveau was sometimes referred to as "*le style Métro.*" While the popularity of Art Nouveau has waxed and waned since its introduction, architectural historians and critics now recognize the fundamental modernity of Guimard's work. Underlying the sinuous curves and often exuberant ornament of his buildings and furnishings is a rejection of classicism in favor of a nature-based aesthetic, a use of industrial technologies, and a unified design of architecture and the arts. Guimard also focused on making modern design affordable, accessible, and a force for social good—an approach that aligned his work with concurrent modern movements in Europe and America.

Details about Guimard's personal life are sparse, and very little personal correspondence survives to provide biographical information or insights.[1] He was born on March 10, 1867, in Lyon, France, the son of an orthopedist and a linen maid and the middle of three children. In 1883, the Guimard family moved to Paris, where Hector was already at school. His studies focused on classic Beaux-Arts training. Accepted to the École nationale supérieure des arts décoratifs in Paris in 1882, when he was fifteen, Guimard was a talented and ambitious student.[2] Within his first six months he advanced to the second year, and he entered the architecture department in December 1883, going on to win a number of student medals, including the school's grand prize for architecture, the Prix Jaÿ, in 1885. His teachers included architects Charles Génuys (1852–1928) and Eugène Train (1832–1903), as well as the decorative artist Victor-Marie-Charles Ruprich-Robert (1820–1887); these instructors introduced Guimard to the study of nature and the intimate relationship between structure and decoration. That same year, he began a program of studies at the École nationale supérieure des Beaux-Arts in Paris, where his academic performance was mediocre. Training was structured around studios headed by renowned artists or architects; Guimard's professor was Gustave Raulin (1837–1910), a follower (as were Guimard's other professors) of the Gothic Revival architect Eugène-Emmanuel Viollet-le-Duc (1814–1879), who would become a profound and lifelong influence on Guimard. One-day sketches were a typical assignment in Raulin's studio. Guimard's drawing of a billiard room, from January 6, 1891, for one of the school's bimonthly sketch competitions illustrates his draftsmanship skills (fig. 2).[3] In 1888, while still in school, and without an apprenticeship or any experience with an established firm, Guimard began working as an architect. While his architectural practice developed

FIG. 1. Photograph of Hector
Guimard, c. 1900. The New
York Public Library.

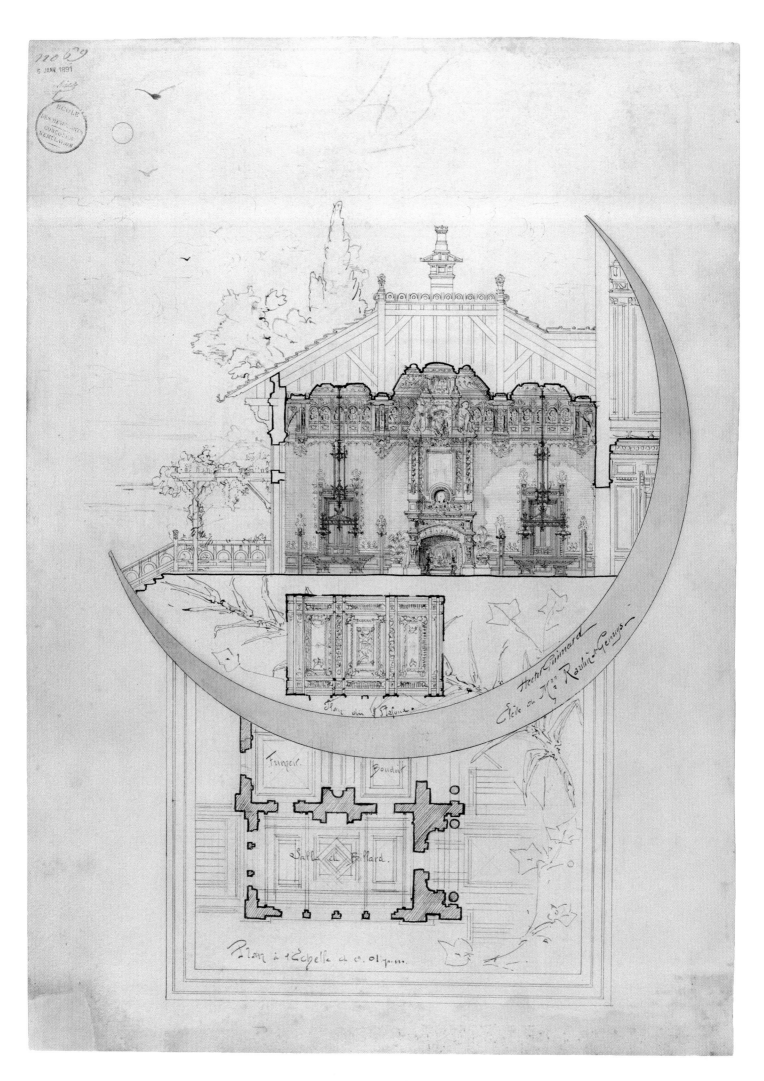

Hector Guimard

Ecole de Mr Raulin et Genuys

Plan du Plafond.

Fumoir.   Boudoir.

Salle de Billard.

Plan à l'Echelle de 0.01 p.m.

between 1891 and 1900, Guimard taught drawing for the girls' section at the École des arts décoratifs.

Guimard had close friendships with some of his clients. The most notable of these was with Léon Nozal, a business associate and important client. Guimard designed several buildings for Nozal, including a house at 52, rue du Ranelagh in the 16th arrondissement. From 1903 to 1914 Nozal made available a studio on avenue Perrichont for Guimard's workshops, Ateliers d'art et de fabrication Guimard. In addition, he served as a witness at Guimard's 1909 wedding. Guimard was also a friend of Léon's son, Paul. When Paul Nozal died in an automobile crash on July 13, 1903, at the age of twenty-seven, Guimard created a memorial marker at the site of the accident, a visual expression of his grief.[4] He designed other funerary monuments for his clients, friends, and their families, including Louis Jassedé and Charles Deron-Levent.

Guimard was a Socialist, and an activist for political and social change. He was involved in the pacifist organization Association for the Study and Propaganda of the International Pax-State.[5] He was a member of the Ligue des droits de l'homme (French Human Rights League), precursor to the League of Nations and an organization that opposed a range of injustices. This quest for social justice is reflected in his designs— from the Métro in 1900 to affordable housing in the 1920s. World War I interrupted Guimard's architectural practice, as construction came to a halt. While residing in Pau in southwestern France during the war, unable to create architecture, he turned to his other great interest: political and social causes. Among a group of pamphlets and publications he wrote was a December 1915 proposal advocating an international peace organization similar to what would become the League of Nations. In fact, he no doubt discussed his idea when he met with President Woodrow Wilson, who was promoting that association. Guimard's proposal required that all countries agree to a rule of law and an international legal code that would have power over rogue nations (like Germany during the war) by means of an international army.[6]

Guimard's interest in modern design was augmented by a group of precursors who adhered to a common theme: design reform based on nature rather than the copying of past styles. Function and materials dictated form, and industrial production was embraced. Among Guimard's most significant design influences were French architect and theorist Viollet-le-Duc; the British Arts and Crafts movement, which flourished between 1880 and 1920; and Belgian architect Victor Horta (1861–1947). Although Guimard found the Beaux-Arts tradition essential in architectural education, he diverged from its general emphasis on grand and ornate classicism in favor of an abstract modern style based on natural forms, which he judged appropriate for the Industrial Age. In so doing, he showed the significance of Viollet-le-Duc's teachings, which advocated the Gothic style with its simplified forms as a way to reform design. Viollet-le-Duc proposed using modern building materials, such as cast iron, and rationalist methods of construction. In his *Entretiens sur l'architecture (Discourses on Architecture)*, a series of essays dedicated to Gothic architecture published in 1863–72, he concentrated in particular on the use of iron and other new materials and on the importance of designing buildings adapted to their function rather than reproducing older styles. In 1898, Guimard wrote, "I always advise my young colleagues to be 'artists' and students of this great master, which should make clear the high esteem to which I hold him."[7] He learned from Viollet-le-Duc the position of the architect as unifying all the arts. Guimard's advanced thinking about new construction methods also reflects his exposure to Génuys, official chief architect for the Commission des monuments historiques as well as teacher. Guimard's angled columns at the 1895

FIG. 2. Guimard, one-day sketch of a billiard room for competition, École des Beaux-Arts, January 6, 1891. Graphite, watercolor on paper. Musée d'Orsay, Paris.

École du Sacré-Cœur, for instance, were inspired by Viollet-le-Duc's design for a covered market beneath a large meeting hall, shown in plate 21 of his *Entretiens*.[8]

Another significant influence on Guimard's work was the British Arts and Crafts movement; in fact, Guimard's interests were more aligned with the British philosopher-designers than with his French compatriots. Contemporaneous with Art Nouveau, the Arts and Crafts movement also shared the objective of reforming design. As Georges Vigne observed, "Great Britain was a much more obvious place for an architect to encounter modernity than the Continent, because in Britain the decorative arts had long been intimately associated with architecture."[9] This unified approach is manifested in the work and writings of William Morris, John Ruskin, and A. W. N. Pugin. With a travel grant he received in 1895 from the Ministry of Public Education and the École des Beaux-Arts, Guimard visited Great Britain and Belgium, followed by a separate trip to the Netherlands and Belgium. At that time, his work already showed a familiarity with and affinity for British Arts and Crafts design: the Hôtel Jassedé of 1893 exemplified a revival of traditional crafts in its ceramic decoration and its garden setting, and the sketches from his visit to Great Britain reflected the growing appeal of the Arts and Crafts cottage style and perhaps a diminished interest in the work of Viollet-le-Duc.[10]

Like British Arts and Crafts designers, Guimard sought an overall unity of design, planning all interior details to be integral to the architecture. This approach, which differed from the more formal French training that Guimard received, was the starting point for a number of modern design movements, including the Wiener Werkstätte's *Gesamtkunstwerk*, or total work of art. However, unlike designer William Morris, who espoused truth through handicraft, Guimard advocated modern technology and materials, aligning his philosophy more closely to British designer Christopher Dresser (1834–1904). With the motto "truth, beauty, power," Dresser sought to reform design, especially after Prince Albert, when establishing the South Kensington Museum (later the Victoria and Albert Museum), spoke about the damage done to "good design" by shoddy craftsmanship and inappropriate use of industrial materials. Dresser had an impact on design reform through his many publications and his domestic, mass-produced objects: ceramics, cast iron, carpets, and wallpaper, including the heavily embossed, high-relief modern wall covering Lincrusta (named after the company that manufactured it), which Dresser had developed and which Guimard used in Castel Béranger. Dresser, who had a doctorate in botanical science, combined a new science- and nature-based aesthetic with more affordable machine-made elements, making his designs accessible to a larger public. The similar approaches meant that Dresser's and Guimard's work shared certain characteristics. Dresser was the first to use cast iron manufactured in Shropshire for decorative furniture. The fanciful and conventionalized ornament in his cast-iron design for a hall stand of c. 1880 (fig. 3), for instance, shows affinities to the cast-iron entrance gate Guimard designed for Hôtel Jassedé (fig. 4). However, Dresser adhered to stylized ornament while Guimard adopted the curves of Art Nouveau. Even so, Dresser's significance as a champion of reform who worked in mass-market materials, such as cast iron and wall coverings, both of which were exhibited in Paris, may have had an impact on Guimard.

Another of Guimard's most profound influences was his contemporary, architect Victor Horta, who introduced Guimard to the newly developing Art Nouveau style. On his second study trip in the summer of 1895, courtesy of the travel grant he had received, Guimard visited Horta's recently completed Hôtel Tassel, a townhouse designed in this style, in Brussels and met the architect himself.[11] This introduction to Horta was a transformative experience for Guimard and an inspiration for his own work, clearly seen in

SARAH D. COFFIN AND DAVID A. HANKS

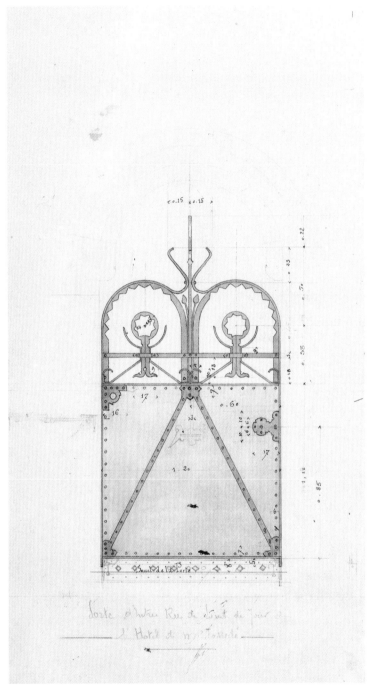

FIG. 3. Christopher Dresser, hall stand, c. 1880. Painted cast iron. Produced by the Coalbrookdale Company, Shropshire, England. Victoria and Albert Museum, London.

FIG. 4. Guimard, design for an entrance gate, Hôtel Jassedé, c. 1893. Watercolor, pencil, red ink with highlights on card stock. Musée d'Orsay, Paris.

FIG. 5. Victor Horta, Hôtel Tassel entrance, Brussels, built 1893.

OPPOSITE: FIG. 6. Guimard, Castel Béranger entrance, built 1895–97.

Castel Béranger.[12] Guimard's letters to Horta expressed great admiration for his work: "In you I have met the architect truly worthy of the name."[13] Before this trip, Guimard's architecture was more Gothic and less organic in appearance. Afterward, the curves of Art Nouveau began to appear in his work, notably in changes to the interior of Castel Béranger. Guimard did not copy the older architect's work as much as he derived inspiration that allowed him to pursue a new, individualized visual language. A comparison of the interiors of Hôtel Tassel (fig. 5) and Castel Béranger (fig. 6) shows that ornamental forms and motifs are similar; the primary difference was the choice of materials, cast iron in Guimard's project, exotic woods in Horta's.

In a 1902 article introducing the Art Nouveau style for the *Architectural Record*, an American architectural magazine, Guimard wrote, "Nature is a big book from which we can draw inspiration, and it is in that book that we must look for principles, which, when found, have to be defined and applied by the human mind according to human needs."[14] Among these principles, Guimard explained, are logic, which considers all conditions and factors in a project; harmony, which unifies exteriors, interiors, and surroundings; and sentiment, which "leads by emotion to the highest expression of the art."[15] At the time Guimard was exploring Art Nouveau, it was flourishing throughout Europe, under different names in different countries. Although specific attributes varied from one interpretation to the next, all were characterized by a rejection of historicism, a unity of design elements, and a focus on nature as formal inspiration. Like Dresser, Guimard wished to make his design aesthetic available, via mass production, to a broad social spectrum—"to put the beautiful within reach of everyone."[16] This attitude was a motivation throughout his career.

Guimard's abstract Art Nouveau designs, often composed of curves and whiplash decorations, were based on natural forms that evoked movement and growth, expressed in novel ways. His work was distinctive in its combination of multiple materials, including cast and wrought iron, lava, concrete, ceramic, multiple colors of brick, and numerous types of stone, such as buhrstone and sandstone. He used these to create surprising forms—for instance, bizarre vegetal and floral forms, or the impression of his own hand for bronze doorknobs. His furniture designs evolved from the dark mahogany of Castel Béranger to lighter pearwood, which he favored because of its color and grain (figs. 7–8). Large openings in the asymmetrical, fluid forms of Castel Béranger furniture contrast to the predominantly symmetrical, tight compositions of the pieces for his own house.

Guimard's early projects were for a relatively small group of loyal clients, most newly rich, living in his neighborhood of Auteuil. His floor plans are distinctive, often carefully worked out to suit awkwardly angled lots. He used mass-production technology, such as

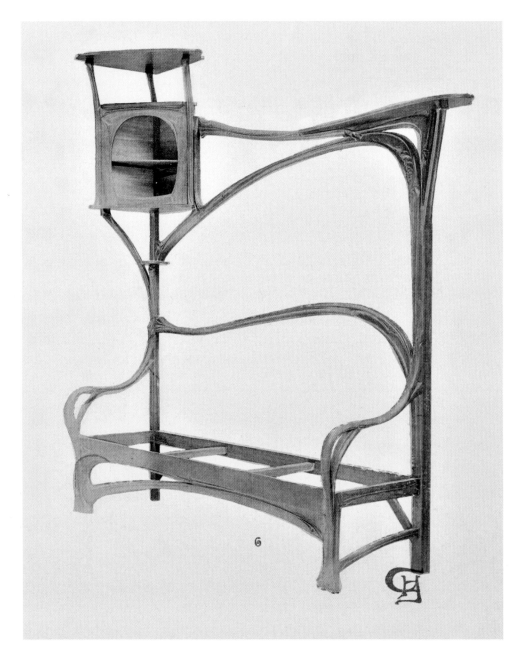

FIG. 7. Detail of plate 64 from Guimard's *Le Castel Béranger* portfolio, showing a mahogany smoking bench. The Collection of Richard H. Driehaus, Chicago.

OPPOSITE: FIG. 8. Guimard, pearwood and gilt-bronze vanity table from Madame Guimard's bedroom in Hôtel Guimard. Musée des Beaux-Arts de Lyon, inv. 1951-37.

SARAH D. COFFIN AND DAVID A. HANKS

standardized building components in cast iron, to promote his vision of modern design for all. At the same time, for some of his commissions, particularly for wealthier and more adventurous clients, he began to introduce interior furnishings. After marrying Adeline Oppenheim (1872–1965, fig. 9), an American artist from a wealthy Jewish banking family in New York, in 1909, Guimard designed Hôtel Guimard, a new house on avenue Mozart, along with the interiors, furnishings, carpeting, draperies, and even table linens. Except for their World War I–era sojourn, during which they stayed at Hôtel Gassion in Pau, the Guimards lived in Hôtel Guimard from 1913 to 1930; they then moved to the fourth floor of an apartment building at 18, rue Henri-Heine, which Guimard had designed in 1921 and completed in 1926, in an area he hoped to develop.

Guimard was as advanced in the ways he promoted his work as he was in the work itself. In 1900, he branded himself "*architecte d'art*" to distinguish his creative ambitions from purely commercial architecture; that same year, he first used the motto "*le style Guimard.*" In 1903, he used both phrases in a collection of twenty-four postcards printed to promote his designs (see Thiébaut, "The First Gesture," fig. 1; cat. nos. 47–55). He seems to have abandoned *architecte d'art* shortly afterward, but he continued to use *le style Guimard* until it was succeeded by "*le style moderne*" around 1910, because he wanted to be associated with the notion of modernity throughout his career. In her communications to museums receiving gifts of Guimard's designs, Mme Guimard repeatedly reinforced the importance of *le style Guimard* brand.

Because of his successful efforts to publicize his own work, and the very visible Métro entrances throughout Paris, Guimard was well known in France. French journalists offered both criticism and praise for his work. In 1899, critic Frantz Jourdain wrote that Guimard had "returned to the conquest of unstoppable beauty, his eyes toward the future, attentive to the rhythmic breaths of the humanity whom he followed and who guided him."[17] In a review of the 1903 Exposition internationale de l'habitation, or Housing Exhibition, another critic described Guimard's pavilion as "a mix of good and bad things," suggested that Guimard needed to "settle down a bit," and judged the excessive promotion strange.[18]

Guimard was less known in the United States at the turn of the century, in part because Art Nouveau never became a dominant style in America. In 1902, the *Inland Architect and News Record* hailed Guimard's work, noting that the recently completed Humbert de Romans concert hall and the Métro followed lines based on natural forms that "are very graceful and striking. Nothing like them was ever seen before, and by all the disciples of the new art they are acclaimed as works of genius."[19] But not all American critics praised French Art Nouveau and Guimard's work. In the magazine the *Craftsman*, Columbia University architecture professor, former student at the École des Beaux-Arts, and respected critic A. D. F. Hamlin characterized the new style as "chiefly a negative movement," describing Castel Béranger as a "jumble of incoherent motives without grace or harmony."[20] By contrast, Samuel Bing, whose pavilion at the 1900 Exposition universelle was called "Art Nouveau," and who was a champion of the new movement, defended the style in a later issue of the same magazine.[21]

In September 1938, the Guimards left Paris, which they both loved, anticipating the approaching war.[22] A Nazi-occupied France would be a threat to Adeline Guimard because of her Jewish heritage and to Hector Guimard because of his liberal political activism. Indeed, less than two years later, in May 1940, the Germans attacked France and, within weeks, defeated the French army and established a de facto Nazi dictatorship that would last more than four years. Before Guimard left France, he corresponded with Alfred H. Barr Jr., founding director of the Museum of Modern Art in New York, who made annual

FIG. 9. Adeline Oppenheim, taken at the Reutlinger Studio in Paris, c. 1909. Cooper Hewitt, Smithsonian Design Museum, New York.

SARAH D. COFFIN AND DAVID A. HANKS

pilgrimages to Europe to see new art and architecture firsthand and to meet artists in preparation for exhibitions at the museum. The two may have met in Europe before the Guimards' move.[23] In March 1936, Guimard wrote to Barr regarding MoMA's upcoming exhibition *Fantastic Art, Dada, Surrealism*, which included the architect's work.[24] Perhaps already thinking of his legacy, Guimard described his artistic production, which he divided into four periods: 1900, "Search for a New Style"; 1910, "Realization of this Style"; 1920, "Evolution of the style due to the elimination of any work requiring artists"; and 1930, "Museum Proposals, where in the reinforced concrete structure, the formwork is preserved, representing a new architectural concept."[25] Barr identified the essential aesthetic significance of Guimard's work and his influence on modern artists: "Guimard has created a new type of biomorphic abstract form. It is a symbolic form that expresses the original rhythms of nature. . . . This is why Guimard's highly simplified and dynamic forms have aroused the admiration not only of surrealist painters but also of Arp and Brancusi, Matisse and Picasso, and even of abstract expressionists! Guimard, Horta, Van de Velde and others gave abstract biomorphic art a formal language one generation before the painters. Guimard had a very special influence because his work was easily accessible. From the twenties to the fifties, all abstract artists look at Guimard's symbolism. As Picasso said, 'Guimard was everywhere.'"[26] Due in part to an exhibition proposal by Barr in 1933, appreciation of Art Nouveau and recognition of Guimard's work in America began even before his move to the United States. Although Barr's exhibition was not approved, in June 1949 MoMA exhibited Art Nouveau acquisitions in a special gallery, including work by Guimard, much of which was part of Adeline Guimard's 1949 gift to the museum after her husband's death.[27]

Hector Guimard died on May 20, 1942, at the Adams Hotel on 86th Street near Fifth Avenue, the Guimards' New York residence. In poor health, he had not been able to work after the move to the United States.[28] A photo of Guimard at a sanatorium in Greenwich, Connecticut, shows an elegantly dressed gentleman seated in the garden with a group (fig. 10). The popularity of his work, which rose and fell throughout his life and after his

FIG. 10. Photo of Adeline and Hector Guimard (seated) in Greenwich, Connecticut, July 1939. Alain Blondel, Garches, France.

death, was at its height in the first decade of the twentieth century, following the design of the Paris Métro. Although he continued to design buildings through the 1920s—including visitors' quarters for the 1925 Exposition internationale des arts décoratifs (World's Fair) in Paris and interiors for his rue Henri-Heine apartment building—*le style Guimard* began to fade with the rise of Art Deco and the International Style. The short-lived Art Nouveau was on the wane by 1910, long before Guimard moved to New York.

Following her husband's death, Mme Guimard devoted herself to preserving his legacy, making important donations to American and French museums, though she did fail to convince anyone in France to set up a Guimard museum in Hôtel Guimard. Her attempt to persuade newspapers to recognize Guimard's career at the time of his death was unsuccessful, even with the help of their friend and advocate Alfred Barr Jr.[29] Happily, Adeline lived long enough to see a revival of interest in Art Nouveau and her husband's work: in 1960, five years before she died, the Museum of Modern Art opened the exhibition *Art Nouveau*. More exhibitions would follow: a monographic show at MoMA in 1970 and a major retrospective at the Musée d'Orsay in 1992. Each of these presentations has taken a step toward a deeper and broader understanding of Guimard's importance in the history of modern design; yet there is much still to be discovered in the work of this *architecte d'art*.

NOTES

1   A chronology of Hector Guimard's life appears on the website of le Cercle Guimard, www.lecercleguimard.fr/en/biography/.

2   A detailed summary of his education can be found in Georges Vigne, *Hector Guimard: Architect, Designer, 1867–1942* (New York: Delano Greenidge Editions, 2003), 21–25. See also le Cercle Guimard's chronology.

3   A crescent shape provides coherence to a detailed rendering in the classical style. The form is signed by Guimard and notes that he was a student of Gustave Raulin and Charles Génuys. Thanks to Isabelle Gournay for bringing this drawing to our attention.

4   Funeral monuments, some for clients, were an important part of Guimard's oeuvre. See Marie-Laure Crosnier Leconte, "Architecture commémorative et funéraire," in Philippe Thiébaut et al., *Guimard,* exh. cat. (Paris: Gallimard/Réunion des musées nationaux, 1992), 267–79.

5   See *Rapport général soumis à la Conférence de la paix sur le projet État Pax* (Paris: État Pax, 1919), and *Association for the Study and Propaganda of the International Pax State Having Object for the Organisation of Universal Peace Obtained Through the Victory of Right* (Paris: Pax State, c. 1919), both in the Adeline Oppenheim Guimard papers, Manuscripts and Archives Division, New York Public Library.

6   Vigne, *Hector Guimard,* 345–46.

7   Vigne, *Hector Guimard,* 124.

8   Yvonne Brunhammer et al., *Art Nouveau: Belgium/France* (Houston: Institute for the Arts, Rice University, 1976), 409.

9   Vigne, *Hector Guimard,* 14.

SARAH D. COFFIN AND DAVID A. HANKS

10 Although there is no known itinerary for this trip, Guimard's drawings at the Musée des arts décoratifs include watercolors for houses on the Isle of Wight and in Sussex. According to Claude Frontisi, Guimard visited Arthur L. Liberty (who sold Dresser's glass and textiles), Aubrey Beardsley, Edward Godwin, and Christopher Dresser himself. Claude Frontisi, "Hector Guimard en son temps," in Thiébaut et al._, Guimard_ (exh. cat.), 31.

11 Guimard arranged an exhibition of sketches of Horta's work in Paris at the Salon de la Société nationale des Beaux-Arts; it opened on April 25, 1896. Among the projects shown were architectural sketches Guimard made in England, Scotland, Belgium, and the Netherlands. Vigne, *Hector Guimard*, 60–61, 100. He also dedicated his portfolio, *Le Castel Béranger,* published in 1898, to Horta.

12 As Philippe Thiébaut notes in his essay in this publication, "The First Gesture."

13 Hector Guimard to Victor Horta, May 8, 1896, reproduced and translated in Brunhammer et al., *Art Nouveau,* 410.

14 Hector Guimard, "An Architect's Opinion of 'l'Art Nouveau,'" *Architectural Record* 12, no. 2 (June 1902): 127.

15 Guimard, "Architect's Opinion," 127–31.

16 Hector Guimard to Fernand Hauser (probably), December 11, 1913, cited in Vigne, *Hector Guimard,* 340.

17 Frantz Jourdain, "Les meubles modernes," *Revue d'art* 1 (November 4, 1899): 5–9.

18 "Supplément: L'Exposition de l'habitation," *Art et décoration*, October 1903, 2.

19 "The Art Nouveau," *Inland Architect and News Record* 40, no. 5 (December 1902): 40.

20 A. D. F. Hamlin, "L'Art Nouveau: Its Origin and Development," *Craftsman* 3, no. 3 (December 1902): 142.

21 Samuel Bing, "L'Art Nouveau," *Craftsman* 5, no. 1 (October 1903): 1–15.

22 The Guimards traveled from Le Havre, France, to New York on the SS *Normandie*, September 7–12, 1938. According to the passenger records from that voyage, Hector had visited New York in 1912. The Statue of Liberty–Ellis Island Foundation, passenger search, accessed September 3, 2019.

23 Alfred H. Barr Jr. to Adeline Guimard, June 6, 1945, Adeline Oppenheim Guimard papers. Barr wrote to Adeline that he remembered her husband with admiration and affection.

24 The Museum of Modern Art, New York, December 9, 1936–January 17, 1937. Guimard's loans included drawings and photographs of the Métro entrances and Hôtel Guimard, as well as color plates from *Le Castel Béranger.*

25 Hector Guimard to Alfred H. Barr Jr., March 10, 1936, MoMA Exhs. 55.4, The Museum of Modern Art Archives, New York. An English translation of this letter appears in Vigne, *Hector Guimard*, 378.

26 F. Lanier Graham, "Guimard, Viollet-le-Duc et le modernism," in *Guimard: Colloque international, Musée d'Orsay, 12 et 13 Juin 1992* (Paris: Réunion des musées nationaux, 1994), 18–19.

27 Philip Johnson to Adeline Guimard, March 30, 1949, Adeline Oppenheim Guimard papers, discusses gifts he wants for the exhibition.

28 Auguste Bluysen to Adeline Guimard, October 7, 1947, Adeline Oppenheim Guimard papers, Mss Col 1264; cited in Bruno Montemat, "Les cercles artistiques, littéraires et philosophiques d'Hector Guimard, 'architecte d'Art,'" *Romantisme* 177 (March 2017): 107.

29 Alfred H. Barr Jr. to Adeline Guimard, May 21, 1942. Barr agreed that "the press did not accord [Guimard] the attention his distinguished career deserved." He telephoned the arts editor for the *New York Times* in an apparently futile attempt to get something published. Adeline Oppenheim Guimard papers.

M. & Mme Guimard

Adeline Guimard's declaration on the occasion of her marriage to Hector Guimard in Paris—"It will be necessary for us to make of our whole life a work of art"—was the focus of their married life. She was from a wealthy Jewish family in New York, an American-born artist who moved to Paris to study painting. He was born in Lyon and moved to Paris, an architect who had achieved considerable fame by the time of their marriage, primarily through Castel Béranger, the Paris Métro, and the Humbert de Romans concert hall.

Guimard applied his philosophy of integrated design to the wedding as much as he did to any work of architecture, designing Adeline's wedding dress, engagement ring, and other jewelry. After the wedding, Guimard embarked on the creation of a residence "according to his dream." He designed every detail of Hôtel Guimard, a four-story (plus attic) townhouse at 122, avenue Mozart in the 16th arrondissement of Paris—including furniture, carpeting, and textiles—to create a total unified design. The radical plan featured an elevator in place of a formal staircase and included both a ground-floor studio for the architect and a fourth-floor studio for Adeline. Financially, the residence was a joint venture with his wife, whose banker father provided funds equivalent to $1.1 million today.

The dovetailing artistic visions of husband and wife were recorded in a series of photographs of Hôtel Guimard. His designs for frames incorporated her paintings into the interiors, since furnishings and works of art were integral to the architecture. Their common endeavor included the placement of objects, whether acquired or designed by Hector, in the rooms of the house. In May 1913, they invited critics, colleagues, and friends to a reception to experience the extraordinary design. The townhouse remained the primary residence of the Guimards until 1930, when they moved to a fourth-floor apartment at 18, rue Henri-Heine, perhaps to economize during the Great Depression.

Mme and M. Hector Guimard, Paris, c. 1909. The Museum of Modern Art, New York.

1
Hector Guimard's Cane
c. 1903–4
Silver, wood
35¼ × 4⅝ × 1 in. (89.5 × 10.3 × 2.5 cm)
Produced by Ateliers d'art et de fabrication Guimard, Paris
ALAIN BLONDEL AND YVES PLANTIN, GARCHES, FRANCE

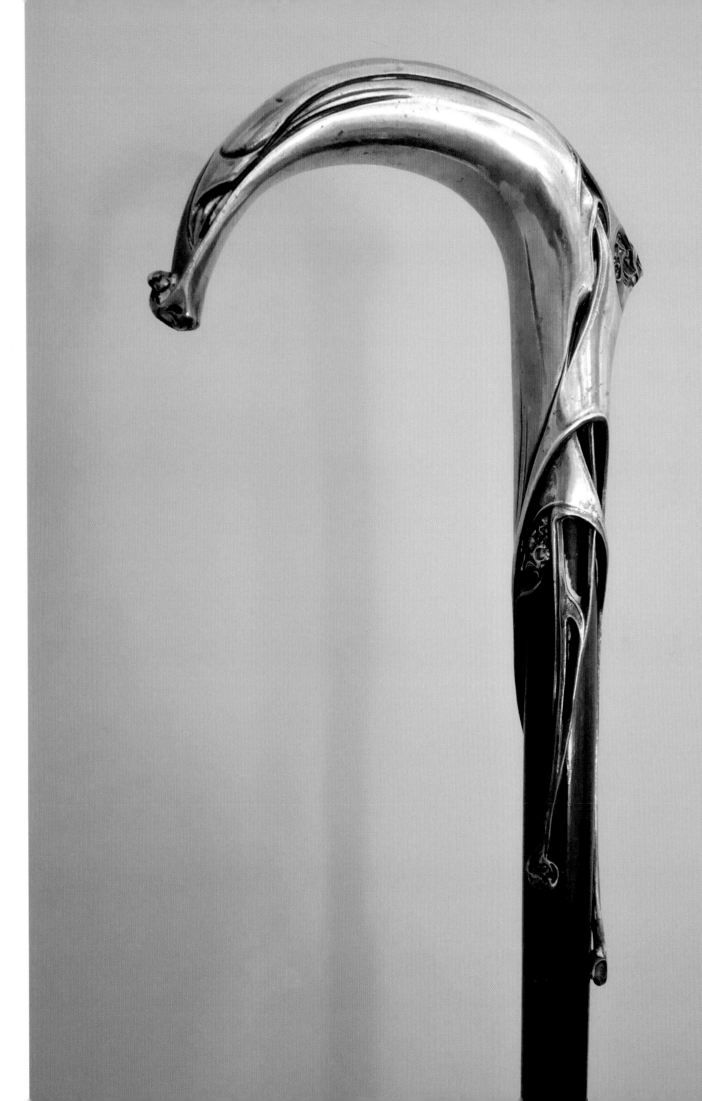

Hôtel Guimard

122, avenue Mozart, Paris, constructed 1909–12

In May 1913, the Guimards moved into an elegant four-story (plus attic) townhouse at 122, avenue Mozart. The couple purchased the corner lot shortly after their marriage in February 1909. The new residence, Hôtel Guimard, included a studio with north-facing windows on the fourth floor for Adeline and offices on the ground floor for Hector and his employees. Although construction was largely complete by 1910, M. and Mme Guimard did not move in until 1913, once custom interior furnishings by Guimard's frequent collaborators—Maison Coudyser (textiles), Paul Philippon (furnishings), and Maison Cottin (hardware)—were in place.

Guimard presided over the design and production of every single detail of the exterior and interior, from the ornate gilt bronze doorbell pull to the gilt and silvered-bronze vases and frames that stood atop side tables and desks. Nothing was too small to escape his attention, even desk accessories, such as letter seals. In the absolute correspondence of style between inside and outside—the supple forms of the tall case clocks and leather-upholstered pearwood chairs, the embroidered curtains, even the writhing lines of the embroidered table linens echoing the fantastic swelling facade—Hôtel Guimard wholly embodied the architect-designer's integrated approach.

YAO-FEN YOU

Hôtel Guimard, c. 1913. Cooper Hewitt, Smithsonian Design Museum, New York, 1956-78-3.

2 (*opposite*)
Front Elevation of
Hôtel Guimard
c. 1909
Photographic print on
sensitized paper
11⅛ × 9 in. (28.2 × 22.8 cm)
COOPER HEWITT, SMITHSONIAN
DESIGN MUSEUM, NEW YORK,
GIFT OF MME HECTOR GUIMARD,
1956-78-3-1

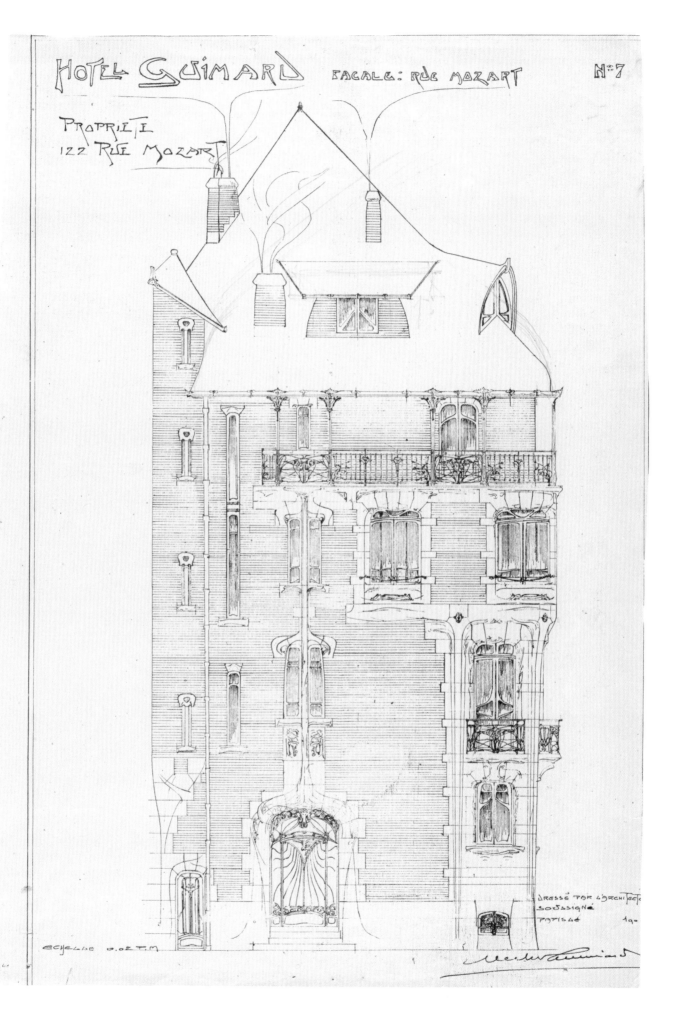

HOTEL GUIMARD   FAÇADE: RUE MOZART   N°7

PROPRIÉTÉ
122 RUE MOZART

ÉCHELLE 0.02 P.M

DRESSÉ PAR L'ARCHITECTE
SOUSSIGNÉ
PARIS LE   19-

3
Tall Case Clock
1910
Oak, copper, metal, glass
92¾ × 17 × 10½ in. (235.6 × 43.2 × 26.7 cm)
THE COLLECTION OF RICHARD H. DRIEHAUS, CHICAGO, 50382

4 (*opposite*)
Side Chair
c. 1912
Pearwood, leather, brass
44¹¹⁄₁₆ × 18⅛ × 18⅞ in. (113.5 × 46 × 48 cm)
Produced by Ateliers d'art et de fabrication Guimard, Paris
COOPER HEWITT, SMITHSONIAN DESIGN MUSEUM, NEW YORK,
GIFT OF MME HECTOR GUIMARD, 1948-114-1

Dining room in Hôtel Guimard, c. 1913. Cooper Hewitt,
Smithsonian Design Museum, New York, 1956-78-11.

5
Doorbell Pull from Hôtel Guimard
c. 1909–13
Bronze, gold
7¾ × 4¾ × 4¾ in. (19.7 × 12 × 12 cm)
Produced by la Maison Cottin, Paris
COOPER HEWITT, SMITHSONIAN DESIGN MUSEUM, NEW YORK,
GIFT OF MME HECTOR GUIMARD, 1948-114-5

6 (*opposite*)
Picture Frame from Mme Guimard's Bedroom at Hôtel Guimard
1909
Brass, silver, plate glass, silk velvet
13½ × 5¹³⁄₁₆ × ¹³⁄₁₆ in. (34.3 × 14.7 × 2 cm)
Produced by Philippon, Paris
COOPER HEWITT, SMITHSONIAN DESIGN MUSEUM, NEW YORK,
GIFT OF MME HECTOR GUIMARD, 1956-76-7-A/C

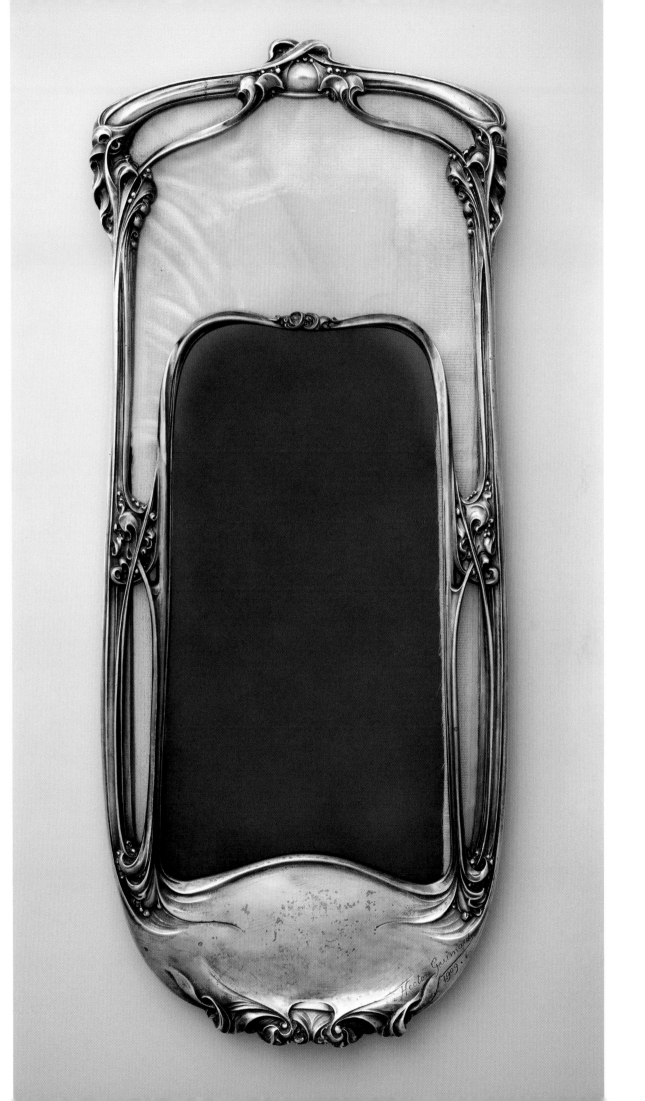

Mme Guimard's bedroom,
c. 1913. Cooper Hewitt,
Smithsonian Design Museum,
New York, 1956-78-11.

7
Vase from Hôtel Guimard
c. 1905
Bronze, gold
10⁷⁄₁₆ × 4¹⁵⁄₁₆ × 4¹⁵⁄₁₆ in.
(26.5 × 12.5 × 12.5 cm)
Produced by Philippon, Paris
COOPER HEWITT, SMITHSONIAN
DESIGN MUSEUM, NEW YORK,
GIFT OF MME HECTOR GUIMARD,
1956-76-2

8 (*opposite*)
Pen Tray
1907
Walnut
2³⁄₈ × 10¹⁄₄ × ³⁄₈ in.
(6 × 26 × 1 cm)
Produced by Ateliers d'art et
de fabrication Guimard, Paris
COOPER HEWITT, SMITHSONIAN
DESIGN MUSEUM, NEW YORK,
GIFT OF MISS CLARE L.
BECKWITH, 1962-132-1

Parlor in Hôtel Guimard, c. 1913. Cooper Hewitt, Smithsonian Design Museum, New York, 1956-78-10.

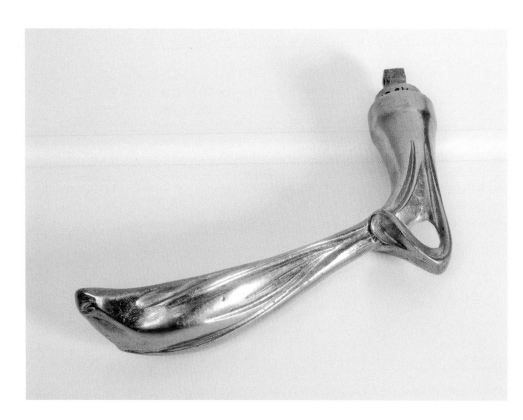

9
Door Handle
c. 1909
Gilt copper alloy
⅞ × 2¾ × 4¾ in.
(2.2 × 7 × 12.1 cm)
PHILADELPHIA MUSEUM OF ART,
GIFT OF MME HECTOR GUIMARD,
P1948-64-5

10
Photograph of Plaster
Models for *le style Guimard*
Door Handles
c. 1909
Gelatin silver print on
cardboard
6⅞ × 9½ in. (17.5 × 24 cm)
MUSÉE DES ARTS DÉCORATIFS
ARCHIVES, PARIS, GIFT OF
ADELINE GUIMARD, JULY 1948,
BAD 7907

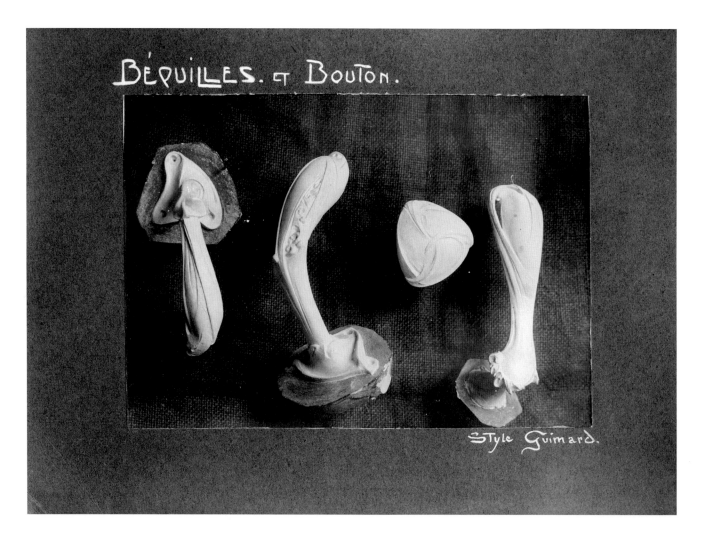

Textiles, Jewelry, and Personal Items

The 1909 marriage of Hector Guimard and Adeline Oppenheim marked an expansion of the French architect's creative prowess and range, with his American-born bride serving as his artistic muse. Guimard's designs for the wedding include not only her delicate silk embroidered wedding dress but also a range of elegant jewelry: the engagement ring, a diamond-studded pendant, and a highly stylized gold-and-agate brooch accented with pearls and moonstones. Each of the unique pieces, all characterized by sinuous flowing lines, embodies the élan of *le style Guimard*. While Mme Guimard parted with components of her wedding attire in 1949, she retained her jewelry, including the model for her engagement ring, until her death. Such personal items must have served as daily reminders of her husband. Adeline bequeathed the pieces to her nephew Laurent Oppenheim Jr., who donated them to the Museum of Modern Art in 1970, five years after her death.

Y. Y.

11
Mme Guimard's Brooch
c. 1909
Gold, agate, pearls,
moonstones
1⅝ × 3¾ in. (4.1 × 9.5 cm)
THE MUSEUM OF MODERN ART,
GIFT OF LAURENT OPPENHEIM
JR., 464.1970

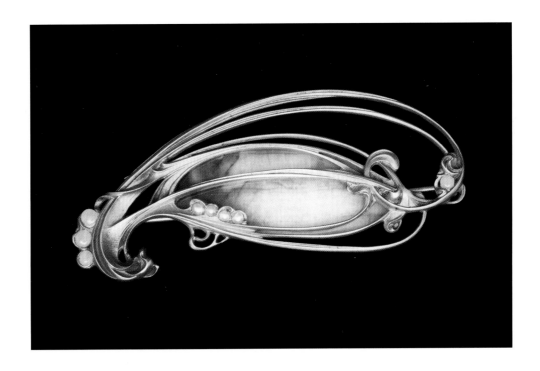

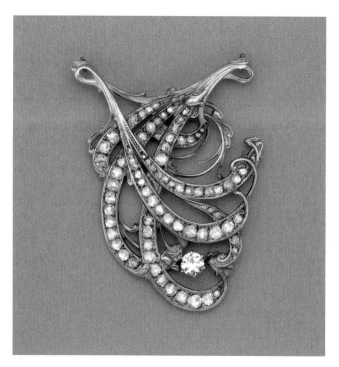

13
Model of Mme Guimard's
Engagement Ring
c. 1909
Gold, replacement gemstone
Height: $^{15}/_{16}$ in. (2.4 cm)
THE MUSEUM OF MODERN ART,
GIFT OF LAURENT OPPENHEIM
JR., 467.1970

14
Mme Guimard's Ring
c. 1907
Gold, pearl, diamond
$1 \times {}^{5}/_{8}$ in. (2.5 × 1.6 cm)
THE MUSEUM OF MODERN ART,
GIFT OF LAURENT OPPENHEIM
JR., 466.1970

12
Mme Guimard's Pendant
c. 1907–12
Gold, diamonds
$2^{1}/_{8} \times 1^{5}/_{8}$ in. (5.4 × 4.2 cm)
THE MUSEUM OF MODERN ART, GIFT OF LAURENT OPPENHEIM JR.,
SC61.1977

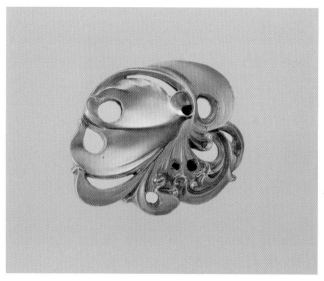

15
Mme Guimard's Hat Pin
c. 1910
Bronze
$1 \times 1^{1}/_{4}$ in. (2.5 × 3.2 cm)
THE MUSEUM OF MODERN ART, GIFT OF MME HECTOR GUIMARD,
325.1949

16
Hector Guimard's Wallet Corner with "HG" Monogram
c. 1910
Gold
$^{5}/_{8} \times 1^{1}/_{16}$ in. (1.6 × 2.7 cm)
THE MUSEUM OF MODERN ART, GIFT OF LAURENT OPPENHEIM JR.,
468.1970

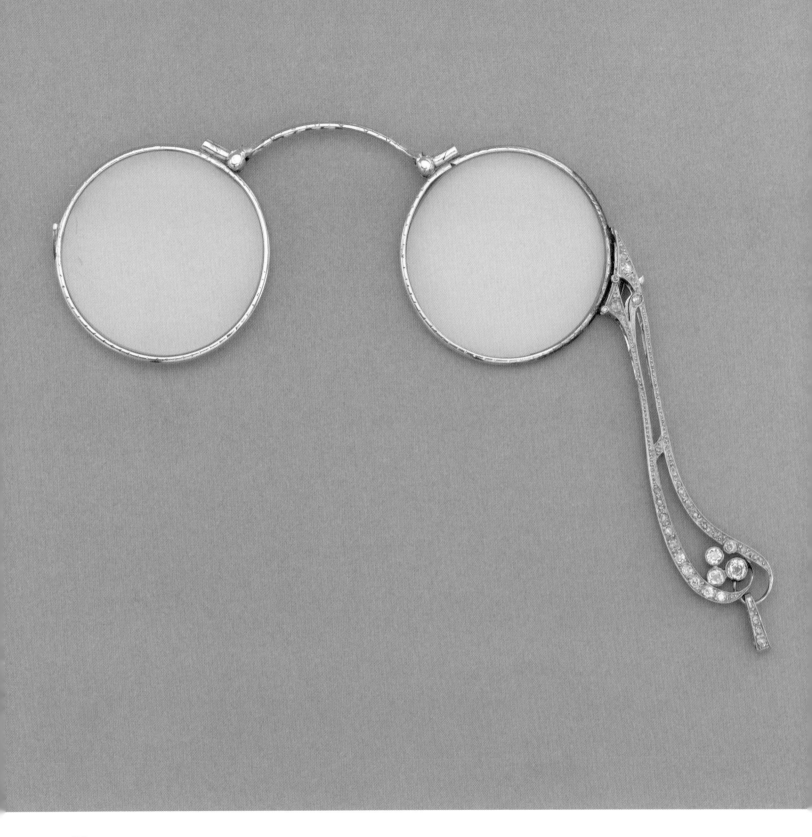

17
Mme Guimard's Lorgnette
c. 1907–12
Glass, platinum, white gold, diamonds
Height, open: 4⅛ in. (10.5 cm)

18
Seal of Adeline Guimard
1909–13
Bronze, gold
$3^{7}/_{16} \times 2^{3}/_{8} \times 2^{3}/_{8}$ in.
(8.8 × 6 × 6 cm)
Produced by Philippon, Paris
COOPER HEWITT, SMITHSONIAN
DESIGN MUSEUM, NEW YORK,
GIFT OF MME HECTOR GUIMARD,
1956-76-3

Detail of Adeline Guimard's
seal, showing "AG" monogram.

19
Picture Frame from Mme Guimard's Desk at Hôtel Guimard
1909–13
Bronze, gold, plate glass
5 × $2^{7}/_{16}$ in. (12.8 × 6.3 cm)
Produced by Philippon, Paris
COOPER HEWITT, SMITHSONIAN DESIGN MUSEUM, NEW YORK,
GIFT OF MME HECTOR GUIMARD, 1956-76-4-A,B

20
Paperweight from Mme Guimard's Desk at Hôtel Guimard
1909–13
Alabaster, bronze, gold
5¹⁵⁄₁₆ × 2½ × 1³⁄₁₆ in. (15.1 × 6.3 × 3 cm)
COOPER HEWITT, SMITHSONIAN DESIGN MUSEUM, NEW YORK,
GIFT OF MME HECTOR GUIMARD, 1956-76-1

21
Panel from Adeline
Oppenheim's Wedding Dress
1909
Silk embroidered with chain
(tambour), stem, satin, padded
satin, speckling, and knotted
stitches on silk net foundation
45¼ × 15⅜ in.
(114.9 × 39.1 cm)
Produced by Maison
Coudyser, Paris
COOPER HEWITT, SMITHSONIAN
DESIGN MUSEUM, NEW YORK,
GIFT OF MME HECTOR GUIMARD,
1949-91-4

22 (*opposite*)
Collar from White Satin
Coat Worn by Mme Guimard
on Her Wedding Day
1909
Silk embroidery on silk
satin weave foundation
16½ × 24⅛ in.
(41.9 × 61.3 cm)
Produced by Maison
Drecoll, Paris
COOPER HEWITT, SMITHSONIAN
DESIGN MUSEUM, NEW YORK,
GIFT OF MME HECTOR GUIMARD,
1949-91-3

Hector Guimard and Adeline Oppenheim's wedding invitation, 1909. Alain Blondel, Garches, France.

23
Embroidery Sample
1909–13
Embroidered silk
26¾ × 11½ in.
(67.9 × 29.2 cm)
Produced by Maison
Coudyser, Paris

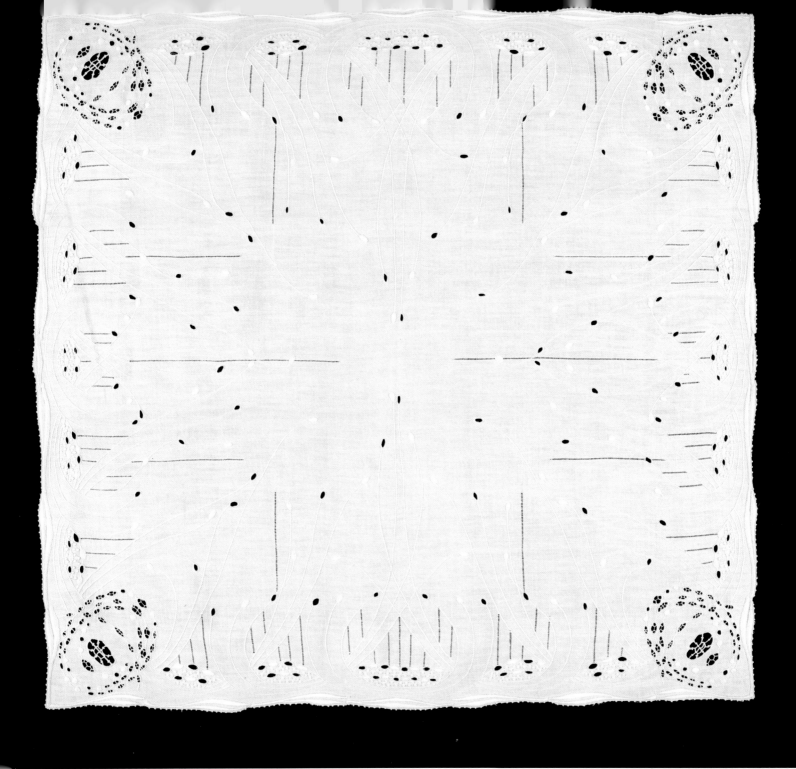

24
Tea Cloth from Hôtel Guimard
1909–13
Cotton embroidery on linen
22 7/16 × 23 5/8 in. (57 × 60 cm)
Produced by Maison Melville et Ziffer, Paris
COOPER HEWITT, SMITHSONIAN DESIGN MUSEUM, NEW YORK,
GIFT OF MME HECTOR GUIMARD, 1949-91-6

25 (overleaf)
Two Curtain Panels from Hôtel Guimard
1909–13
Embroidered silk, brass rings
26 3/4 × 19 11/16 in. (68 × 50 cm) each
Produced by Maison Coudyser, Paris
COOPER HEWITT, SMITHSONIAN DESIGN MUSEUM, NEW YORK,
GIFT OF MME HECTOR GUIMARD, 1949-91-2-A,B

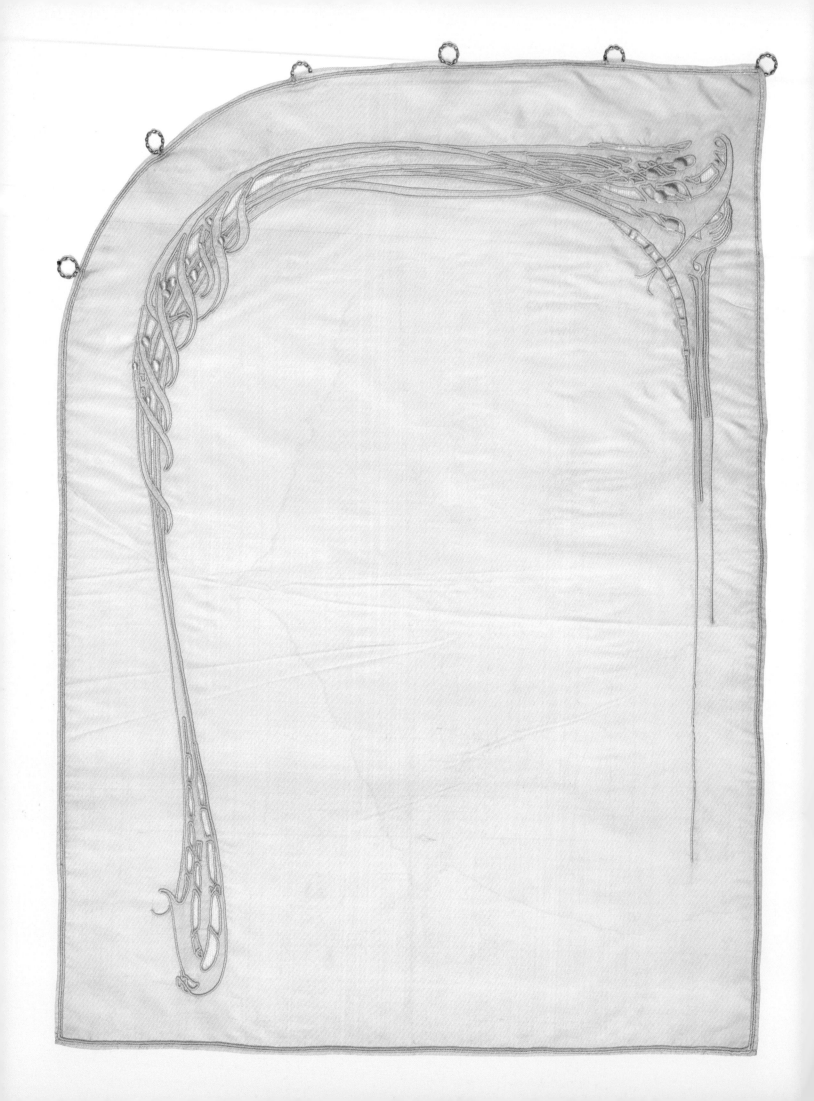

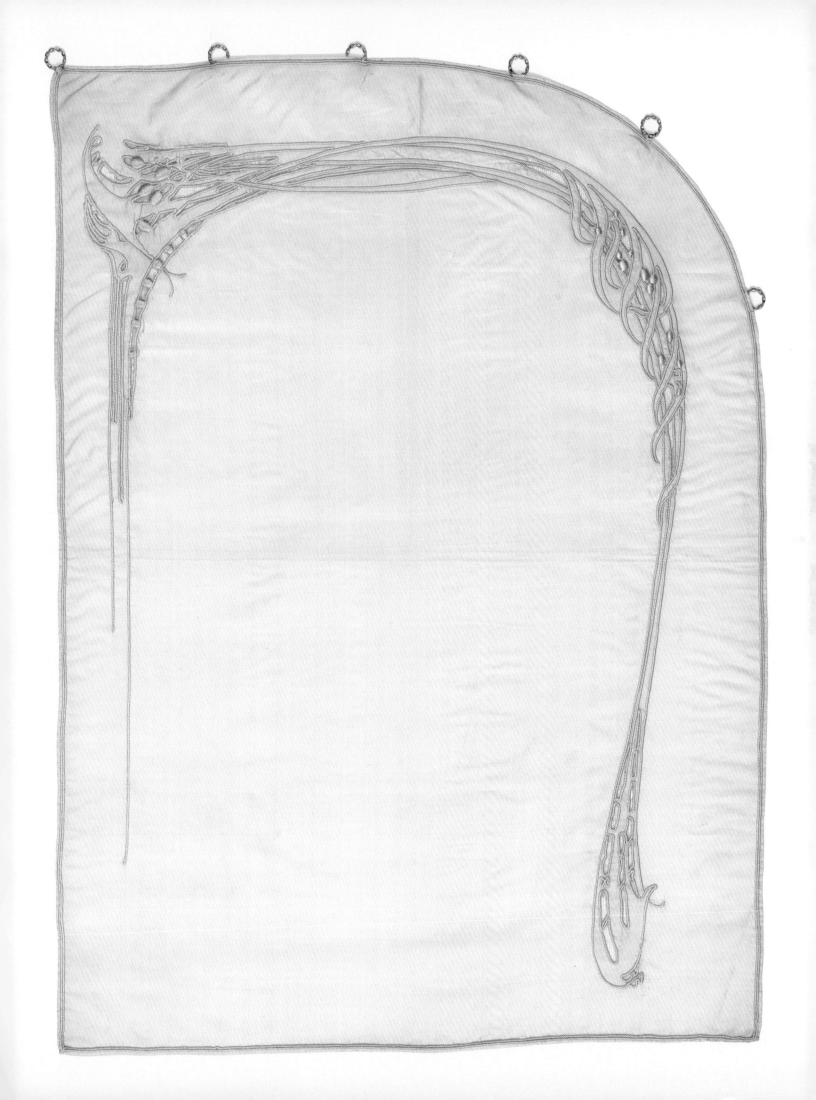

Revisiting Guimard's Auteuils
Isabelle Gournay

Hector Guimard spent his professional life in Auteuil, the southernmost area of the 16th arrondissement, and a majority of his surviving work is located there (fig. 1). Indeed, residency in Auteuil was a key factor in his twofold career: local practitioner, on the one hand, and "*architecte d'art*" with international ambitions and a unique approach to total design, on the other.[1] As evidenced by Frank Lloyd Wright's beginnings in Oak Park, Illinois, outside of Chicago, at about the same time, securing clients among like-minded, or at least sympathetic, neighbors was not an uncommon approach for a progressive architect establishing his own practice.

Auteuil has a multifaceted planning and architectural legacy. Similarly, it is a multidimensional lens through which to contextualize Guimard's work. A journey through Auteuil, imaginary or real, is a path of discovery—virtual and concrete, intellectual and physical—that suggests numerous sociological and topographical connections.[2] Guimard's linked but distinctive worlds are visible in various clusters of buildings. Beyond its current NAP reputation for posh traditionalism,[3] Auteuil is a fascinating palimpsest, an overlay of surviving "sites of memory" from the ancien régime to the Jazz Age; from the mansion where Abigail and John Adams, fleeing the hustle and bustle of Paris, chose to live with their two sons to the house Le Corbusier designed for art collector Raoul La Roche.[4]

In Auteuil, some of Guimard's works have been lost or irretrievably altered: his earliest building, the gritty Point-du-Jour *café-concert*, was lost to the great flood of 1910, which resulted in a complete restructuring of the banks of the Seine, and his charming, quasi-suburban Hôtel Roy (fig. 2), tucked between a fortification and a sunken railroad, was demolished (without anyone noticing) around 1960. Yet at the same time, delightful surprises abound for the curious flaneur, such as the juxtaposition near rue La Fontaine between Guimard's 1910 Immeuble Trémois and a 122-year-old daycare center.[5]

The land-owning middle class of Auteuil commissioned Guimard for personal residences and rent-producing apartment houses (*immeubles de rapport*); such patronage extended to funerary monuments and suburban and seaside villas. At age eighteen, Guimard decided not to live with his parents in the 17th arrondissement or near his schools (École des arts décoratifs and École des Beaux-Arts) on the Left Bank. Instead, he moved in with a distant relative at 147, avenue de Versailles and continued to live in the area until emigrating to America in 1938.

"Le Far West" of Paris, Auteuil had experienced growth as dramatic as that of American frontier towns: it had 1,077 residents in 1800; 6,270 in 1856, five years before it was annexed by Paris; and 29,134 in 1901.[6] In 1912, when Hector and Adeline Guimard moved to their new townhouse on avenue Mozart, Auteuil's population reached 40,000; it doubled again as they were leaving rue Henri-Heine in 1938. Bastioned fortifications dating from the 1840s (not demolished until after 1910) separated the district from the Bois de Boulogne, while a mighty railroad viaduct (fig. 3) dating from the 1860s extended

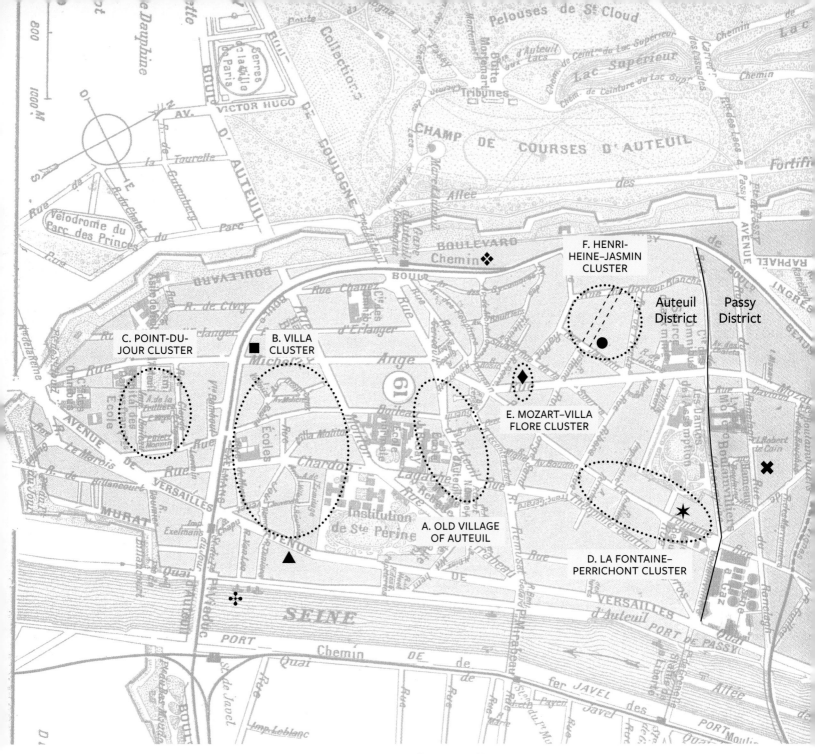

FIG. 1. Map of Auteuil, c. 1899, showing Guimard's residences and clusters of his local buildings.

A. OLD VILLAGE OF AUTEUIL

B. VILLA CLUSTER
Hôtels Roszé, Jassedé, Delfau, 1893–95
Villas Roucher, 1898
Hôtel Deron-Levent, 1905

C. POINT-DU-JOUR CLUSTER
École du Sacré-Cœur, 1895
Dejardin Plant, 1901
Deron-Levent Tomb, 1912

D. LA FONTAINE–PERRICHONT CLUSTER
✶ Castel Béranger, 1897
Ateliers Guimard, 1903
Immeuble Trémois, 1910
Hôtel Mezzara, 1910
Apartment complex, rues La Fontaine, Agar, and Gros, 1910–12

E. MOZART–VILLA FLORE CLUSTER
◆ Hôtel Guimard, 1909–12
Immeuble Houyvet, 1926

F. HENRI-HEINE–JASMIN CLUSTER
Hôtel Nicolle-de-Montjoye, 1914
Industrialized House, 3, square Jasmin, 1922
Garage Bastien, 1922
● Apartment building, 18, rue Henri-Heine, 1926

ADDITIONAL SITES
✛ Grand Neptune café-concert, 1888
❖ Hôtel Roy, 1898
✖ Hôtel Nozal, 1902–6
▲ 147, avenue de Versailles
■ 64, boulevard Exelmans

FIG. 2. Guimard, *Le style Guimard* postcard, number 20, Hôtel Roy, 81, boulevard Suchet, 1898 (demolished), printed 1903. Frédéric Descouturelle, Montreuil-sous-Bois, France.

FIG. 3. Paul Signac, *Viaduct and Bateau-Mouche at Auteuil*, 1927. Watercolor and black crayon on paper.

ISABELLE GOURNAY

along boulevard Exelmans—where Guimard maintained an office in the mid-1890s, at number 64—to the Gare d'Auteuil. Building activity took off around 1892, which entailed widening and straightening various country trails (fig. 4). It is not difficult to picture a twenty-five-year-old Hector Guimard, dapper in top hat, inquiring about opportunities to build along such a modernized street.[7] Auteuil's reconstructed parish church was also consecrated in 1892: fifteen years in construction, this new landmark in the predominantly Catholic district was a compelling example of Romano-Byzantine style (fig. 5). It is not improbable that Guimard met its designer, Émile Vaudremer: Vaudremer was the master of Guimard's own design instructor, Gustave Raulin, and lived until the late 1890s in a house of his own design at 93, boulevard Exelmans.[8]

Auteuil was a land of artistic and financial opportunity for several generations of architects.[9] Guimard's great patron, Léon Nozal, whose commissions ranged from a modern-day chateau on the rue du Ranelagh (officially located in the adjacent quartier de La Muette, but a three-minute walk from Castel Béranger) to suburban warehouses, selected a local colleague for his brother's house-studio (fig. 6): Charles Blanche, an *architecte diplômé*, who had also studied under Raulin. Blanche produced an elegant design for the wedge-shaped site facing

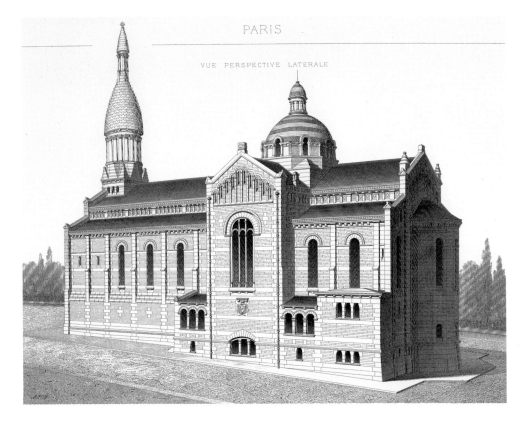

FIG. 4. Jules-Adolphe Chauvet, *Groundbreaking on the Right Side of rue des Perchamps at the Corner of rue d'Auteuil,* April 7, 1892. Lead pencil and white gouache on paper, with the handwritten note at bottom, center, "The streets of the future." Musée Carnavalet, Paris.

FIG. 5. Émile Vaudremer, *Perspective of the Church of Notre-Dame d'Auteuil, Paris,* engraving by Bury, c. 1877–83. DeA Picture Library.

HÔTEL PARTICULIER
Quai d'Auteuil a Paris
Façade sur la Seine

FIG. 6. Charles Blanche, Alexandre Nozal Studio, quai Louis Blériot, Paris, completed 1910.

FIG. 7. Henri Tassu, rue Chapu apartment block at avenue de Versailles, built 1893.

ISABELLE GOURNAY

the river, a scheme reminiscent of the more restrained version of Art Nouveau promoted by Charles Plumet. Designers with no academic training enjoyed local success: the work of Ernest Toutain, a native and resident of Auteuil, evolved, like Guimard's, from single-family houses to apartment buildings.[10] Architect Henri Tassu was active in elegant sections of the 16th and 17th arrondissements and near the Luxembourg Gardens, where he settled in a townhouse of his own design; in 1893, he developed and designed in Auteuil lower-middle-class apartment buildings on either side of the newly opened rue Chapu (fig. 7) between avenue de Versailles and boulevard Exelmans.[11]

Guimard's own buildings and residences gravitated around the relatively untouched historic village at the center of the area.[12] His single-family homes are mostly found in Auteuil's "villa district," which originated with the rustic hameau Boileau and the exclusive Villa Montmorency, both planned by architect Théodore Charpentier. Picturesque houses, which may have been used originally as second homes and escapes from the congestion of central Paris but had mostly become primary residences, lined private streets, typically gated and often ending in culs-de-sac. Restrictive deeds excluded retail enterprises, as well as the industrial activities that had developed in nearby Javel and Billancourt. Large estates dating back to Auteuil's preannexation years that had not been subdivided accommodated retirement and convalescent homes and schools. Greenery was abundant, but, as elsewhere in Auteuil, there were no public gardens. In this villa district, Ernest Toutain and other architects built mansarded homes; many of these residences bore touches of *pierre meulière* (the rough buhrstone so ubiquitous in the Paris suburbs), low stone enclosures, and artistic ironwork, which would be reinterpreted by Guimard in the taut freestanding homes he inserted in this fabric. Paul Sédille raised the artistic bar at Villa Weber (fig. 8), which offers parallels to Guimard's Hôtel Jassedé in its facade composition and fenestration.[13] In addition to promoting polychromy and terracotta, Sédille would have served as an inspiration for Guimard, both as a proponent of

FIG. 8. Paul Sédille, front elevation of Villa Weber, 9–11, rue Erlanger, Paris, 1884. From Pierre Chabat, *La brique et la terre cuite: Étude historique de l'emploi de ces matériaux; fabrication et usages; motifs de construction et de décoration choisis dans l'architecture des différents peuples,* 2nd ser. (Paris: Vᵉ A. Morel et Cie, 1886), plate 66.

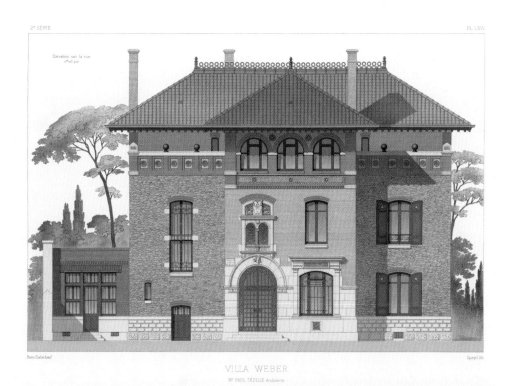

3. — **PARIS-POINT-DU-JOUR.** *Avenue de Versailles, emplacement du Marché.* G. B.

contemporary English architecture and as a campaigner to elevate the prestige of private commissions to the level of those sponsored by the French government.

Beyond the railroad viaduct, a cluster around the Point-du-Jour neighborhood (fig. 9) offered a sharp physical and sociological contrast.[14] Scarred by the Prussian Army siege and the Paris Commune of 1870–71, this former hamlet interspersed vernacular housing with small factories, such as one designed by Guimard that produced blood-orange syrup.[15] Another commission was the fittingly industrial-looking, economically built École du Sacré-Cœur, which was not a full-time school but an organization (a *patronage*) that taught catechism and provided activities for local boys. These youths may have lived in the small houses in the nearby Villa Mulhouse, Auteuil's singular foray into well-designed, low-density working-class housing.[16] The local bourgeoisie on the other side of the viaduct ventured into this lower-class area to visit its intimate walled cemetery. Originally located in front of the parish church in the old village, this graveyard contained the tomb of Guimard's client Charles Deron-Levent, a collaboration between the architect and his avenue Perrichont neighbor sculptress Jeanne Itasse.[17]

Guimard's contribution to Auteuil's growth was most significant in a cluster centered on rue La Fontaine (fig. 10) close to the Pont de Grenelle, where he designed eight apartment buildings and a townhouse as well as his own workshop. Irregular in contour and heterogeneous in land use, this old road was an unpretentious, leafy foil for Castel Béranger, where Guimard dared to adopt the rustic mix of brick and *pierre meulière* at a much larger scale than in Auteuil's villa district. Guillaume Apollinaire (who moved to rue Gros to be close to his beloved, the painter Marie Laurencin, who herself lived at numbers 10 and 32, rue La Fontaine) described the nearby gas factory (currently Maison de la

FIG. 9. Postcard showing the open-market area on avenue de Versailles in Auteuil's Point-du-Jour section, c. 1900. The market still operates there today. The Richard H. Driehaus Museum Archives, Chicago.

ISABELLE GOURNAY

8. PARIS XVIe. — Rue de la Fontaine
prise du Rond-Point de Boulainvilliers

Ch. Barillot, Paris

FIG. 10. Postcard showing rue La Fontaine, c. 1900; on the right is the tree-lined block where Castel Béranger was built. The Richard H. Driehaus Museum Archives, Chicago.

radio) in his *Le flâneur des deux rives* (The flaneur along two riverbanks) of 1918: "mountains of coal," gigantic chimney stacks ablaze at night, and vegetable gardens. The poet also described a "courtyard cluttered with statues and roaming chickens" at the Municipal Fine Arts Repository, across from Castel Béranger. Further along rue La Fontaine was a compound occupied by a Catholic charity housing and training working-class orphans, well known in Guimard's years for its gymnastics pageants.[18] The adjacent rue Ribéra, ascending toward avenue Mozart, was the "fiefdom" of architect Jean-Marie Boussard, a master of bombastic eclecticism.[19] Across from the avenue Perrichont workshops, Joachim Richard settled in an apartment building where he layered Guimard's cast-iron balconies over concrete trabeation in a striking manner; in 1923, he joined Guimard in the Groupe des architectes modernes.[20]

Auteuil, despite its many streets named after painters and sculptors, was not an avant-garde mecca like Montmartre or Montparnasse, while established artists preferred building house-studios in the 17th arrondissement. While Paul Signac moved to Castel Béranger primarily for its cheap rents and comfort,[21] another early tenant, architect Pierre Selmersheim, was attuned to, and inspired by, Guimard's work.[22] Literary neighbors included Xavier Privas, the "prince of songwriters," and Pierre Louÿs. In 1896, Fernand Mazade settled at 17, rue de Boulainvilliers: it is possible that simple neighborliness explains why this poet, with no known connection to architects, or to America, wrote articles on the work of Guimard and others for the *Architectural Record*.[23]

Avenue Mozart was the only thoroughfare Baron Haussmann had envisioned for Auteuil; even so, it was a modest enterprise compared with boulevard Malesherbes, where Adeline Oppenheim lived before her marriage.[24] In the miniature cluster formed

33. PARIS — Rue d'Auteuil - Place du Marché

by his own townhouse and the Immeuble Houyvet, Guimard rose to the challenge of not only maximizing impossibly narrow footprints but celebrating the corner sites by means of an original wall treatment and decorative syntax. His arrival at the southern end of avenue Mozart coincided with those of the Métropolitain two blocks away and of popular entertainment in the form of the Mozart Palace, a 1,300-seat movie palace next to the Michel Ange–Auteuil station.[25] Ernest Herscher designed an elegant apartment building between Guimard's townhouse-office and this new transit and commercial hub (fig. 11), its top floor clearly inspired by the latter; both architects belonged to the Société du Nouveau-Paris, a group that placed a premium on expressive balconies.[26]

While avenue Mozart and its streetcar line embodied belle epoque vibrancy, the newly opened rue Henri-Heine, where Guimard designed his most upscale apartment building, had no trees, shops, or through traffic. His effort to counteract the safe, even sedate, elegance that well-heeled residents of the manicured residential areas were beginning to favor informed other buildings at the intersection with rue Jasmin: the prewar Telephone Exchange Building designed by Paul Guadet, himself an Auteuil resident, and adjoining designs by Pol Abraham, another member of the Groupe des architectes modernes.[27] As Auteuil's last frontier of exclusivity, this cluster presented an intriguing paradox: while Guimard was intent on demonstrating his solution for low-cost construction at square Jasmin,[28] nearby upscale residences by Le Corbusier and Robert Mallet-Stevens responded to the neighborhood's snob appeal.

FIG. 11. Postcard showing the intersection of rue d'Auteuil and rue Michel Ange, two blocks from Hôtel Guimard, c. 1910, just before the arrival of the Métro and construction of a movie palace. The striking steeple of Émile Vaudremer's Notre-Dame d'Auteuil rises in the background. The small triangular plaza on the left still hosts a biweekly market. The Richard H. Driehaus Museum Archives, Chicago.

ISABELLE GOURNAY

Imaginative and buoyant, yet never estranged from their surroundings, Guimard's works were clustered in multiple Auteuils with specific growth patterns and visual and social identities to which he responded and reshaped in return. He was influenced—professionally, typologically, and in terms of decoration—by the work of architects active in the same clusters; at the same time, he provided incentives for forward-looking designs by others. In Auteuil, as Guillaume Apollinaire almost says in his famous "Le pont Mirabeau" of 1912:

> Vienne la nuit sonne l'heure
> Les jours s'en vont Guimard demeure
> (Comes the night sounds the hour
> The days go by Guimard endures)

NOTES

1. It may be an exaggeration to assert, like Claude Frontisi did [in "Hector Guimard entre deux siècles," *Vingtième siècle, revue d'histoire* 17 (Jan.–March 1988): 61], that Guimard was the "prisoner of a geographic area"; it is certain, however, that he enjoyed few opportunities for commercial and religious commissions and none for government buildings.

2. Such an approach helps explain why, in bourgeois Auteuil, Guimard's Métro entrances, which would have been considered his trademark by most early twentieth-century Parisians, were standardized and rather inconspicuous—a far cry from Guimard's iconic Porte Dauphine pavilion, which was located at the end of the ultraexclusive avenue du Bois (currently Foch) and led Métro riders through the bastioned 1840s fortifications toward the grandest entrance to the Bois de Boulogne.

3. The abbreviation *NAP* refers to the upper-class districts of Neuilly-sur-Seine, Auteuil, and Passy and implies that the subject has been born with a silver spoon in his or her mouth.

4. *The Adams Family in Auteuil, 1784–1785: As Told in the Letters of Abigail Adams*, ed. Howard C. Rice Jr. (Boston: Massachusetts Historical Society, 1956), accessed November 22, 2019, https://archive.org/details/adamsfamilyinaut00adam.

5. Designed by Charles Dupuy, who lived near the Trocadéro, this daycare is discussed in *L'architecture* 10, no. 40 (October 20, 1897): 362–63.

6. Léo Claretie, "Le Far West de Paris," *Société historique d'Auteuil et de Passy: Première exposition d'histoire et d'archéologie du XVIᵉ arrondissement au Musée Guimet (du 1ᵉʳ au 27 juin 1904)* (Paris: à la bibliothèque de la société, 1905), p. iii; Auguste Doniol, *Histoire du XVIᵉ arrondissement de Paris* (Paris: Hachette, 1902), 167. From 1878 to 1888, Auteuil's elected municipal councilor was an architect, Léopold Cernesson.

7. For a photograph of a top-hatted, lean-looking Guimard in front of Castel Béranger, see Philippe Thiébaut et al., *Guimard,* exh. cat. (Paris: Gallimard/Réunion des musées nationaux, 1992), 166.

8. See Alice Thomine, *Émile Vaudremer 1829–1914* (Paris: Picard, 2004), 156–57. Vaudremer moved near the Palais du Trocadéro; Charles Girault, designer of the Petit Palais, and Auguste Perret lived nearby, like Vaudremer, in apartment buildings of their own design.

9. For a systematic study of architects working in the western suburbs of Paris, including Guimard, see C. Jubelin-Boulmer, F. Hamon, D. Hervier, and P. Ayrault, *Hommes et métiers du bâtiment, 1860–1940: L'exemple des Hauts-de-Seine*, Cahiers du patrimoine 59 (Paris: Éditions du patrimoine, 2001).

10. For a substantial listing of Ernest Toutain's work, see Anne Dugast and Isabelle Parizet, *Dictionnaire par noms d'architectes des constructions élevées à Paris aux XIXᵉ et XXᵉ siècles: Première série, période 1876–1899*, 5 vols. (Paris: Service des travaux historiques de la Ville de Paris, 1990–2003), 4:108–9. Toutain lived at 32, rue Molitor and 4, rue Erlanger. Several of his Auteuil houses and stables were published in J. Lacroux and C. Détain, *Constructions en briques: La brique ordinaire au point de vue décoratif* (Paris: Ducher et Cie, 1878). The fine 1913 apartment building designed with his son Edmond at 133, boulevard Exelmans (backing on boulevard Murat) is illustrated in Gaston Lefol, *Immeubles modernes de Paris: Facades-plans-sculptures* (Paris: Ch. Massin, 1928), plates 56–58.

11 On rue Chapu, see Doniol, *Histoire du XVIe arrondissement*, 224. Tassu (see listing in Dugast and Parizet, *Dictionnaire par noms*, 4:100) is remembered for his opulent 1906 block on rues Spontini, Benjamin Godard, and Mony in the Porte Dauphine district of the 16th arrondissement. Maxime Decommer illustrates Tassu's townhouse on rue le Verrier in his discussion of the live-work accommodations of Guimard and his peers; Decommer, *Les architectes au travail: L'institutionnalisation d'une profession, 1795–1940* (Rennes: Presses Universitaires de Rennes, 2017), 234.

12 Supervised by the Société historique d'Auteuil et de Passy, to which he applied for membership in 1892, Guimard assembled remains from the old church in the parish presbytery, as illustrated in Georges Vigne, *Hector Guimard: Architect, Designer, 1867–1942* (New York: Delano Greenidge Editions, 2003), 52.

13 Charles Naudet, who lived at 71, rue d'Auteuil, was also active on rue Erlanger. See Lacroux and Détain, *Constructions en briques*, plate 31, and Dugast and Parizet, *Dictionnaire par noms*, 4:7.

14 Architect Charles Devinant lived on rue Claude Lorrain. Associated with Boulogne-based Henri Désiré Poigin, he was active throughout Auteuil from about 1880 to 1905. See Thiébaut et al., *Guimard* (exh. cat.), 57, for an Art Nouveau detail by Devinant's firm at 77, rue Boileau. See also Dugast and Parizet, *Dictionnaire par noms*, 2:28–29.

15 From 1873 to 1882, Haviland maintained a ceramic workshop at 116, rue Michel Ange, and Maximilien Luce (who also painted the Viaduc d'Auteuil) lived at 102, rue Boileau around 1900. In 1914, Auguste Perret completed a house-studio for Théo Van Rysselberghe, at 14, rue Claude Lorrain (see drawings, Cité de l'architecture et du patrimoine, Objet PERAU-063; https://archiwebture.citedelarchitecture.fr/fonds/FRAPN02_PERAU/inventaire/objet-7770, accessed November 22, 2019), which has been much altered.

16 See essays by Françoise Hamon, "Maisons ouvrières," and Pauline Prévost-Marcilhacy, "Villa Mulhouse," in Isabelle Montserrat Farguell and Virginie Grandval, eds., *Hameaux, villas et cités de Paris* (Paris: Action artistique de la Ville de Paris, 1998), 166–70 and 182–85; Marie-Jeanne Dumont [*Le logement social à Paris 1850–1930: Les habitations à bon marché* (Liège: Mardaga, 1991), 179] mentions only two examples of social housing in the 16th arrondissement (53, rue Chardon Lagache and 87, rue Boileau), both of 1911.

17 See Vigne, *Hector Guimard*, 328. Itasse was born the same year as Guimard and died a year earlier. In 1893, her work was exhibited at the Women's Building at the World's Columbian Exposition in Chicago.

18 See Maxime Du Camp, "La charité privée à Paris," pt. 4, "L'orphelinat des apprentis," *Revue des deux mondes* 58, no. 3 (August 1, 1883): 578–612, where this well-known writer, like many outside observers, predicted the complete demise of historic Auteuil. This foundation (see https://www.apprentis-auteuil.org/) still exists on the premises.

19 Boussard (see Dugast and Parizet, *Dictionnaire par noms*, 1:64–65), whose office is recorded at 26, rue Ribéra in 1888 and 38, rue Ribéra in 1891, also worked for the postal administration and was a regular contributor to *Le moniteur des architectes*. His "protected" apartment buildings—on rue Ribéra; 5, rue Dangeau; 76–78, avenue Mozart; and 1, rue de l'Yvette—all near Guimard's last two residences, are concisely but ably appraised in *Protections patrimoniales: 16ème arrondissement* (downloadable at http://pluenligne.paris.fr/plu/sites-plu/site_statique_37/pages/page_783.html). The apartment buildings at 8ter, rue La Fontaine near Castel Béranger and at 64, rue La Fontaine, adjacent to Guimard's Hôtel Mezzara, are surprisingly restrained examples of the work of Gustave Rives. An architect employed by the Département de la Seine, François-Albert Allain, was a longtime resident of 6, rue La Fontaine; he performed odd jobs and designed small structures in Auteuil, tasks Guimard also resorted to when other employment sources were limited.

20   A student of both Victor Laloux and Anatole de Baudot, Richard had lived on rue du Ranelagh since the late 1890s. The 1906 *hôtel particulier* he designed with Eugène Audiger at 40, rue Boileau for painter Lucien Simon has been altered for the worse. See *Joachim Richard: Notice biographique (Mathilde Dion); Notice sur le fonds et sur l'architecte (Éric Furlan),* Cité de l'architecture et du patrimoine; https://archiwebture.citedelarchitecture.fr/pdf/asso/FRAPN02_RICJO_BIO.pdf, accessed November 22, 2019.

21   See Philippe Thiébaut, "Art nouveau et néo-impressionnisme: Les ateliers de Signac," *Revue d'art* 92 (1991): 72–78.

22   Guimard's influence on Pierre Selmersheim, who was enrolled at the École des Beaux-Arts in the same years and whose younger brother Tony was an interior designer and collaborator of Charles Plumet, is noticeable in Selmersheim's fireplace and house porch designs, published in Victor Champier, *Documents d'atelier: Art décoratif moderne* (Paris: Librairie de la revue des arts décoratifs et industriels, 1898); and Champier, *Modèles nouveaux pour les industries d'art . . .* (Paris: Librairie de la revue des arts décoratifs et industriels, 1899). (Found in the Selmersheim files, Documentation, Musée d'Orsay.) Pierre's wife, Jeanne, a painter, would leave him for Signac.

23   In *Architectural Record,* Mazade wrote "A French Dining Room of the Upper Middle-Class Type," July–September 1895, 33–34; "Sculpture as Applied to the External Decorations of Paris Houses," October 1896, 134–43; "An 'Art Nouveau' Edifice in Paris: The Humbert de Romans Building: Hector Guimard, Architecte," May 1902, 53–66; "The Mairies of Paris," April 1898, 401–25; and "Living in Paris on an Income of $3000 a Year," pt. 1, April 1903, 349–57, pt. 2, May 1903, 423–32, pt. 3, June 1903, 548–54.

24   Because it was lined with trees for its entire length, rue Mozart became avenue Mozart in 1911.

25   The Mozart Palace has been transformed into a Monoprix.

26   A 1898 École des Beaux-Arts *diplômé,* Herscher lived near the Trocadéro, where his best-known and more ornate Art Nouveau apartment building is located at 39, rue Scheffer.

27   In the 1925 *hôtel particulier* directly adjacent to Guimard's apartment building, Félix Dumail and Jean Hébrard were markedly uninspired by the eighteenth-century "néo-Gabriel" idiom upon which their client must have insisted.

28   See Barry Bergdoll's essay in this publication, "Signature vs. Standardization: Guimard and Prefabrication."

Visionary Architect

Guimard's architecture may be considered modern, even radical, in France in two specific ways: first, in the conceptualization of exterior architecture, interior architecture, and the decorative arts as an integrated whole; and second, in the rejection of classicism and incorporation of forms based on nature and new materials. His revolutionary approach earned him the nickname "Ravachol of Architecture," after a notorious French anarchist.

Along with Hôtel Guimard, two key works designed by Guimard—Castel Béranger and Castel Henriette—demonstrate a dedication to the *Gesamtkunstwerk*, or total work of art. This overall unity of exterior and interior was sought more by architects in other parts of Europe, such as Charles Rennie Mackintosh in Scotland, than by Guimard's contemporaries in France. For these three buildings, Guimard designed everything the client's budget permitted, from doorknobs to wallpaper. The objects that have survived, as well as photographs and drawings, help to re-create Guimard's original intent. In later commercial investment properties, however, Guimard had to settle for less of his signature style on the interiors.

Architecturally, Guimard was always an advocate for modernism and maintained that the classical style he learned in school was primarily useful for the education of young architects. Guimard's architecture evolved from the wild gestures of Castel Béranger to the controlled appearance of Hôtel Guimard. After World War I, Guimard abandoned the decorative arts, which had been so important to the oneness of his earlier work, and focused on the technical aspects of architecture, such as the construction systems he developed for mass housing.

Photograph of building exterior, plate 1 from *Le Castel Béranger*, 1898. The Collection of Richard H. Driehaus, Chicago.

Castel Béranger

14, rue La Fontaine, Paris, constructed 1895–97

Guimard was twenty-seven in 1894 when he received the commission for Castel Béranger, named for the popular poet and songwriter Pierre-Jean de Béranger. Client Anne-Elisabeth Fournier, a widow interested in an investment property, engaged Guimard to design a rental apartment building with thirty-six units at 14, rue La Fontaine in Auteuil. Castel Béranger was Guimard's first large-scale project, and one of his most important. The project comprises three main structures around an interior court. On the ground floor were boutiques, private apartments, and Guimard's own office and studio (illustrated in a *Le style Guimard* postcard; see Thiébaut, "The First Gesture," fig. 1); on the sixth floor, artists' studios and maids' rooms. Built between 1895 and 1897 in the Art Nouveau style, Castel Béranger is picturesque, with an asymmetrical arrangement of rich materials. In 1899, the building won a Facade Competition award from the City of Paris. Among the materials used are brick, stone, cast iron, and stained glass.

Inside, Guimard designed a wide range of fittings, including wallpaper. The complete set of drawings is preserved in the Guimard archives at the Musée d'Orsay. In addition to depictions of the architecture, the collection contains drawings for the interior decorative elements.

DAVID A. HANKS

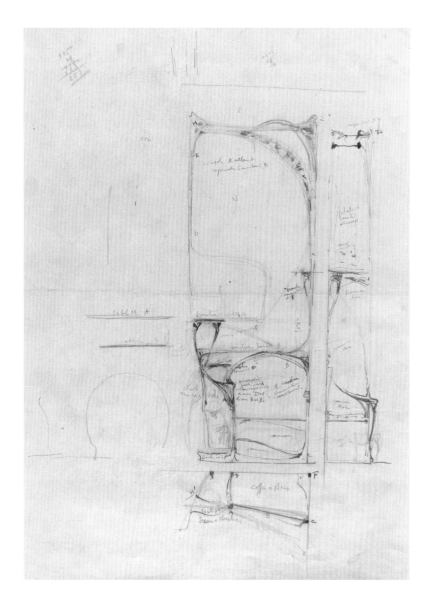

26
Sketch for Interior of the Salon (Wall with Fireplace) for Castel Béranger
c. 1897–98
Pencil and red ink on tracing paper
19¹¹⁄₁₆ × 14⁹⁄₁₆ in. (50 × 37 cm)
MUSÉE D'ORSAY, PARIS, GP 553

VISIONARY ARCHITECT

CP 554

27
Sketch for Interior of the Salon (Wall with Fireplace)
for Castel Béranger
c. 1897–98
Pencil and red ink on tracing paper
18 × 23⁷⁄₁₆ in. (45.7 × 59.5 cm)
MUSÉE D'ORSAY, PARIS, GP 554

28 (*overleaf*)
Elevation of Entry Gate for Castel Béranger
July 1896
Black and red ink on tracing paper
13¹³⁄₁₆ × 25³⁄₁₆ in. (35.1 × 63.9 cm)
MUSÉE D'ORSAY, PARIS, GP 424

Vue de la Porte   Vue de la Grille

Elevation

d 0.05 par Metre

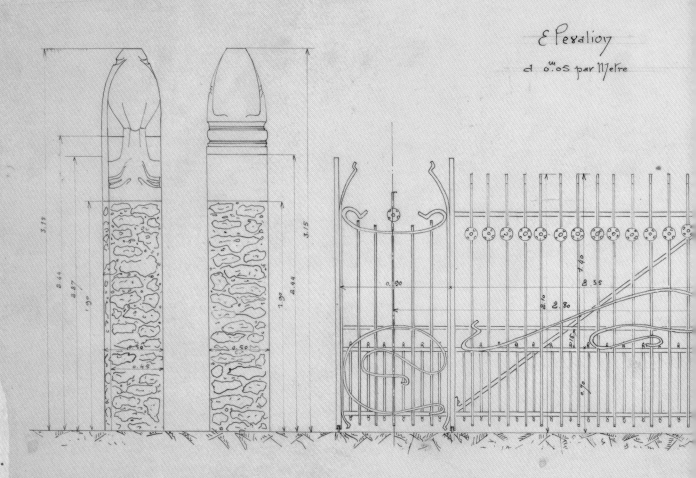

taine

Hameau

Coupe
sur le mur bahut

0.47

0.62

0.60

0.65
0.60

1.25

2.299

7.60

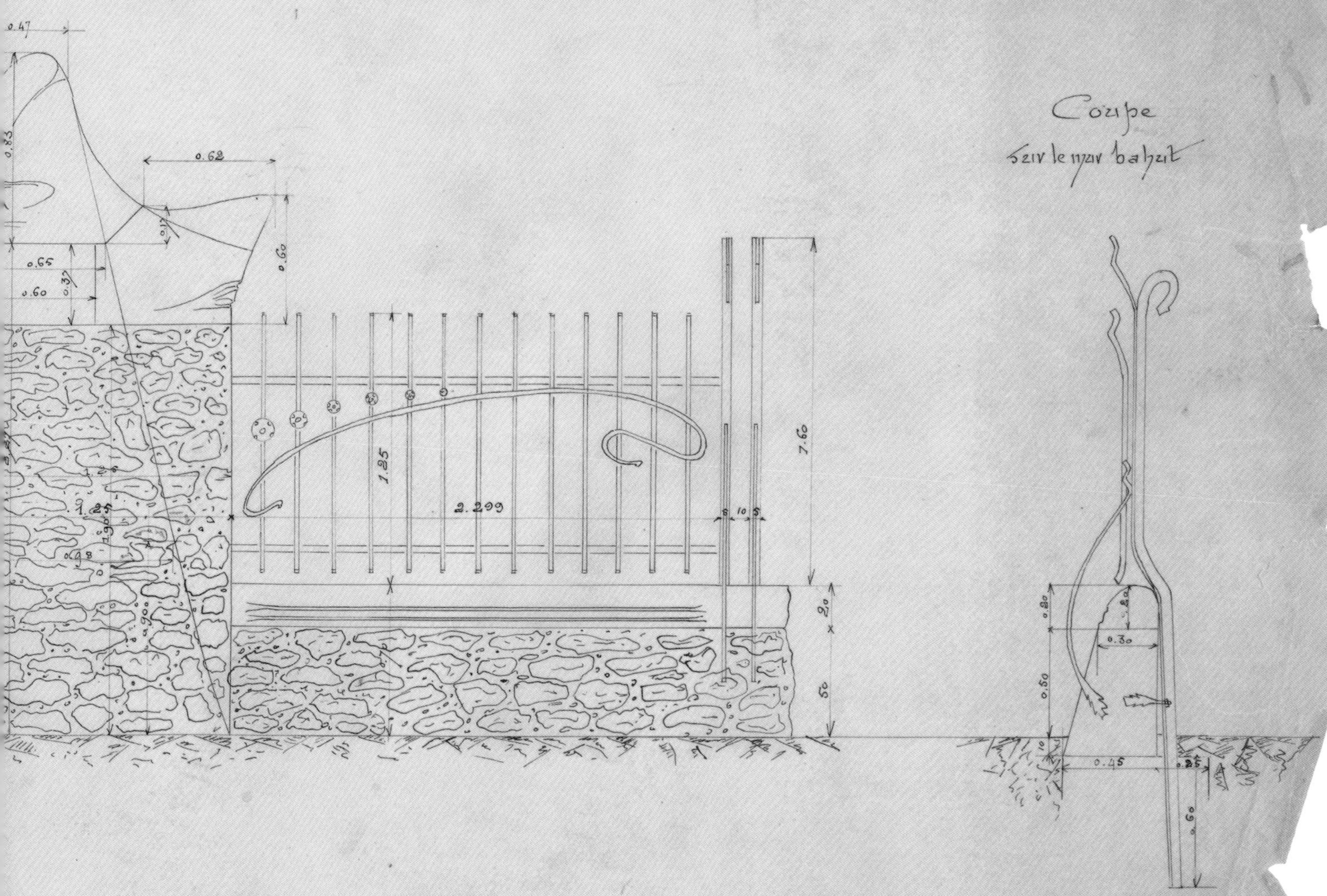

Paris le Juillet 1896.

l'Architecte:

Hector Guimard

Guimard's most important furniture design was his own desk, which consists of two pedestal cabinets positioned at a right angle and supporting an asymmetrical, free-form top. The cabinets are embellished with shaped panels and drawers. He used an armchair as his desk chair. Shown in one of Guimard's famous postcards of 1903—the view of the architect's Castel Béranger studio—the desk exemplifies the new, abstract Art Nouveau.

In 1910, he moved the desk to a first-floor studio in Hôtel Guimard, and when the Guimards immigrated to New York in 1938, the aging and sick architect ensured that the prized desk was shipped with their belongings. Guimard said, in an 1899 interview with Victor Champier, "When I design a piece of furniture or sculpt it, I reflect upon the spectacle of the universe. . . . For construction do not the branches of trees, the stems, by turn rigid and undulating,

furnish us with models? . . . These dominant lines that describe space, sometimes supple and sinuous arabesques, sometimes flourishes as vivid as the firing of a thunderbolt, these lines have a value of feeling and expression more eloquent than the vertical, horizontal, and regular lines continually used until now in architecture."

D. A. H.

29
Hector Guimard's Desk
c. 1899
Olive wood, ash, metal
28¾ × 101 × 47¾ in.
(73 × 256.5 × 121.3 cm)
THE MUSEUM OF MODERN ART,
GIFT OF MME HECTOR GUIMARD,
310.1949.A–C

31
Espagnolette
1897–98
Gilt bronze
7 × 2 × 4 in.
(17.8 × 5.1 × 10.2 cm)
THE COLLECTION OF RICHARD H.
DRIEHAUS, CHICAGO, 20263

32
Doorknob
1897–98
Porcelain, metal
3 × 2 × 2 in.
(7.6 × 5.1 × 5.1 cm)
THE COLLECTION OF RICHARD H.
DRIEHAUS, CHICAGO, 20045

30 (*opposite*)
Hector Guimard's Armchair
c. 1899–1900
Walnut, leather
32³⁄₈ × 30³⁄₄ × 21 in. (82.3 × 78.1 × 53.3 cm)
THE MUSEUM OF MODERN ART, GIFT OF MME HECTOR GUIMARD,
311.1949

As part of his quest for a total unified interior—a lifelong goal for the architect—Guimard developed four Art Nouveau wallpapers for the Castel Béranger apartments, one for each room type—living room, dining room, bedroom, and vestibule—as well as a Lincrusta (embossed wall covering) design for the dining room. All five compositions are illustrated in the *Le Castel Béranger* portfolio; in addition, the Lincrusta example is shown in a catalogue for the Lincrusta-Walton company.

The wallpaper designs were a remarkable departure from the elaborate, realistic floral patterns of the day. The most exuberant of Guimard's patterns incorporate repeated whiplash curves, an abstract motif inspired by a similar design in Victor Horta's Hôtel Tassel, which Guimard visited in 1895. The same swooping motifs are repeated throughout Castel Béranger—in the wrought-iron entrance gate, stained-glass windows, and papier-mâché ceiling decoration—in the service of unity of design. The wallpapers were manufactured by the Parisian firm le Mardelé by means of an artisanal printing technique, not mechanical production. Although none of the papers survives in Castel Béranger, three original examples are preserved in the Bibliothèque Fornay in Paris, and two of the designs have been reissued.

D. A. H.

33
Lincrusta Wall Panel for Castel Béranger
c. 1896–98
Linoleum
39 × 23⅝ in. (99 × 60 cm)
Produced by Lincrusta-Walton, Pierrefitte, France
MUSÉE D'ORSAY, PARIS, OAO 481

34
Wallpaper for Castel Béranger
c. 1898
Machine printed
49¾ × 18½ in. (126.5 × 47 cm)
ALAIN BLONDEL, GARCHES,
FRANCE

35
Plate 45 from *Le Castel
Béranger,* Showing Wallpaper
1898
Hand-painted photo-mechanical
collotype and bronze paint
on paper
17 × 12³⁄₈ in. (43.2 × 31.4 cm)
Published by Librairie Rouam
et Cie, Paris
THE COLLECTION OF RICHARD H.
DRIEHAUS, CHICAGO, 140138.A

36
Plate 44 from *Le Castel
Béranger*, Showing Lincrusta
Wall Covering
1898
Hand-painted photo-mechanical
collotype and bronze paint
on paper
12³⁄₈ × 17 in. (31.4 × 43.2 cm)
Published by Librairie Rouam
et Cie, Paris
THE COLLECTION OF RICHARD H.
DRIEHAUS, CHICAGO, 140138.A

Pl. 44

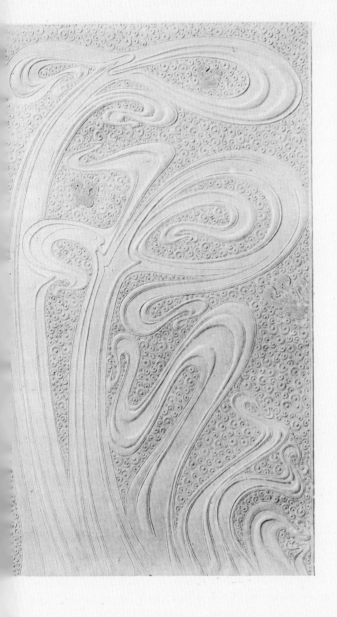

Castel Henriette

46, rue des Binelles, Sèvres, 1899 (demolished 1969)

Castel Henriette was a picturesque stone-clad villa designed in 1899 for Caroline Henriette Hefty, a widow who lived in the neighborhood of another of Guimard's designs, Hôtel Roy. In addition to the building, the project included a garden, garage, small chalet, plus access roads and an artificial grotto and stream, all devised by the architect. The plans for Castel Henriette, dated August 1, 1899, are in the Guimard archives at the Musée d'Orsay. The tower was removed after a violent storm in 1903; Guimard made other changes to the building at the same time. The house was demolished in 1969, on the eve of the Art Nouveau revival, although furniture and architectural fragments have been preserved in museums and private collections.

The exterior of the castlelike residence was asymmetrical and complex; the flexible interior was decorated by Guimard between 1900 and 1903 to achieve a complete unity. Rustic materials, such as stone and abundant cast iron, appear on the facades, which, like the interior, strive for unity. Guimard signed the house twice and also designed the graphic name of the house on a signpost of glazed lava, now in the Musée d'Orsay. A side chair in the dining room relates to other furnishings in the room. Guimard devoted three *Le style Guimard* postcards to this commission, an indication of its importance to him.

D. A. H.

Postcard no. 6 from *Le style Guimard* series, "Castel Henriette à Sèvres," 1903. Nicolas Horiot, Auberville, France.

37 (opposite)
Door Plate from
Castel Henriette
c. 1900
Enameled ceramic and
lava stone
$43\,^5/_{16} \times 42\,^3/_{16}$ in.
(110 × 107.2 cm)
MUSÉE D'ORSAY, PARIS, OA01268

38
Fence Section from Castel Henriette
1899–1903
Wrought iron
45½ × 48½ × 6 in. (115.6 × 123.2 × 15.2 cm)
THE MUSEUM OF MODERN ART, GIFT OF JOSEPH H. HEIL, BY EXCHANGE,
AND AGNES GUND, 960.2010

Dining Room, Castel Henriette. Musée des arts décoratifs, Paris.

39 (*opposite*)
Side Chair
1900–1903
Walnut, tooled leather, gilding
38⅛ × 18⅛ × 21 in. (96.8 × 46 × 53.3 cm)
THE COLLECTION OF RICHARD H. DRIEHAUS, CHICAGO, 2017.142

40
Doorbell Plate
1900–1903
Gilt bronze
2³⁄₈ × 2 × 2 in. (6 × 5.1 × 5.1 cm)
THE COLLECTION OF RICHARD H. DRIEHAUS, CHICAGO, 20156

41
Door Handle
1900
Gilt bronze
3½ × 4 × 4 in. (8.9 × 10.2 × 10.2 cm)
THE COLLECTION OF RICHARD H. DRIEHAUS, CHICAGO, 20168

The First Gesture
Philippe Thiébaut

His drawing board is an inextinguishable crucible.
  —Alain Blondel and Yves Plantin, "Le monde plastique de Guimard"

The celebrated set of *Le style Guimard* postcards published by Hector Guimard in 1903, at the time of the Housing Exhibition, included among the building photographs of private commissions only one interior view. The subject of card number 10 was the architect in his office, situated since June 1897 in Castel Béranger (fig. 1).[1] The evocative power of this image is considerable. Not only does it constitute an essential document in any study of Guimard's professional surroundings, it also puts viewers in direct contact with his practice and his imagination. Seated at his drafting table, pencil in hand, could the artist perhaps be in the very act of drawing one of the curved lines that gave rise to the organic evolution of the furnishings of the room (fig. 2)?

The layout of the Guimard studio corresponds perfectly to the plans that have been preserved in the archive of the Musée d'Orsay.[2] The desk was composed of a large, free-form work surface supported by cabinets at either end; a drafting table was attached to the work surface. When he transferred his office to his townhouse at 122, avenue Mozart in 1910, Guimard made radical changes to the desk, which was given to the Museum of Modern Art in New York by Adeline Guimard in 1949.[3] At Castel Béranger, the office was set up on the ground floor of the main building and opened onto both rue La Fontaine and the hamlet Béranger. Another room, with views of the hamlet through three windows, housed the workshop. Given the relatively small space, there could not have been many workers, possibly three at most. Later, at avenue Mozart, they would work in another ground-floor studio, this one with windows looking out on Villa Flore. According to the drawings that accompanied the request for a building permit for 122, avenue Mozart, filed in June 1909, three or four stations were planned for a drafting room that would connect to Guimard's office, situated at the corner of the building.[4] Thus, the layout replicated that of Castel Béranger. Indeed, despite the existence of his workshops on avenue Perrichont, Guimard wanted to keep his team of draftsmen nearby so that he could communicate with them at any time of day. Such a choice for the daily work environment signals the importance of drawing in the architect's creative process.

Drawing had played a fundamental role in Guimard's education.[5] He had been affected by the teaching at the École des arts décoratifs—the success he achieved there shows that the course of study suited him to perfection—to such a degree that at the École des Beaux-Arts he enrolled in the atelier of Gustave Raulin, no doubt because Raulin was also an alumnus of the École des arts décoratifs. Guimard himself was to join the faculty there in 1891. In 1890, the École des arts décoratifs merged with the École nationale de dessin pour les jeunes filles, on rue de Seine, founded in 1803, which led to a reorganization of the curriculum. Louvrier de Lajolais, the director at the time, split the courses,

FIG. 1. Guimard, *Le style Guimard* postcard, number 10, showing the architect in his office at Castel Béranger, 1903. Cooper Hewitt, Smithsonian Design Museum, New York.

FIG. 2. Guimard, furniture plan for the Guimard office at Castel Béranger, 14, rue La Fontaine. Black lead and ink on tracing paper. Musée d'Orsay, Paris.

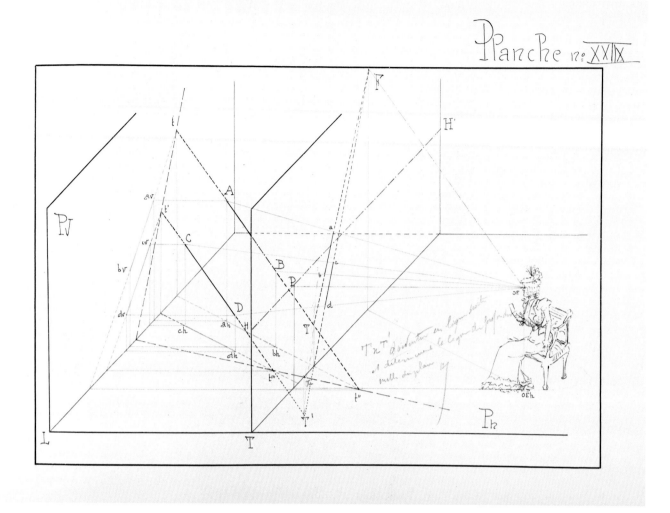

and entrusted geometric and perspective drawing to Guimard, who took up his functions at the beginning of the fall semester in 1891 (fig. 3).

In 1896, he was charged with instructing the young men as well. Two years later, given the demands of his career, and the refusal of school administrators to assign him a teaching assistant, he gave up the course for young women. Two years later still, he ceased all teaching activity: he resigned from the school, to the great regret of the administrators, on July 21, 1900.[6]

The extensive archive of Guimard's firm affords an exceptional abundance of material through which to understand his drawing. Less than a month after the end of World War I, the architect asked Paul Léon, the director of civil monuments at the Ministry of Fine Arts, whether Léon could lend him some sheds adjacent to the former *orangerie* of the estate of Saint-Cloud. In a 1918 letter he wrote: "The art workshops that I had on avenue Perrichont for research for my work have been such an expense to me that I was obliged to close them at the beginning of the war, and today I must immediately clean out the premises. These sheds would help me avoid difficulties and permit me to safely store the things that I must move out."[7] There the collection, consisting of 2,285 items, would stay for approximately four decades.

In fact, it would have been impossible to move the drawings and models stored in these workshops, the work of more than twenty years of activity, to his house on avenue

FIG. 3. Alice Cathalifaud (known 1898–1906), sketch from Perspective and Shadow course taught by Hector Guimard to the women's division at the École des arts décoratifs, 1898. Ink on paper. Musée d'Orsay, Paris.

PHILIPPE THIÉBAUT

Mozart. The rediscovery of the trove in 1968 is due to Alain Blondel and Yves Plantin. As early as 1959, while students in the atelier of Louis Arretche at the École des Beaux-Arts, the two young men set out on the trail of Guimard. At a symposium organized in 1992, at the time of the landmark exhibition at the Musée d'Orsay, where the drawings are now preserved,[8] they described their unearthing of these hundreds of rolls of drawings: "We contacted the administration of the park. The building in question—a gardener's shed—that was soon going to be torn down, had just been cleaned out. Luckily, an official, having noticed that certain rolls of drawings 'reminded him of the Métro,' had piled them up temporarily in the boiler room of the administration buildings."[9] Between the Orsay archive and the gifts made by Mme Guimard to various American institutions, the drawings and other materials are extensive and exceptionally important in understanding Guimard's career—even though, as he once declared to Victor Horta: "As you know, with me, architecture isn't drawn, it is built."[10]

It is necessary to be aware of the context of Guimard's letter to Horta in order to avoid misunderstanding the meaning of that declaration. Guimard was alluding to the drawings that he had executed after Horta's engravings related to the Hôtel Tassel. Guimard would exhibit these works at the Salon de la Société nationale des Beaux-Arts in 1896 along with sketches he made during a study trip funded by the Ministry of Public Education and the École des Beaux-Arts the previous summer. From Guimard's point of view, there was no doubt that formulating a creative idea required the support of graphic activity. That conviction, in fact, led Guimard to call himself "*architecte d'art.*"[11] He was thereby claiming not only for himself, but for architects in general, the right to create with a freedom comparable to that accorded to painters, poets, and musicians. Architecture was, according to him, like the other arts, a field of creation open to the artistic imagination. Furthermore, he claimed for architecture the right to express feelings. Indeed, feeling is the third principle, after logic and harmony, that guided his architectural practice, as he declared in 1899 in "La renaissance de l'art dans l'architecture moderne," his famous talk at Salon du Figaro, given in conjunction with an exhibition at the newspaper.[12] Feeling is the principle that, related to emotion, permitted Guimard to take the first step toward art, taking for his medium a pencil.

The drawings in the various archives cover architecture, interior decoration, and furniture. Diverse in nature (plans, elevations, prints, tracings, hand-marked blueprints, spontaneous sketches), they allow scholars to follow the genesis of the most famous projects—Castel Béranger, Castel Henriette, the Humbert de Romans concert hall, the Métro entranceways (fig. 4), Hôtel Nozal—from the first rough sketch all the way to the final sheets given to the contractors, manufacturers, and craftsmen. The drawings also provide details about some lesser-known projects—the Coutolleau gun shop in Angers and the Melrose tearoom in Paris, for example—or unfinished ones, such as the Champs-Élysées garden or the Folk High School in the 15th arrondissement. A comprehensive analysis of the drawings is the subject for a book, not an essay. Even so, a study of Guimard's distinctive line, a key component of his creative process, illuminates one of the major features of *le style Guimard.*

A significant change to Guimard's line followed his encounter with Horta in the summer of 1895. After this trip to Belgium, the French architect transformed his plans for Castel Béranger. The transformation affected only the surfaces of the facades, not the structures; the elevations were animated by means of graphic manipulation of the stone and the metal components. Meandering, incised lines trace the stone of the semicircular or low arches of the openings and the termination of the pillars at the entrance leading to

FIG. 4. Guimard, motif plan for cast-iron elements for the Wagram-MacMahon Métro station, 1900.
Charcoal and lead pencil on card stock. Musée d'Orsay, Paris.

PHILIPPE THIÉBAUT

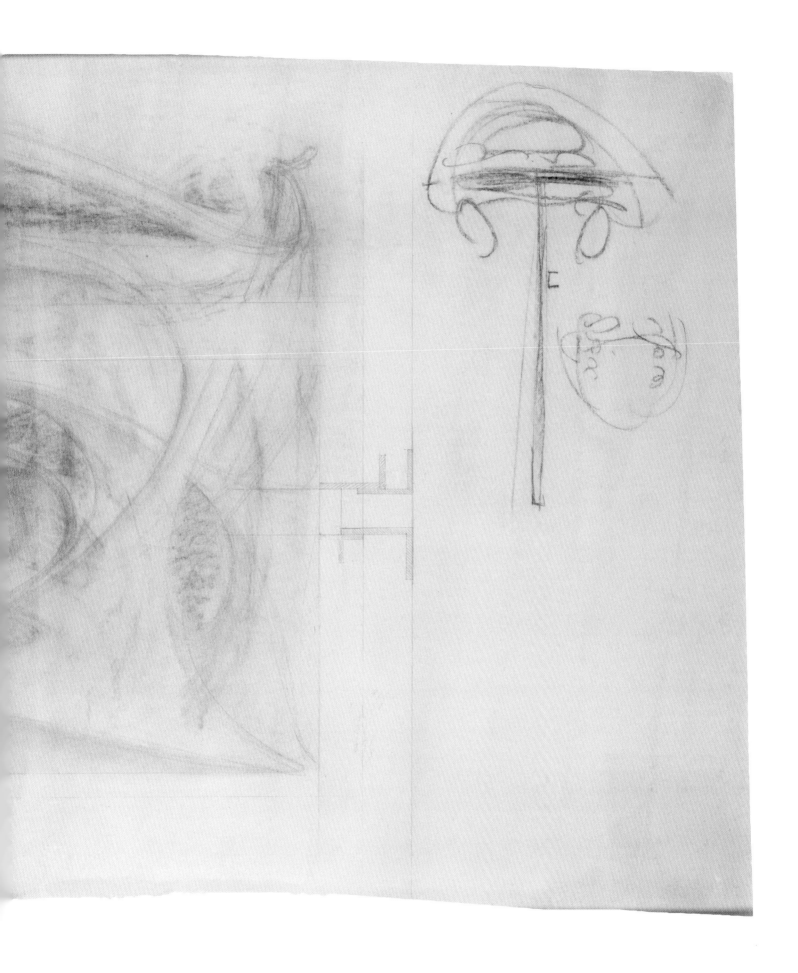

the hamlet (see cat. no. 28). The sheet-metal cutouts for the window valances are more supple. The ironwork of the window grilles, including those for the basement, bends into curves and countercurves with a virtuosity that culminates in the design of the principal entrance door, the first true masterpiece of Guimardian linearism. Inside the apartment building, the design of the mosaics, stained-glass windows, wall paneling in the common areas, and wallpaper in the apartments pertains to the same uplifting inspiration. The ornamentation bears witness to Guimard's ability to work at different scales and to seize on diverse materials and impose on them a unique rhythm. This work must be called an artistic gesture, recognized as such by the architect Louis-Charles Boileau, who wrote in the professional journal *L'architecture*: "M. Guimard will not hold it against me, I hope, if I state that his stance is graceful, always distinguished, often suggestive."[13]

In his 1899 lecture at Salon du Figaro, Guimard spoke at length about his inspiration: the contemplation of natural developments and the study of vegetal growth:

> You see, it is from nature that one must always seek guidance. When I construct a house, when I design a piece of furniture or when I sculpt it, I think of the spectacle bequeathed to us by the universe. . . . No parallelism or symmetry; forms are born with movements that are never the same. . . . And what a lesson for the architect, for the artist who knows how to look in this admirable repertory of forms and colors! For construction, don't the branches of trees, the twigs sometimes stiff, sometimes wavy, provide our models? . . . These dominant lines, that draw in space now supple arabesques, now dazzling swashes like bolts of lightning, these lines have a sentimental and expressive value far more eloquent than the perennial vertical, horizontal, and regular lines used continuously until now in architecture. I repeat, there is no formal symmetry in nature, I mean neither in appearances nor in forms.[14]

Informed by the École des arts décoratifs, Guimard's design vocabulary was considerably enriched by the adoption of the principle that Horta had revealed to him as his own—that is, the banishment, in the study of nature, of the leaf and the flower to focus exclusively on the stem, a concept that implied considering naturalistic ornament superfluous and a plastic language founded on orthogonality arbitrary.

From the months that followed his encounter with Horta until the years 1902–3, many of the forms drawn by Guimard, notably those for fixed or movable furniture, evoke the knotty branches of a tree and their offshoots. The furniture created for Castel Béranger, then for the Maison Coilliot or Castel Henriette, shares with the entrance lamps of Guimard's Métro stations a fluid and treelike aspect, while the framework of the Humbert de Romans concert hall spreads in powerful branches imbued with a lyricism in harmony with the purpose of the building. Rationalism and fantasy, structural rigor and formal invention coexist within these organic works, as Frantz Jourdain, one of the earliest observers, noted: "In an elegant tangling, the tree, the branch, the vine cooperate in the arrangement of the whole, to the exclusion of any other element. This is not the result of chance, but the application of a reasoned principle . . . the capricious strangeness of the dreams of a smoker of opium."[15] After 1903, the forms in Guimard's drawings lose their audacious fervor in favor of more enveloping contours, but without giving up the sinuous inflections and swells of the material (fig. 5). This evolution befits an artist possessed of a profound desire to always advance toward something new, though without betraying the distinctive character of his work. Father Abel Fabre, enthusiastic about the connections between Gothic and modern art, had foreseen such an evolution when

PHILIPPE THIÉBAUT

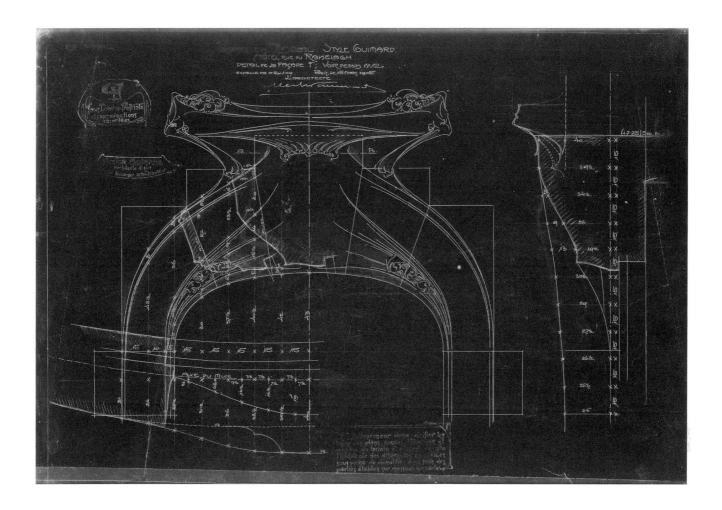

he affirmed in 1901 that Guimard had but one concern: "to have serene simplicity follow what had been the tormented disquiet of a feverish temperament."[16]

That a piece of furniture designed in 1899 is different from a piece of furniture designed in, say, 1907 cannot be disputed. The spirit, however, is rigorously the same, and the conception immediately identifiable, because of the role played by line and also the nature of the line. Whether drawn in fine lead, thick, greasy lead, or blurry charcoal, the line remains the fundamental element of Guimard's creative process, the element on which his architectural and decorative language depends. His visual explorations, carried on simultaneously in these two fields, in reality inseparable, both abolish the disconnect between exterior and interior but also make structure and decoration grow from the same movement, and to such a degree that the very notion of ornament loses its meaning. In addition to marrying structure and decoration, Guimard's line also combines dynamism and abstraction. As the eminent specialist in handwriting and typography Jérôme Peignot has so judiciously remarked, "Something in these elongated movements is akin to the strokes of a pen or rather to the flourish of a signature. They seem to hesitate between abstraction and this gestural aspect that any handwriting still preserves in itself."[17]

Thus, the same line that, on the outside, animates the surface of the facades with bands of stone that undulate, swell, hollow out, and are bordered with motifs suggesting sea foam or spring burgeoning, on the inside, spreads over wood paneling, plaster ornaments, textiles, and more, generating a fluid play of forms and materials into which the furniture is effortlessly integrated. Long ribs run over facades and emphasize the construction lines of furniture before melting softly back into the material or giving birth to a

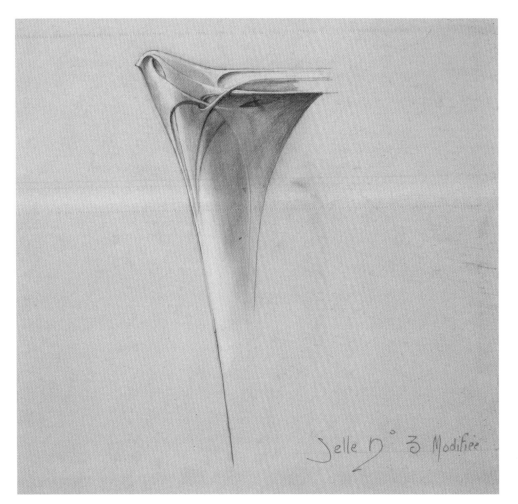

delicately sculpted organic motif. What is truly remarkable in Guimard's drawn line is that it shows all the planes on a single sheet of paper, determining beforehand the modeling in relief (fig. 6). The construction lines that constitute the armature of a piece of furniture converge toward junction points that are sculpted with elegant sensuality and great refinement, making the sculpture participate in the structure of the piece. In certain cases, the opposite impression emerges—that is, that the lines constituting the armature of the piece of furniture or the object escape from a piece of sculpture without at any time giving a feeling of entanglement in the material (fig. 7). To make these objects, Guimard relied on gifted artisans and craftsmen who were able to produce, in the objects, the feeling of wood swollen with sap.

Beyond his achievements in architecture and interior decoration, Guimard has a significant body of work as a graphic designer. He exhibits, both in the composition of the printed page and in the design of the typefaces, a personal virtuosity, as shown in his studies for *Le Castel Béranger,* an album released by Librairie Rouam et Cie at the end of 1898. The publication bears the stamp of the artist throughout: he drew the lettering of the presentation box and the title page as well as the HG monogram stamped on each of the plates.[18] A few months later, he designed the poster and invitation announcing the exhibition at Salon du Figaro. The graphic design work continued with covers for the *Revue d'art* and the catalogue for the Saint-Dizier Foundries (see cat. nos. 63, 83).[19]

Guimard's print work presents deep stylistic similarities to any signage or other text applied to his architectural creations, whether the signs for the pavilions and railings of the Métro, on a background of metal or enameled lava stone, or the plaques in enameled lava stone that announce in bright, shiny colors the names of suburban or seaside villas

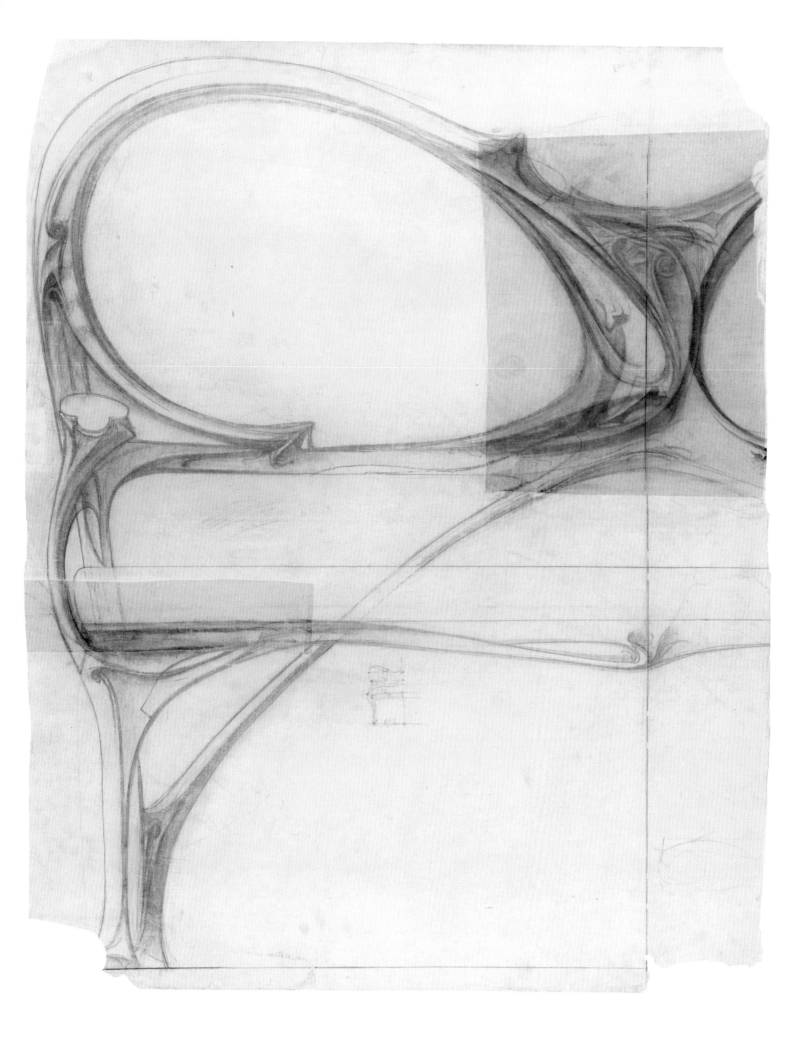

such as Castel Henriette in Sèvres, Villa "La Bluette" in Hermanville, and Chalet Blanc in Sceaux. The lettering is as much an element of the architectural decoration as the surface of the facades or the motifs on the furniture. Swollen, flaring, stretched out, the letters respond to the rhythm of the architecture; their dynamism contributes to the stylistic unity of the facade. This new form of writing, perhaps unsurprisingly, gave rise to violent condemnations, of which the most famous is by the journalist André Hallays. Lashing out at "the disastrous fantasy" of the Métro stations, he demanded as early as 1901 the removal of the signage: "What would be possible, at least, would be to have the names of the stations written in *French letters*. . . . These disorderly hieroglyphics cause excusable mirth to little children and stupefaction to foreign visitors to Paris. To quiet the children, to reassure the Cook tourists, and most of all for the honor of French taste, these ridiculous inscriptions must be done away with."[20]

Drawing is, assuredly, the first gesture Guimard uses to express his desire to occupy all fields of creation. His activity as a draftsman reveals an artist who wants to reinvent architectural and decorative language but also a patient artisan who is careful not to let any element of that language escape his imagination. The language is intensely personal, but at the same time it is related to the aspiration of the creators of Art Nouveau: to restore to "modern" humankind an intimate rhythm, by means of an environment that creates both material and spiritual well-being. It is an artist absorbed in that task who appears on beautiful postcard number 10, the image that shows the creator in complete harmony with his environment. To live in a space conceived by Guimard was assuredly a new experience, that some, such as the critic and art historian Gustave Soulier, claimed was pivotal to a satisfying private life: "The ensemble of these sinuous forms, in which a too rapid glance sees only a bursting of turbulent rockets, seems to draw around us little by little an irresistible embrace. The lines slide harmoniously upon each other, weave and unweave themselves, creating the background for the play of our movements and our thoughts; they seem to draw our actions and our attitudes into the same necessary rhythm."[21]

PHILIPPE THIÉBAUT

NOTES

1   Guimard's previous offices were also in Auteuil, at 64, boulevard Exelmans. He set up there in August 1893.

2   Fonds Hector Guimard, Musée d'Orsay, Paris, GP 1949-1950-1951.

3   See on this subject Yvonne Brunhammer, "Guimard concepteur de meubles," in *Guimard: Colloque international, Musée d'Orsay, 12 et 13 Juin 1992* (Paris: Réunion des musées nationaux, 1994).

4   Archives de Paris et de la Seine, Paris, VO 23/26.

5   See Thiébaut, *"Le style Guimard,"* in this catalogue.

6   During his years as a professor, Guimard engaged in an active correspondence with Louvrier de Lajolais (see Archives nationales, Paris, AJ 53/130).

7   Guimard to Paul Léon, December 6, 1918, Adeline Oppenheim Guimard papers, Manuscripts and Archives Division, New York Public Library. What Guimard does not say in this letter is that he no longer had the support of Léon Nozal, who had died on August 15, 1914, and who had been, in fact, the owner of the avenue Perrichont building.

8   See Philippe Thiébaut, "Hector Guimard: Ensemble de dessins," *48/14: La revue du Musée d'Orsay* 2 (February 1996): 32–35.

9   See Alain Blondel, "Blondel et Plantin à la redécouverte," in *Guimard: Colloque international*, 11. All those responsible for the rediscovery of Guimard, except Ralph Culpepper, who had died, and Henri Poupée, participated in this symposium: Alain Blondel and Yves Plantin, Roger-Henri Guerrand, Luciana Miotto-Muret, Lanier Graham, and Yvonne Brunhammer.

10   Guimard to Victor Horta, May 8, 1896, Horta Museum Archives and Library, Saint Gilles, Brussels, XV-G-3-3.

11   For his justification of this claim, see Guimard's letter to the editors, published in *L'art décoratif* 65 (February 1904).

12   Hector Guimard, "La renaissance de l'art dans l'architecture moderne," *Le moniteur des arts* 91 (July 7, 1899): 1465–75.

13   Louis-Charles Boileau, "Causerie," *L'architecture*, April 1899, 131. A pioneer in the use of iron and metal in French architecture as well as an architect, Boileau worked in collaboration with his father, Louis-Auguste Boileau, and Gustave Eiffel of the *grand magasin* le Bon marché. He contributed a column called "Causerie," which described current architectural developments, to *L'architecture*, the journal of the Société centrale des architectes français.

14   "La renaissance de l'art," 1467.

15   Frantz Jourdain, "Les meubles modernes," *Revue d'art* 1 (November 4, 1899): 8–9.

16   Abel Fabre, "Du gothique au moderne," *Le mois littéraire et pittoresque* 33 (September 1901): 297.

17   Jérôme Peignot, "Guimard, son graphisme est du grand art," *Connaissance des arts* 217 (March 1970): 74.

18   The monogram was also used on a label with the notice "All rights reserved" attached to architectural projects and furniture.

19   The *Revue d'art*, founded in November 1899 by Maurice Méry, used Guimard's cover until issue 7 in December 1899. The "modern" character of the Saint-Dizier Foundries is asserted in the typefaces chosen for the names of the items: Auriol Labeur and Robur Pâle.

20   André Hallays, "En flânant," *Le journal des débats*, July 5, 1901. Hallays takes up arguments made by members of the Commission du vieux Paris, minutes of the meeting of June 27, 1901, 121–22.

21   Gustave Soulier, "La décoration moderne et le Castel Béranger," *Études sur le Castel Béranger, œuvre de Hector Guimard, architecte, professeur à l'École nationale des arts décoratifs* (Paris: Librairie Rouam et Cie, 1899), 15.

Le style Guimard
Philippe Thiébaut

A dwelling by Guimard becomes a palace where our eyes are enchanted, where our soul rests. It is the poetry of architecture.

—Maffeo-Charles Poinsot, "Un exemple pour les jeunes: Hector Guimard"

"I love architecture because it contains, in its essence and in all its expressions, all the other arts, without exception," wrote Hector Guimard in a French journal in 1899.[1] Still in the early years of his career, Guimard defined architecture as the collaborative union of all the arts in a spirit of harmonious subordination. His profession of faith dates from May 12, 1899, when the architect spoke publicly on the premises of the newspaper *Le Figaro* where an exhibition on Castel Béranger had been on view since April 5 (fig. 1). Castel Béranger, a large investment property at 14, rue La Fontaine in the neighborhood of Auteuil, was one of six privately owned structures that had recently won prizes in the first Facade Competition established by the city of Paris.[2] In the same talk, Guimard stated that architecture was a perfect expression of a given era and that it was incumbent upon the architect to express through his creations the spirit of the age. Clearly, he was motivated by a strong sense of modernity and by an obligation to "work as a man of his own time."[3]

Such a way of thinking and acting could not have arisen solely from the values professed at the École des Beaux-Arts, where the professors relied on composition and on the distribution and harmony of architectural forms. Guimard had been admitted to the school in the spring of 1885, specifically, to the atelier of Gustave Raulin.[4] However, he proved to be an inconsistent and average student, earning honorable mentions but no medals in the various competitions that punctuated the curriculum. In 1892, Guimard failed in the second round for the Prix de Rome competition; five years later, having reached the age limit of thirty without accumulating the necessary points to obtain the government-granted *architecte diplômé*, he left the institution. Raulin did not hold it against him. In fact, as one of the small group of artists who, in 1911, solicited the cross of the Legion of Honor for Guimard, he described a tenacious young man: "I saw his beginnings, witnessed the formation of his personality, recognized his courage. While still young, he set the goal that he has pursued for many years with unfailing energy. While using none of the traditional forms of architecture, he also wanted the architect to be in his building, both for the exterior and the interior [*le contenant et le contenu*], more the master of the work than he had ever been. He cultivated all the decorative arts, he created workshops that he directs himself and from which emerge with a new artistic form all kinds of objects whatever the material."[5]

It is striking to consider the contrast between the difficulties the young man encountered in the course of his studies at the École des Beaux-Arts and the brilliant results he had obtained previously, between 1882 and 1885, at the École des arts décoratifs.[6] It was while at the latter institution that the adolescent Guimard had decided to embrace the

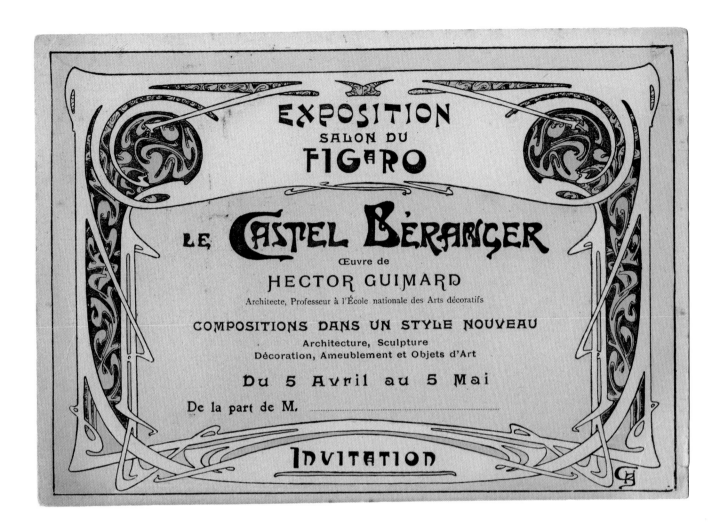

career of architect and that he met his first true master: the architect Charles Génuys.[7] In fact, it was Génuys who taught Guimard the many styles of architecture and introduced him to the writings of Eugène-Emmanuel Viollet-le-Duc.[8] Viollet-le-Duc led the way to personal structural inventions by openly opposing the rules and aesthetic values of academic training, by relying on the rationalism of Gothic architecture, and by linking the use of traditional materials (stone and brick) with new ones (iron and cast iron) and choosing those most appropriate for the building function. Moreover, at the École des arts décoratifs, prominence was given to the study of nature. It is important to remember that Victor-Marie-Charles Ruprich-Robert, a disciple of Viollet-le-Duc and author of the famous *Flore ornamentale* (*Ornamental Floral*), which he worked on from 1866 to 1876, taught at the institution from 1850 to 1887 and was its first professor of architecture. Thus, it was from the study of the Gothic style and of nature together that Guimard acquired his methodology. Guimard's encounter with Victor Horta[9] in Brussels in the summer of 1895 also made a decisive contribution to this approach—not so much from the use Horta made of the curved line as from Guimard's desire to proclaim himself the sole author of his architectural output. In February and June 1895, before traveling to Brussels, Guimard had filed plans with the Paris authorities to obtain a building permit for Castel Béranger; as soon as he returned, he revised those plans. He barely touched the structure; the interior decor, on the other hand, whether common areas or the thirty-six apartments in three portions of the building, became the focus of intense scrutiny that neglected no element, however tiny.

Guimard's personal language would continue to evolve until just before World War I. The expression rests upon a continuous line that simultaneously determines the framework of the exterior spaces and the decoration of the interior spaces. Through a lyrical play of curves and countercurves, this line generates both structure and ornament; it also institutes a powerful dialectic between solids and voids and, additionally, imposes a flexibility on the materials. Such creative vitality appears to be, without question, a transposition of the organic forces that circulate in the botanical world, though not the force of any specific organism. Guimard's transposition of the organic to the abstract is accomplished instantaneously, accentuating the dynamism of his creations. After 1903, the forms become calmer and more delicate in character, but they lose nothing of their vigor or their elusive mystery. The architect labeled this mode of design *"le style Guimard."*

He coined this expression at the time of the Paris Exposition universelle of 1900. Guimard, who showed in several sections, had obtained permission to add, as an addendum to the official catalogue, a pamphlet that listed all the places at the event where creations in *le style Guimard* were displayed.[10] The most emblematic and complete one was unquestionably the booth of the F. Millot perfume company (fig. 2).[11] A portfolio assembled by the architect Théodore Lambert gives an idea of this ensemble, temporary as were nearly all the fair pavilions.[12] Plate 20 of the album gathers several photographs that bear witness to the plastic unity of the F. Millot booth. Guimard designed the wall paneling, display cases, seating, printed silk wall fabric, and a large stained-glass window; the bottles (in two different sizes for each of the four fragrances) for the most recent of the perfumer's creations—Kantirix eau de toilette, Primalis eau de cologne, and Kantirix and Violi Violette perfumes; and the boxes for the perfume bottles and for soap and rice powder. Even the labels for the products—all abstract motifs and lettering—were designed by Guimard.

Surprisingly, the elegant and refined ensemble provoked hardly any commentary; nor, in fact, did the other designs that the architect sent to the exposition. The almost total neglect must have been due to Guimard's creations being scattered across the exposition pavilions, a direct consequence of how such exhibitions classified products. Indeed, Guimard was already famous by the time the Exposition universelle opened. Castel Béranger had generated significant coverage throughout 1899, whether in the daily press or in specialized publications. Moreover, railings and entrance structures designed by Guimard had begun to be installed on line 1 of the Paris Métropolitain,[13] which was built to bring visitors to the fair and introduced entirely novel forms into the landscape of Paris. The press had been mostly favorable and sometimes enthusiastic since the presentation of the Métro project in February 1900; *Le Figaro*, for example, continued to support the young architect: "Very simple and very elegant, the small pavilions designed by M. Guimard are entirely of iron, ceramic and glass. As light as the bubbles of champagne! . . . As for the form, indescribable—the modern architectural style lacking terms of comparison—but, graceful: a strangely jagged roof decorated with shell-like canopies of an unexpected effect, that pleases. What is essential is that Paris won't become uglier; on the contrary."[14] When, in November 1900, the entrance at the Place du Palais-Royal was causing some controversy—all the other line 1 entries had been installed—*Le Figaro* hastened to mock the protest: "Supporters of street art have found, it seems, that the aesthetics of this square will be gravely offended. Well, and the newsstands, and the fake-bronze street lights, and the horse cabs parked there, don't they tease the aesthetics of the Place du Palais-Royal a little bit?"[15] By the end of 1900, *le style Guimard* had literally descended into the streets.

　　　　　　　　　　　　　　　　　　　　　　　PHILIPPE THIÉBAUT

FIG. 2. Display of F. Millot perfume bottles on a stand designed by Hector Guimard, at the Exposition universelle, Paris, 1900. From Théodore Lambert, *Das moderne Möbel auf der Pariser Weltausstellung* (1900), plate 20. Smithsonian Libraries, Washington, D.C.

Nevertheless, it would take nearly three more years for the characteristics of the style to become clear. This would occur at the Housing Exhibition, which opened at the Grand Palais in Paris on July 30, 1903. At the center of the building, which had been built for the Exposition universelle, Guimard presented a structure with the title Pavilion for a Summer Gathering in a Park.[16] In the professional journal *Le bâtiment*, Stanislas Ferrand described the pavilion as "the synthesis of the architectonic doctrines that, for at least fifteen years, Guimard has been trying to materialize."[17] The playful assemblage of Guimardian forms—it is easy to recognize elements borrowed from the Métro, from the loggias of the Maison Coilliot in Lille and the Villa Canivet in Garches, and from the masonry piers of the Humbert de Romans concert hall—was hardly appropriate, unlike the other projects presented by defenders of Art Nouveau and friends of Guimard,[18] for an event that was officially dedicated to affordable housing and low-cost construction. Guimard's ideas on that topic would be presented the following year at the Salon d'automne by means of an ensemble of fourteen villa projects, some of which were quite affordable.[19] The pavilion was nonetheless widely discussed and appreciated for what it truly was: a brilliant embodiment of *le style Guimard*: "M. Guimard has generated a very personal style that is rightly called today: Style Guimard, a very sincere expression of an Art Nouveau born at the dawn of the XXth century! . . . Visit the 'Summer Pavilion,' inspect all its details, and I remain convinced that, unless you are biased, you will be enthralled by the aesthetic ensemble of this work realized by a man of very artistic temperament, who has left nothing to routine, but followed, unfailingly, the path he has set for himself" (fig. 3).[20] The pavilion even earned the praise of French President Émile

FIG. 3. L. E., "Le Pavillon d'été: Style Guimard," in *Gil Blas*, illustrated supplement on the Housing Exhibition, October 12, 1903. Bibliothèque Nationale de France.

Le Pavillon d'Été

STYLE GUIMARD

Lorsqu'on entre au Grand Palais par la façade de l'avenue Nicolas II, le Pavillon de M. Guimard est la première construction qui attire et retient l'attention, autant par son élégance et son style nouveau que par la richesse des tons et la variété des formes, quis'allient dans un ensemble raisonné d'une rigoureuse logique.

Pavillon d'Été (style Guimard)

Fort remarquable en son tout, cette construction n'a d'autres prétentions, sous sa modeste appellation de « Pavillon d'Été », que de présenter groupés dans une pure esthétique, les trois principes absolus contenus dans la nature : la Logique, l'Harmonie et le Sentiment.

C'est en s'attachant à cette règle immuable que M. Guimard a créé un style spécial portant fort justement son nom, style que l'on peut critiquer, mais qu'il faut bien admettre, même en le discutant.

Or, si de la discussion jaillit la lumière, M. Guimard est sûr de la victoire, car à une vive sympathie. il joint encore un don de persuasion bien personnel ; ses discours et conférences sont parsemés de citations dont il tire des déductions fort originales et très justes ; elles s'appuient sur l'observation absolue des lois de la nature qui devraient toujours servir de modèle et d'exemple à toutes les manifestations artistiques.

C'est fort judicieusement que dans une de ses conférences il constate que :

« La difficulté de créer un ensemble homogène est telle que la Maison la plus cossue forme, le plus souvent, un ensemble incohérent depuis l'antichambre gothique jusqu'au boudoir art nouveau, en passant par la chambre Louis XV, le salon Louis XVI, le cabinet de travail Empiré et la salle à manger Henri II. »

Et, peu après :

« Tous ceux qui s'intéressent à la rénovation de l'art, et qui voudraient se créer une habitation dans un style en harmonie avec les conditions de notre époque, pourront se rendre compte qu'avec les ressources dont on dispose ordinairement, on peut réaliser cette conception de l'habitation suivant la vraie et belle tradition française qui veut que tout, depuis le heurtoir de la porte, d'entrée, jusqu'au plus petit bibelot usuel, porte comme un orgueilleux blason, la marque de l'art contemporain. »

Un premier obstacle se dressait devant M. Guimard : le manque de collaborateurs. Si quelques-uns se sont rencontrés qui n'ont pas cru déchoir en apportant leur concours technique à l'œuvre du maître, dont ils ont suivi strictement les indications sans faux amour-propre, combien en est-il qu'il fallut éduquer, guider et styler ?

C'est de ces difficultés que naquirent les ateliers Guimard, où tout se trouve aujourd'hui centralisé : meubles d'art, rampes d'escaliers, modèles divers aux formes multiples, etc.

C'est là que s'appliquent immuablement les principes posés par M. Guimard, principes qu'il a puisés dans l'étude raisonnée des lois de la nature et dans les axiomes émis par son maître, Viollet-Leduc, et dont il a su tirer les conclusions normales et les approprier aux besoins de notre époque en s'appuyant sur les règles de l'harmonie et de la logique.

Viollet-Leduc avait dit, dans un de ses entretiens sur l'architecture : « Les Arts qui cessent d'exprimer le besoin qu'ils ont en vue de satisfaire, la nature de la matière employée et le moyen de la façonner cessent d'avoir du style. » C'est en s'inspirant de cet axiome et en en tirant toutes les conséquences que M. Guimard a procréé un style bien personnel où toutes les règles et les lois de l'Harmonie et du Sentiment sont religieusement observées et qu'on désigne fort justement aujourd'hui sous le nom de : Style-Guimard,

manifestation très sincère d'un Art Nouveau qui prend naissance à l'aurore du XX· siècle!

Il serait injuste de ne pas signaler ici les principaux collaborateurs qui ont prêté à M. Guimard un très précieux concours, tels M. Gillet, dont les pilastres et panneaux en lave émaillée sont très remarqués, M. Balet qui a exécuté la serrurerie d'art, M. Toussaint qui a appliqué à la peinture les produits portant son nom, et la Société Française des Ornements en Zinc, qui a posé la

Pavillon d'Été.
Vitrine. — Style Guimard.

couverture en métal repoussé. Très remarqués aussi les papiers d'art pour tentures de M. Sauvage, les étoffes d'art pour ameublement fournies par MM. Cornille frères et les belles et artistiques broderies de M. Coudyser.

Visitez le « Pavillon d'Été », visitez-le dans tous ses détails et je reste convaincu, qu'à moins de parti pris, vous serez séduit par l'ensemble esthétique de cette œuvre réalisée par un tempérament très artiste, n'ayant rien abandonné à la routine et suivant sans faiblesse, la voie qu'il s'est tracée. — L. E.

Pavillon d'Été.
Intérieur et cheminée. — Style Guimard.

Loubet: "Then passing from the useful to the agreeable, [Loubet] went to see the pretty pavilion built, decorated and furnished by the master architect Guimard. This true masterpiece seemed to please him very much, and he didn't hide from M. Guimard that his works had managed to reconcile him with what we have agreed to call modern art."[21]

Guimard created a great deal of publicity material to accompany the pavilion. One flyer repeated the information from the exhibition's official catalogue of the event along with an excerpt from Ferrand's article in *Le bâtiment* and a statement by Guimard: "The principal concern of an artist must be to create a dwelling appropriate for the needs of man and a setting for his active life. The arts of domesticity cannot thrive or develop unless they issue from and are subject to a general, perfectly defined aesthetic. All renewal, all invention of detail will perish at birth if it does not belong to an ensemble, that is to say architecture."[22] In addition, Guimard produced a series of twenty-four postcards—black-and-white photos hand-tinted with color—that brought together the principal architectural stages of *le style Guimard.* The architect most likely got the idea from Ferrand who, a few months earlier, had published a comparable series of twenty-four postcards titled "Art in the Street." Ferrand's cards were presented as "genuine professional documents" striving toward "a formula, as yet imprecise, but which should achieve definitive expression as what is known as 'the style' of an age."[23] Finally, Guimard put forth his artistic program in numerous public lectures. On October 7, at the restaurant of the Grand Palais, for instance, he offered a guided visit of the pavilion followed by two talks, one by the architect Frantz Jourdain, the other by Stanislas Ferrand, "supporters who braided a friendly garland for Guimard into which a few thorns were adroitly hidden under the flowers."[24]

The well-engineered publicity campaign around the exhibition, in general, and the Guimard pavilion, in particular, without doubt benefited from the savoir faire and energy of the Société du Nouveau-Paris, a group of artists, art critics, and journalists that had just formed at the initiative of Frantz Jourdain.[25] Jourdain, who led the group, set out its program in an open letter: "We want the Paris of tomorrow to remain worthy of the Paris of yesterday; we want to no longer let reign as masters bad taste and anonymous indifference that seem to take pleasure in dishonoring the marvelous decor of our streets."[26] The association published, beginning in October 1903, a monthly bulletin that reflected on projects of Parisian urbanism from a viewpoint that combined respect for the past with an acknowledgment of the demands of modern life. For Guimard, many of whose acquaintances were members of the association, this support was all the more welcome because the Housing Exhibition coincided with the beginning of a polemic about the entrances and edifices of the Métro. Throughout 1903, the press covered this controversy, fueled by the fight against Guimard's works led since 1901 by the Commission du vieux Paris that the following year would bring about a rupture between the Métropolitain Railway Company and its architect.[27]

Thus, just when Guimard was prepared to present to the public a controlled example of what he meant by *le style Guimard,* his architectural accomplishments in the capital were confronting a wave of opposition. Guimard was not the only victim. Beginning in the years 1902–3, Art Nouveau was denigrated more and more frequently, a fact that a few lucid minds, such as the art critic François Thiébault-Sisson, did not fail to deplore: "It is fashionable to disparage Art Nouveau. The same snobs who, just recently, proclaimed its virtues with enthusiastic ardor and were delighted by its piquant inventions, are now up in arms against it. With a touching unanimity, they tear down the movement, denying it any value or purpose."[28]

It must be thought of as ironic that it was in a period of disaffection for Art Nouveau that Guimard was able to show his greatest achievements in the field of interior design, achievements that fully justified the use of the expression *le style Guimard*. In other projects, Guimard had not been able to fully realize his vision of a union of the arts. At Castel Béranger, only the decoration of the common areas and the fixed decor of the apartments had been taken into account. At the Exposition universelle in 1900, Guimard had shown just fragments of interiors, with furniture playing a secondary role. No private interiors were included in his series of postcards, with the exception of one showing the architect in his office on the ground floor of Castel Béranger. But, in 1903, in the interior of his pavilion, Guimard was finally able to present real domestic spaces he had designed in their entirety. From then on, he made a point of promoting his work in decorative arts in national and international exhibitions.[29] In Paris, the architect was present at the first two Salons d'automne, in 1903 and 1904, and was associated with the Société des artistes décorateurs, which was created in 1901 and where he was named vice president in 1905. At the first exhibition of the Société des artistes décorateurs, which opened on January 15, 1904, he presented a vitrine of bronze and ceramic objects. He directed the installation of the Société's second exhibition, which opened at the Musée des arts décoratifs in November 1906. His work was included in every Société exhibition until 1914, with the exception of 1909, a year when he was particularly busy with architectural projects.[30] Furthermore, his role in the society offered him the opportunity to speak publicly more and more frequently.

If the Housing Exhibition is a decisive moment in the elaboration of *le style Guimard,* it is first of all because the interior spaces of Guimard's pavilion had been conceived and carried out in large part by the architect's own recently created workshops (fig. 4). Before this time, Guimard depended on manufacturers to fabricate models based on drawings he supplied. In the spring of 1903—thanks to the financial support of his friend Léon Nozal, a wealthy metal trader whose home, Hôtel Nozal, he designed (fig. 5)— Guimard built workshops at 12, avenue Perrichont (fig. 6), where the models of decorative art objects designed by the architect (though not the objects themselves) and the

FIG. 4. Guimard, detail of business letterhead of Ateliers Guimard, 12, avenue Perrichont, designed c. 1903. Musée d'Orsay, Paris.

OPPOSITE: FIG. 5. Guimard, perspective of entrance hall and elevator vestibule, Hôtel Nozal, December 27, 1902. Musée d'Orsay, Paris.

PHILIPPE THIÉBAUT

HOTEL NOZAL

VUE PERSPECTIVE
DU VESTIBULE DE L'ASCENSEUR

Paris le 27 Dec.1902
L'Architecte.

Hector Guimard
Architecte d'Art
Castel Béranger 16 Rue Lafontaine

furniture were constructed and stored. The workforce was small, only five employees: draftsman, modeler, and three artisans.[31] But each was a collaborator who worked directly with Guimard himself, by now in a position to supervise the essential step of realizing in plaster the designs he had traced on paper. The workshops were a considerable improvement, as an article in the newspaper *Gil Blas* pointed out: "M. Guimard faced a first obstacle: the lack of collaborators. If he found a few who didn't think they were lowering themselves by offering their technical support to the master, whose instructions they followed without false pride, how many others had to be trained, guided, formed? It is from these difficulties that the Guimard workshops were born, where everything is now centralized: artistic furniture, stair railings, models of various kinds and forms, etc."[32] Only furniture was fabricated in the Guimard workshops. For objects other than furniture, Guimard continued to call upon manufacturers.[33] Some of them had worked with him since the days of Castel Béranger, as in the case of the woodworking firm le Coeur, part of the French branch of the Lincrusta-Walton company, or the enameled- and reconstituted-lava specialist Gillet. The Housing Exhibition marked the beginning of lasting collaborations with the modeler Paul Philippon and two textile firms, Cornille Frères and Jules Coudyser. In the course of the following years, other companies joined the distribution outlets of *le style Guimard,* such as the Saint-Dizier Foundries in Haute-Marne, the carpet manufacturer Aubert, and the electric lighting fabricator Langlois, which produced lamps, chandeliers, and sconces under the brand name Lustre Lumière.[34]

    Furniture presented difficulties of its own, even once Guimard had established the workshops on avenue Perrichont. The workshops never found a way to produce furniture commercially; in fact, the best their small workforce could assure was the production of orders related to Guimard's architectural projects[35] along with a few isolated

FIG. 6. Guimard, elevation of Ateliers Guimard, 12, avenue Perrichont, print on blue paper, number 4, 1903. Archives de Paris.

PHILIPPE THIÉBAUT

pieces made for the Société des artistes décorateurs exhibitions. For this reason, in 1913, Guimard turned to Olivier et Desbordes, a furniture maker in Faubourg Saint-Antoine. A contract between the fabricator and the architect set forth the steps and conditions of creation and production. Olivier et Desbordes was to pay for Guimard's workshops to create drawings and models; the manufacturer would then produce twelve exemplars of each.[36] This arrangement was not to be realized. In 1914, the death of Léon Nozal, Guimard's faithful financial supporter, and the declaration of war forced the architect to close the workshops. *Le style Guimard* was condemned to disappear just after having produced its finest outcome—the private house of the architect and his wife at 122, avenue Mozart—and just as this outcome drew the admiration of the architect's former critics. In 1911, the art critic Arsène Alexandre, whose diatribes against Art Nouveau are still famous,[37] saw in Guimard the leader of a new decorative order: "M. Guimard has kept the personal accent that won him much success for his first inventive designs for villas, but he has purged his style of its excesses and the fireplace that he displays along with a few other fragments has nothing in common with the skeletal forms [*ostéologies*] of the Métro. This very sympathetic and lively artist must now show us an ensemble of real importance; if it is conceived in his current spirit, it can have a very rapid, very unexpected—and very French—influence."[38] Two years later, dazzled by the elegant urbanity of the house on avenue Mozart, writer Maffeo-Charles Poinsot saw in this achievement "the undisputed dawn" of a truly new style.[39]

A comparison between these testimonials of the early 1910s and the positive assessments formulated in the late 1890s, at the time of Castel Béranger and the projects for the Métro, indicates that Guimard was, at the turn of the twentieth century, truly a man of his time. After personifying the detonating blast of Art Nouveau, he became a model for the new, very Parisian elegance to which the period aspired. Yet, Guimard would never turn away from his long-stated goal: to use his singular aesthetic principles to unify *le contenant et le contenu.*

NOTES

1. Hector Guimard, "La renaissance de l'art dans l'architecture moderne," *Le moniteur des arts* 91 (July 7, 1899), 1465.
2. The results of the competition were announced on March 28, 1899.
3. On the subject of this commitment, see Luciana Miotto-Muret, "Morale et architecture chez Guimard," in *Guimard: Colloque international, Musée d'Orsay, 12 et 13 juin 1992* (Paris: Réunion des musées nationaux, 1994), 130–39.
4. On Guimard's course of study, see Marie-Laure Crosnier Leconte, "Les années d'étude," in Philippe Thiébaut et al., *Guimard,* exh. cat. (Paris: Gallimard/Réunion des musées nationaux, 1992), 5–85.
5. Archives nationales, Paris, F12 8615.
6. The school opened in 1766 as the École royale gratuite de dessin. It was founded to give artisans a solid apprenticeship in drawing in order to assure the highest quality in industrial products. At the time Guimard was a student, the school taught and practiced all the techniques of drawing: life drawing, ornamental drawing, architectural drawing, shadow study, perspective, and elementary and descriptive geometry.
7. Charles Génuys, former student of the École impériale de dessin and of the École des Beaux-Arts, was the professor of the course on architectural drawing and, from 1890 to 1913, assistant director. Guimard was admitted to the architectural section in December 1884.
8. Guimard never failed to acknowledge the importance for his own architectural practice of Viollet-le-Duc's *Entretiens sur l'architecture,* published between 1863 and 1872.
9. By that date, Victor Horta had designed three private structures that marked the flowering of Art Nouveau in Brussels: the Hôtels Tassel (1893), Frison (1894), and Winssinger (1894). Horta may also have shown Guimard the plans for the future Van Eetvelde and Solvay houses (both completed 1900).

10 This pamphlet is extremely rare. The example consulted was sent by Guimard to Louvrier de Lajolais, director of the École des arts décoratifs (Archives nationales, Paris, AJ 53/130).

11 Founded in 1860, F. Millot had been managed since 1899 by the two grandsons by marriage of the founder, Henri Desprez and Félix Dubois. In all likelihood, it was the architect Frantz Jourdain, a friend of Guimard's, committed to the cause of Art Nouveau, and the party responsible for introducing the category of perfumery to the Exposition universelle, who suggested that F. Millot commission the architect of Castel Béranger.

12 Théodore Lambert, *Meubles de style moderne: Exposition universelle de 1900; sections française et étrangères* (Paris: Charles Schmid, 1900), plate 20.

13 On the Métro, see the very detailed study by Frédéric Descouturelle, André Mignard, and Michel Rodriguez, *Guimard: L'Art nouveau du Métro* (Paris: Éditions la vie du rail, 2012).

14 *Le Figaro*, February 10, 1900.

15 *Le Figaro*, November 12, 1900.

16 The critics were somewhat baffled by this architectural program; some called it a "hunting lodge" (see *Le Figaro*, August 9, 1903).

17 Stanislas Ferrand, "A travers l'Exposition: Pavillon style Guimard," *Le bâtiment*, August 9, 1903. A few weeks earlier, Ferrand had suggested to his readers that the Guimard pavilion, still under construction, would be one of the highlights of the show (see *Le bâtiment*, July 19, 1903). Ferrand, an architect by training and director of the professional journal *Le bâtiment: Journal des travaux publics et particuliers*, also assumed political responsibilities as deputy of the *département* of Seine between 1898 and 1902. Additionally, he was a member of the Société du Nouveau-Paris.

18 Notably two constructions by Jules Lavirotte (Workers' Pavilion and Small Middle-Class House) and one by Charles Plumet (Small Country House), which had interior furnishings by Tony Selmersheim.

19 The list is in a small folder titled "Construction villas 'style Guimard' pour la campagne, les bords de la mer et le midi de la France." See Philippe Thiébaut, *Guimard: L'Art nouveau* (Paris: Gallimard/Réunion des musées nationaux, 1992), 104–7.

20 Illustrated supplement to *Gil Blas* on the Housing Exhibition, October 12, 1903.

21 G. Davenay, "Le président de la République au Grand Palais," *Le Figaro*, November 6, 1903.

22 Hector Guimard, *Pavilion le style Guimard: Exposition de l'habitation 1903* (exh. pamphlet, 1903). Le Cercle Guimard archive.

23 See *Le bâtiment*, March 1, 1903.

24 See the account published in *Le bâtiment* on October 8, 1903. Another lecture took place on October 27; Léon Sabatier published an account in *Gil Blas* on October 29.

25 The association was founded in May 1902, announced in November 1902, and published in the *Journal officiel* on November 11, 1903. By the first of January 1904, it had more than 160 members.

26 *L'architecture*, June 6, 1903, 226–27; *Art et décoration*, supplement of July 1903, 1–2.

27 See, for example, the *Gil Blas* of August 20, 1903: "It has been declared that the Guimard structures adorning the entrances to the Métro, are no longer in favor. Will the commission of the Municipal Council that adopted this elegant and artistic design, allow its choice to be contested and destroy the harmony of an ensemble that the public has greeted so favorably? We hope that it will know how to defend its decisions." The Commission du vieux Paris, formed in 1897, fosters the preservation and appreciation of historic buildings and sites.

28 François Thiébault-Sisson, "Choses d'art: A propos de l'exposition lorraine; Le bilan de l'Art nouveau," *Le temps*, March 5, 1903. Thiébault-Sisson was an art critic for *Le temps*, a conservative daily newspaper. He was also among the founders of the magazine *Art et décoration*, which gave unwavering support to Art Nouveau.

29 Among the international exhibitions were the Franco-British Exhibition in London (1908), the French Exhibition of Decorative Art in Copenhagen (1909), and the International Exhibition of Industry and Labor in Turin (1911).

30 That year, Guimard, who had married Adeline Oppenheim on February 17, filed for two building permits (one for his own house at 122, avenue Mozart, the other for the Immeuble Trémois at 11, rue François-Millet) and signed the first plans for the group of buildings on a site bounded by rue Gros, rue La Fontaine, and rue Agar.

31 The names are given in Guimard, *Pavilion le style Guimard*: Vedy (draftsman); Godin (modeler); Chaput, Sablé, and Landre (artisans).

32 Supplement to *Gil Blas*, October 12, 1903. The unsigned article is accompanied by three photographs: a view of the whole pavilion and two partial views of the interior, one showing the fireplace in Gillet lava and the other a corner cabinet against a wall hung in silk by the firm of Cornille Frères. The cabinet is part of two other handsome ensembles in *le style Guimard*—the living room of Castel Val in Auvers-sur-Oise built in 1903 for the Chanu family and the living room executed in 1907 for the Villa Jules Desagnat in Saint-Cloud (from the donation by Ferdinand Neess of his remarkable collection of Art Nouveau to the Wiesbaden Museum).

33 The album devoted to Castel Béranger and the catalogue of the Housing Exhibition include lists of the firms Guimard used to have his models fabricated. These industrial firms, or most of them, were the subject of notices written by Marie-Madeleine Massé for Thiébaut et al., *Guimard* (exh. cat.).

34 On the Saint-Dizier Foundries, see Philippe Thiébaut, "Un ensemble de fontes artistiques de Guimard," *La revue du Louvre et des musées de France* 3 (1983): 212–21. The draft agreement signed between Guimard and Aubert on November 16, 1908, is among the Adeline Oppenheim Guimard papers, Manuscripts and Archives Division, New York Public Library. It was published in its entirety in Thiébaut, *Guimard: L'Art nouveau*, 100–101. Carpets in *le style Guimard* were sold at le Bon marché. On Lustre Lumière, see Philippe Thiébaut, "Guimard et les industries d'art," in Thiébaut et al., *Guimard* (exh. cat.), 361–62.

35 Starting with the architect's own house.

36 The contract is preserved among the Adeline Oppenheim Guimard papers. It is published in its entirety in Thiébaut, *Guimard: L'Art nouveau*, 101–2.

37 "It all smells of the vice-ridden Englishman, the morphine-addicted Jewess, or the crooked Belgian, or a jolly mixed salad of all three of these pests," Alexandre declared on the front page of *Le Figaro*, December 28, 1895, a few days after merchant Siegfried Bing opened a gallery called l'Art nouveau.

38 Arsène Alexandre, "Chez les décorateurs," *Comœdia*, March 4, 1911.

39 Maffeo-Charles Poinsot, "Un exemple pour les jeunes: Hector Guimard," *Les pages modernes* 64 (May 1913): 187.

Entrepreneur

As an energetic and gifted entrepreneur and marketer, Guimard was a century ahead of his time: like many present-day architects, he recognized the awesome power of the press. He produced exhibitions, publications, posters, and postcards of his work. Many of these pieces showcased his distinctive graphics, including the typeface he created and used, with variations, for all his work. Perhaps nothing better illustrates Guimard's inventive promotional efforts than his attempts to capitalize on the success of Castel Béranger. In 1899, he organized an exhibition about the apartment house at the Salon du Figaro in Paris—effective marketing since *Le Figaro* was the most important Parisian newspaper that had given Guimard favorable publicity. Both the invitation to the opening and a large poster featured his distinctive calligraphy. The presentation of architectural drawings and models was unusual for its time; augmenting its news value, the exhibition launched with a lecture by Guimard. The architect would have been very much at home in today's world of social media.

Around 1900, Guimard began to call himself "*architecte d'art*"—sophisticated branding a hundred years before the concept entered popular consciousness. Like works of art, his buildings were signed and dated in prominent locations, usually near the entrance, to acknowledge his artistic role. At the same time, he started to use the term *le style Guimard* to promote his work. He sought, with limited success, to promote *le style Guimard* as a trade name, inscribing it on many of his drawings, photographs, and designs. He prepared a lavish publication, *Le Castel Béranger*, and further publicized his work by creating a set of twenty-four hand-tinted postcards of his designs, all inscribed on the front with both "*architecte d'art*" and "*le style Guimard.*"

"Pavillon le style Guimard,
Exposition de l'habitation"
postcard, c. 1903. Nicolas
Horiot, Auberville, France.

42
Picture Frame
1907
Bronze, plate glass; modern photo reproduction
10⅝ × 6¹¹⁄₁₆ × ⅞ in. (27 × 17 × 2.3 cm)
Produced by Philippon, Paris
COOPER HEWITT, SMITHSONIAN DESIGN MUSEUM, NEW YORK,
GIFT OF MME HECTOR GUIMARD, 1956-53-1-A,B

43
Picture Frame
1907
Bronze, gold, plate glass; modern photo reproduction
9¾ × 6½ × 6½ in. (24.8 × 16.5 × 16.5 cm)
Produced by Philippon, Paris
COOPER HEWITT, SMITHSONIAN DESIGN MUSEUM, NEW YORK,
GIFT OF MME HECTOR GUIMARD, 1948-114-4-A,B

44
Picture Frame
1907
Bronze, silver, plate glass
10⁹⁄₁₆ × 6⁵⁄₈ × 1⁹⁄₁₆ in. (26.8 × 16.8 × 4 cm)
Produced by Philippon, Paris
COOPER HEWITT, SMITHSONIAN DESIGN MUSEUM, NEW YORK,
GIFT OF MME HECTOR GUIMARD, 1956-76-6-A/C

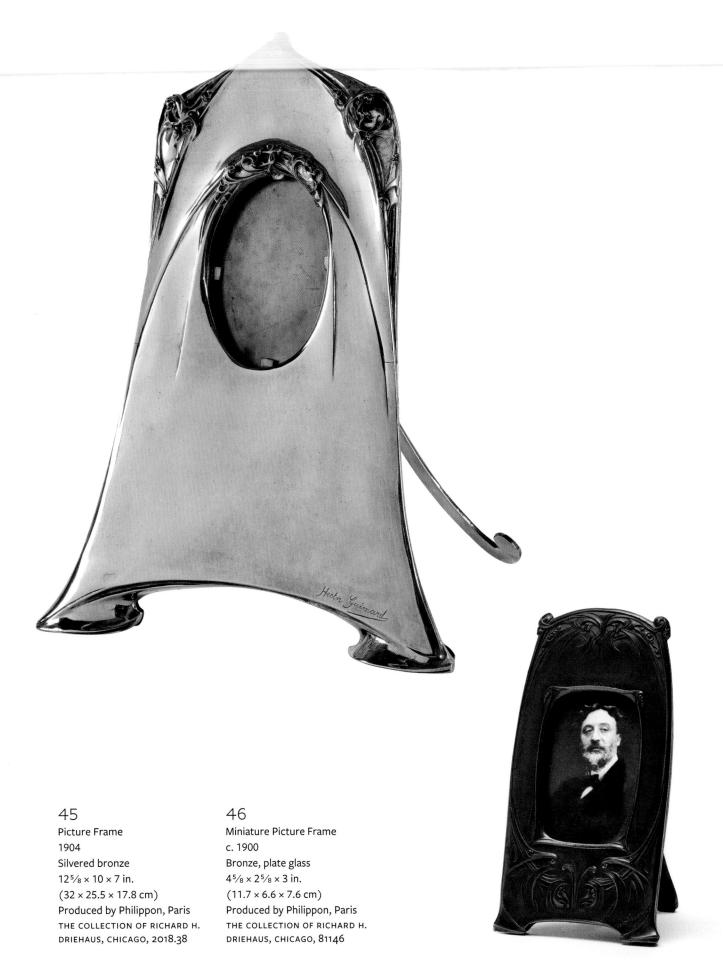

45
Picture Frame
1904
Silvered bronze
12⅝ × 10 × 7 in.
(32 × 25.5 × 17.8 cm)
Produced by Philippon, Paris
THE COLLECTION OF RICHARD H.
DRIEHAUS, CHICAGO, 2018.38

46
Miniature Picture Frame
c. 1900
Bronze, plate glass
4⅝ × 2⅝ × 3 in.
(11.7 × 6.6 × 7.6 cm)
Produced by Philippon, Paris
THE COLLECTION OF RICHARD H.
DRIEHAUS, CHICAGO, 81146

Le style Guimard Postcards

The Pavillon le style Guimard, formerly Pavilion for a Summer Gathering in a Park, at the 1903 Housing Exhibition, held at the Grand Palais, was the architect's first major presentation of *le style Guimard* as a brand name that encompassed all his designs. To mark the occasion (and to promote his work up to that time), he issued a set of twenty-four inexpensive hand-tinted photographic postcards; twenty-three of the cards have been identified, but no complete set is known to exist. Each card is numbered, with *"le style Guimard"* and the subject at the top; at the bottom is a brief rights statement and "Hector Guimard/Arch[te] d'Art/Paris," all in red ink. The postcards came in a wrapper that listed Guimard's collaborators. He also designed a display cabinet for the postcards, though it was never built.

Most of the postcards showed building exteriors, but two showed interiors: his office in Castel Béranger, which recorded Guimard at work, and the Humbert de Romans concert hall. Five featured his Métro entrances. Guimard was probably the first architect to promote his work in this way, using the striking photographs much as contemporary architects use websites.

D. A. H.

47
Postcard No. 1 from
Le style Guimard Series,
"Pavillon le style Guimard,
Exposition de l'habitation"
1903
Letterpress
5½ × 3½ in. (14 × 9 cm)
NICOLAS HORIOT,
AUBERVILLE, FRANCE

48

Postcard No. 2 from *Le style Guimard* Series,
"Le Métropolitain station des Champs-Élysées"
1903
Letterpress
5½ × 3½ in. (14 × 9 cm)
NICOLAS HORIOT, AUBERVILLE, FRANCE

49

Postcard No. 3 from *Le style Guimard* Series,
"Ville dans le Parc de Beauveau-Craon à Garches"
1903
Letterpress
5½ × 3½ in. (14 × 9 cm)
NICOLAS HORIOT, AUBERVILLE, FRANCE

50
Postcard No. 6 from *Le style
Guimard* Series,
"Castel Henriette à Sèvres"
1903
Letterpress
5½ × 3½ in. (14 × 9 cm)
NICOLAS HORIOT,
AUBERVILLE, FRANCE

51
Postcard No. 9 from
Le style Guimard Series,
"Villa 'La Bluette' à
Lions-sur-Mer"
1903
Letterpress
3½ × 5½ in. (9 × 14 cm)
NICOLAS HORIOT,
AUBERVILLE, FRANCE

52
Postcard No. 11 from
Le style Guimard Series,
"Le Métropolitain—Station
de l'Étoile"
1903
Letterpress
3½ × 5½ in. (9 × 14 cm)
NICOLAS HORIOT,
AUBERVILLE, FRANCE

53
Postcard No. 12 from
Le style Guimard Series,
"Hôtel particulier, rue
Chardon-LaGache, Paris"
1903
Letterpress
3½ × 5½ in. (9 × 14 cm)
NICOLAS HORIOT,
AUBERVILLE, FRANCE

54

Postcard No. 15 from
Le style Guimard Series,
"Maison de M. Coilliot à Lille"
1903
Letterpress
5½ × 3½ in. (14 × 9 cm)
NICOLAS HORIOT,
AUBERVILLE, FRANCE

55

Postcard No. 22 from
Le style Guimard Series,
"Intérieur de la Salle de
Concert, 60, rue St-Didier"
1903
Letterpress
3½ × 5½ in. (9 × 14 cm)
NICOLAS HORIOT,
AUBERVILLE, FRANCE

Typography & Graphic Design

HECTOR GUIMARD
Ancien Professeur à l'École Nationale des Arts Décoratifs
Ancien Vice-Président de la Sté des Artistes Décorateurs
Ancien Vice-Président de la Sté des Architectes Modernes

18, Rue Henri Heine, 16ᵉ

56
Hector Guimard's Business Card
After 1926
Letterpress
2 3/8 × 4 in. (6 × 10.2 cm)
COOPER HEWITT, SMITHSONIAN DESIGN MUSEUM, NEW YORK,
GIFT OF UNKNOWN DONOR, 2003-1-1-B

57
Printing Plate for Guimard's Business Card
After 1926
Copper
2 1/2 × 4 1/8 in. (6.4 × 10.4 cm)
COOPER HEWITT, SMITHSONIAN DESIGN MUSEUM, NEW YORK,
GIFT OF UNKNOWN DONOR, 2003-1-1-A

Guimard published a splendid portfolio to celebrate his first architectural masterpiece: Castel Béranger, an apartment complex built between 1895 and 1897. In one of his many promotional initiatives, Guimard sought to generate new work opportunities by creating the equivalent of one of today's luxe coffee-table tomes, which impress through size, weight, and extensive photography. The release of the portfolio in November 1898 coincided with his exhibition and lecture on Castel Béranger in the offices of the newspaper *Le Figaro*.

The portfolio contains sixty-five mechanically produced plates of photographs and drawings, all hand-tinted or colored with stencils. Guimard included a broad survey of the exterior and interior architecture as well as details of wallpaper, fabrics, mosaics, carpeting, stained glass,

and hardware. The final plates illustrate furniture that Guimard designed for the building, though in the end the apartments were rented unfurnished. He also listed the artisans and contractors responsible for the realization of his design. The book was advertised in decorative arts magazines with a prepublication price of 60 francs (about $685 today).

Critic Yvanhoé Rambosson praised *Le Castel Béranger* in the June 1899 issue of *Le mercure de France* as "revolutionary. . . . Whichever facade you look at, no matter what detail stops you, you will be struck by the author's desire to avoid or obscure straight lines. The result is an overall impression of movement, life, and gaiety that seems new in this order of conceptions."

58
Portfolio *Le Castel Béranger*
1898
Plates: Hand-painted photo-mechanical
and bronze paint on paper
13 × 17⅜ in. (33 × 44.1 cm)
Published by Librairie Rouam et Cie, Paris
THE COLLECTION OF RICHARD H. DRIEHAUS, CHICAGO, 140138.A

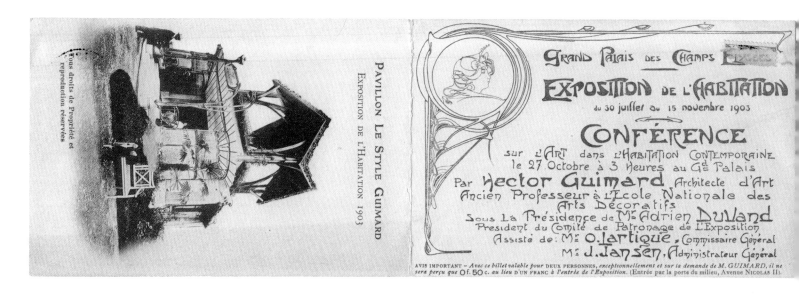

Verso of Housing Exhibition invitation, 1903.

59
Invitation to the Housing Exhibition at the Grand Palais, Paris
1903
Letterpress
3½ × 5½ in. (9 × 14 cm)
NICOLAS HORIOT, AUBERVILLE, FRANCE

60 (*opposite*)
Announcement Card for Pavilion le style Guimard at the
Housing Exhibition at the Grand Palais des Champs Élysées,
July 30–November 15, 1903
1903
Letterpress
3½ × 5½ in. (9 × 14 cm)
NICOLAS HORIOT, AUBERVILLE, FRANCE

Verso of Housing Exhibition announcement card, 1903.

61
Working Drawing for Guimard's Sign at the Housing Exhibition
1903
Graphite and watercolor on tracing paper
$12^{11}/_{16} \times 21^{5}/_{8}$ in. (32.2 × 55 cm)
MUSÉE D'ORSAY, PARIS, GP 1641

Hector Guimard

Architecte

1903

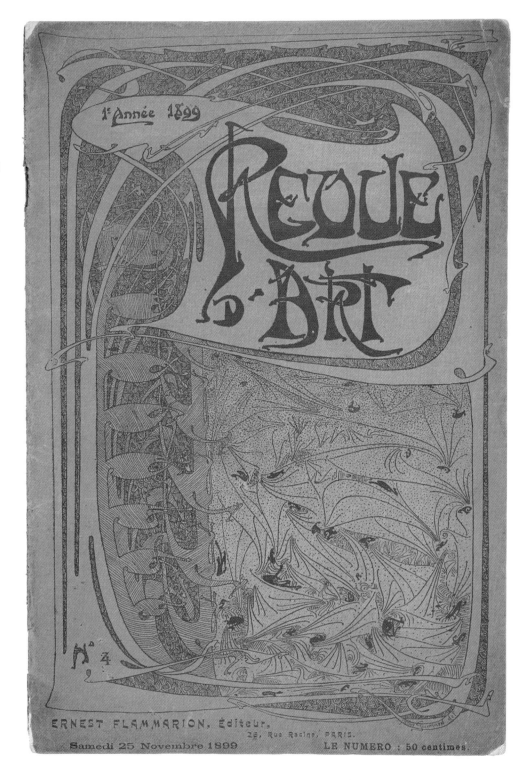

62 (*opposite*)
Working Drawing for the
Cover of *Revue d'art*
c. 1899
Black ink, watercolor, and
pencil on tracing paper
15¾ × 10⅞ in. (40 × 26.5 cm)
MUSÉE D'ORSAY, PARIS, GP 526

63
Revue d'art Magazine, No. 4
November 25, 1899
Letterpress
11¹⁵⁄₁₆ × 8¹⁄₁₆ in.
(30.3 × 20.5 cm)
Published by Ernest
Flammarion, Paris
COOPER HEWITT, SMITHSONIAN
DESIGN MUSEUM, NEW YORK,
GIFT OF DAVID A. HANKS IN
HONOR OF RICHARD H.
DRIEHAUS, 2019-4-1

In the fall of 1899, the established journal of art criticism *Moniteur des arts: Revue des expositions et des ventes publiques* was succeeded by *Revue d'art*. Guimard's lecture "La renaissance de l'art dans l'architecture moderne" had been published in the second-to-last issue of *Moniteur des arts,* and the "*architecte d'art*" was tapped to design the cover of the new journal. Guimard labored tirelessly to achieve his vision of an animated, almost undulating, cover page featuring his original, flourishing lettering. The iterations—at least eight are preserved—reveal Guimard's perfectionist tendencies.

Printed on both orange and green paper, Guimard's daring and innovative cover design was used only for the first seven issues. Subsequent issues, with a traditional cover design based on floral motifs, attest to the dramatic reduction of interest in Art Nouveau starting about 1910.

Y. Y.

Villa Hemsy Plans of House and Garden as Graphic Design

Villa Hemsy was one of many private residences that Guimard built in the French countryside, in this case in Saint-Cloud, a western suburb of Paris. The three-story villa was commissioned on the eve of World War I by Léon Hemsy, an affluent Jewish dealer of fine pearls. Guimard modified his design of Villa Hemsy more than once, as evidenced in blueprints for the project. In the initial scheme, the main entrance is slightly off center. All of the rooms connect to a large, irregularly shaped vestibule, which has a dramatic staircase and a bay window that swells out toward the rear side of the property. The asymmetry is retained in the built design, but the entrance is at the left corner and initiates a clearer, L-shaped sequence of rooms.

Guimard's dynamic use of line, fundamental to his creative process, evolves along with his design. Profuse fluid, undulating curves meant to depict garden foliage appear in the first scheme as natural forms that have been reduced to abstract patterns, recalling the elegant lines of his furniture designs. Loose, gestural arcs evoke nature's sense of movement and perpetual variety. The flourishes at the corners of the villa and the lettering contribute to the unified aesthetic. Guimard's final design, just months later, has simplified typography, taut and elongated curves in the garden, and no corner flourishes. The garden's sinuous lines, still evocative of movement, delineate a clear circulation route from the property's southern gates to the villa.

ALISA CHILES

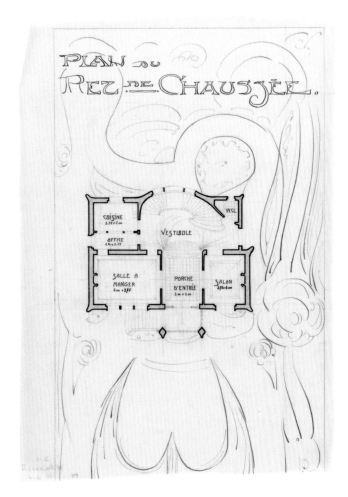

64
Plan of Ground Floor for Villa Hemsy, Saint-Cloud
1913
Pen and black ink, graphite on paper
12¾ × 9¹/₁₆ in. (32.4 × 23 cm)
COOPER HEWITT, SMITHSONIAN DESIGN MUSEUM, NEW YORK,
GIFT OF MME HECTOR GUIMARD, 1950-66-14

65
Plan of Ground Floor for
Villa Hemsy, Saint-Cloud
May 1913
Blueprint on white wove paper
21½ × 10¹³⁄₁₆ in.
(54.6 × 27.5 cm)
COOPER HEWITT, SMITHSONIAN
DESIGN MUSEUM, NEW YORK,
GIFT OF MME HECTOR GUIMARD,
1950-66-18

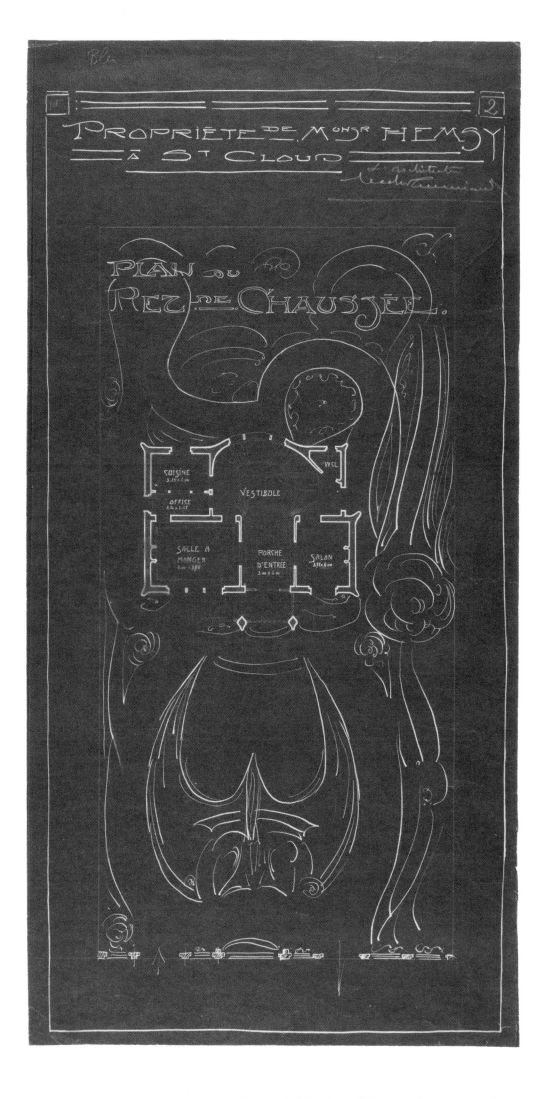

Commercial Architecture

No longer wanting to rely solely on private commissions, Guimard aimed to venture into commercial real estate as early as 1906, when he created the initial designs for a large ensemble of buildings along rues Gros, La Fontaine, and Moderne. It was only after his 1909 marriage to Adeline Oppenheim, however, that he was able to create a real estate company to finance such enterprises, the Société générale de constructions modernes. Guimard welcomed the opportunity to experiment with modern design in a commercial context. The Société financed several building projects in the 16th arrondissement, including that ambitious early project. A 1911 block plan shows eleven buildings, designated A through L (there is no J), clustered around an internal street Guimard labeled rue Moderne.

Building C was to be located at 4, rue Moderne, in the middle of the site. Its facade, which wrapped around the corner of rue Moderne, featured regular fenestration. The subtle curves of the sculptural stone carving on the facade were less dramatic than those of the dynamic cast-iron balconies. The mansard roof was punctuated by a series of regularly spaced, elegant dormer windows. The rear facade was similarly restrained and orderly. It employed simple brick and rubble masonry as well as three types of windows. The plans of the ground and upper floors show that Guimard positioned the main rooms, including the bedrooms, salon, and dining room, along the street facade to ensure ample natural light.

Although Building C was never realized, six of the eleven were, including 43, rue Gros; 17–21, rue La Fontaine; and 8 and 10, rue Agar (formerly Moderne).

A. C.

66
Development on rue Moderne
Photograph of Immeubles Agar
After 1911
Photographic print on sensitized paper
7 × 8½ in. (17.8 × 21.6 cm)
COOPER HEWITT, SMITHSONIAN DESIGN MUSEUM, NEW YORK,
GIFT OF MME HECTOR GUIMARD, 1951-160-1-1

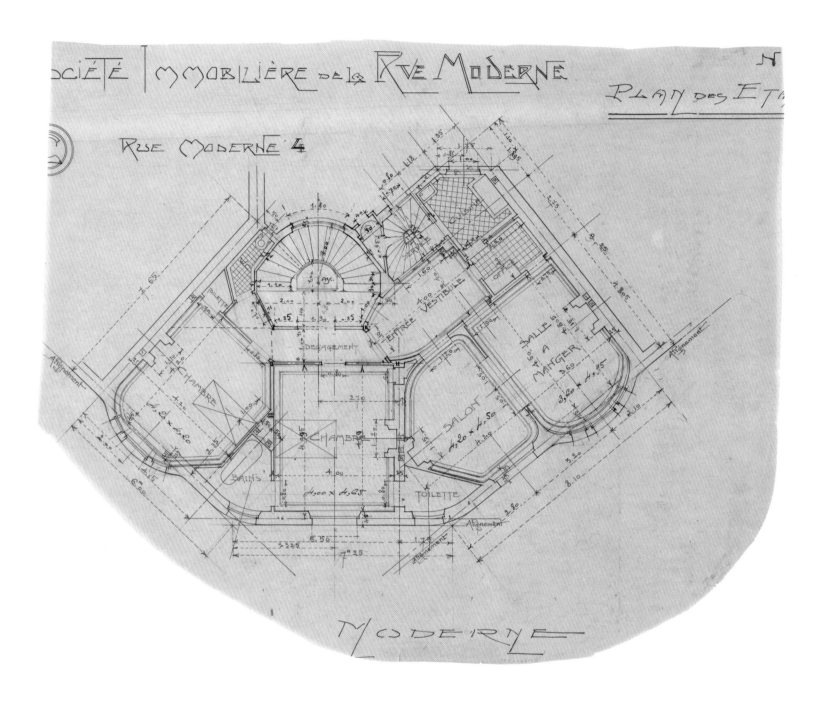

67
Immobilière de la rue Moderne
Floor Plan of Building No. 10, Immeubles Agar
c. 1907
Pen and black ink, graphite on brown paper
15 5/16 × 19 3/16 in. (38.9 × 48.7 cm)
COOPER HEWITT, SMITHSONIAN DESIGN MUSEUM, NEW YORK,
GIFT OF MME HECTOR GUIMARD, 1950-66-10

68 (opposite)
Immobilière de la rue Moderne
Front Elevation of Building No. 6, Immeubles Agar
November 20, 1909
Pen and black ink, graphite on heavy tracing paper
24 3/8 × 18 3/8 in. (61.9 × 46.7 cm)
COOPER HEWITT, SMITHSONIAN DESIGN MUSEUM, NEW YORK,
GIFT OF MME HECTOR GUIMARD, 1950-66-12

Société Immobilière de la Rue Moderne

Dessiné par l'architecte soussigné
Paris le 20 Novembre 1909

Income Housing

The apartment building at 38, rue Greuze—conceived of as an income project—was one of Guimard's last realized buildings in Paris. Guimard excelled at rationalizing small and irregularly shaped sites, and this seven-story building, which occupied an extremely narrow lot at the corner of rue Greuze and rue Decamps, was no exception. There were two apartments per floor, each with an entry, kitchen, dining room, central room, bedroom, and bathroom. A compact central stairwell provided access to the small but efficiently laid out units.

The overall restraint and crisp geometric forms of the building are characteristic of a mid-1920s change in Guimard's decorative vocabulary, as are his simplified design for the "French village town hall" at the 1925 Exposition internationale des arts décoratifs and the stark angular forms of his 1926 apartment on rue Henri-Heine. The ornamental austerity at 38, rue Greuze results in part from simple, inexpensive building materials: cream-colored brick, asbestos cement Eternit pipes (developed by his friend and fellow modern architect Henri Sauvage), and a small amount of cut stone on the ground floor. The cement pipes function decoratively, helping to animate the facade: they punctuate the fenestration, which is more regular and symmetrical than that of Guimard's earlier projects; express the bay windows, also enlivened by rippled braided brickwork; and emphasize the building's verticality. The building's cast-iron balcony fronts and window grilles, produced by the Saint-Dizier Foundries, also exhibit unusually controlled linearity.

A. C.

69
Front Elevation, Immeuble rue Henri-Heine
December 1925
Blueprint
$27^{15}/_{16} \times 14^{7}/_{16}$ in. (70.9 × 36.6 cm)
COOPER HEWITT, SMITHSONIAN DESIGN MUSEUM, NEW YORK,
GIFT OF MME HECTOR GUIMARD, 1950-66-43

⑫

IMMEUBLE RUE H. HEINE

FAÇADE SUR RUE

Xbre 1925   L'ARCHITECTE

ÉCHELLE DE 0.02 P.Mᵉ

IMMEUBLE 38 RUE GREUZE

FAÇADES

ECHELLE DE 0,02 p. M.

Dressé par l'Architecte soussigné
Paris, Janvier 1928

70 (*opposite*)
Front Elevation of 38,
rue Greuze
January 1928
Graphite, pen and black ink
on tracing paper
22 7/16 × 20 11/16 in.
(57 × 52.5 cm)
COOPER HEWITT, SMITHSONIAN
DESIGN MUSEUM, NEW YORK,
GIFT OF MME HECTOR GUIMARD,
1950-66-53-1

71
Cross Section of 38,
rue Greuze
April 1929
Pen and ink, graphite on paper
23 7/16 × 7 3/16 in.
(59.6 × 18.2 cm)
COOPER HEWITT, SMITHSONIAN
DESIGN MUSEUM, NEW YORK,
GIFT OF MME HECTOR GUIMARD,
1950-66-52

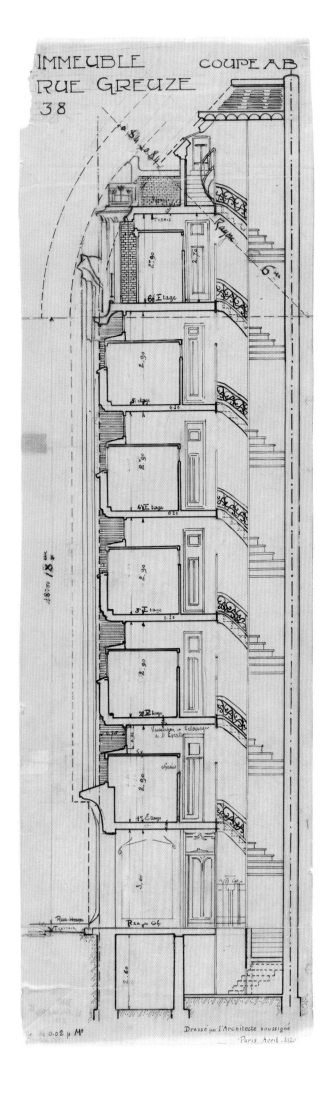

72
Design for the Entrance of 38, rue Greuze
c. 1928
Graphite, pen and ink, blue crayon on paper
20⅝ × 15⅛ in. (52.4 × 38.4 cm)
COOPER HEWITT, SMITHSONIAN DESIGN MUSEUM, NEW YORK,
GIFT OF MME HECTOR GUIMARD, 1950-66-54

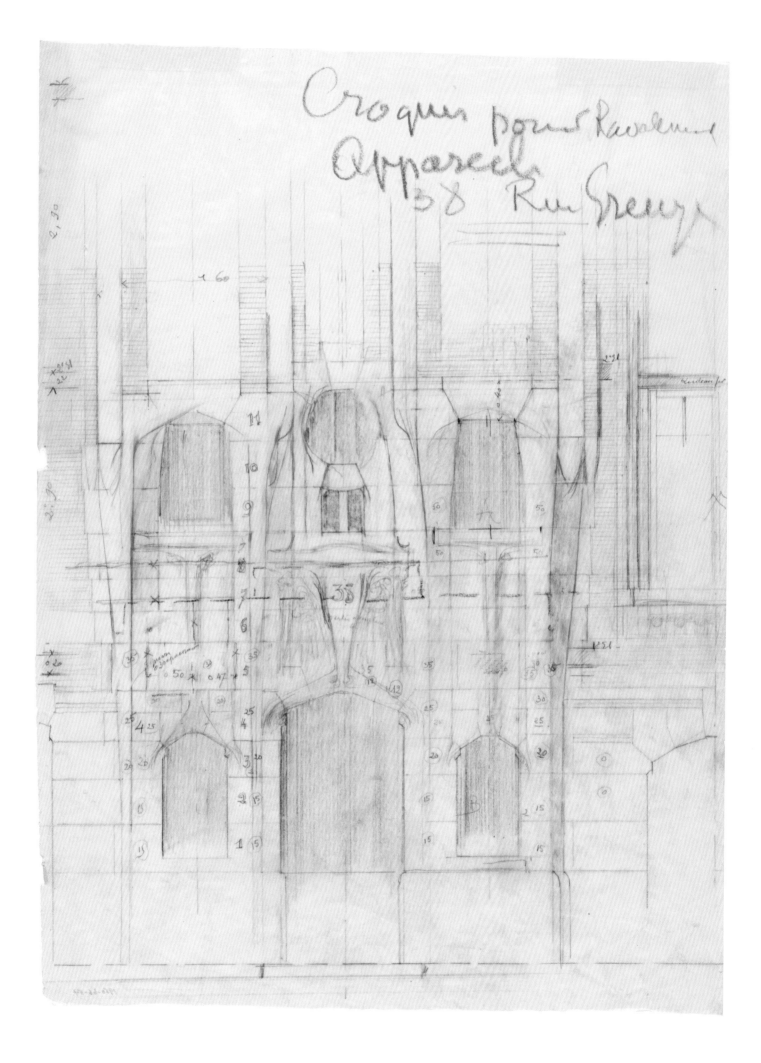

Production, Promotion, Publicity
Georges Vigne

Even in the earliest years of his career, Hector Guimard paid equal attention to both the interiors and exteriors of his buildings, ensuring a unity of style. At the time, roughly 1890, Art Nouveau in France was emerging in the decorative arts, but not yet in architecture. Thus, recognition for the ambitious young man came about only gradually. In fact, it was at Castel Béranger, the imposing apartment building at 14, rue La Fontaine, that Guimard conceived decorative arts in a wide range of materials—stained-glass windows, mosaics, ceramics, stair carpets, wall paneling, wallpaper, fireplaces, ironwork—down to the smallest details of woodwork, hardware, or decorative door and window fixtures (fig. 1). The building met with considerable success, as much for its novelty as for its strange, abstract, almost aggressively graphic dynamic.

Guimard likely thought he could promote the designs for that project by applying to prestigious manufacturers to produce them. But the singularity of his creations seems to have frightened off his admirers, even with considerable publicity from a luxury monograph published in 1898, a prize in Paris's first Facade Competition in 1899, and an exhibition opening on April 5 of that year on the premises of the newspaper *Le Figaro*. Guimard strove to position himself as a genuine "designer"—the word did not yet exist—but without commercial backing. He did not change his methods in other house commissions—in Sèvres, Lille, Hermanville, or Garches—always continuing to invent, to renew himself. Born during the Second Empire, he was true to the ethos of his time, insisting on asserting himself as a creator, not as a purveyor of designs for industry.

By 1900, Guimard had become the architect everyone was talking about. Even so, he was not invited to build a single pavilion for that year's Exposition universelle, participating only in a few displays. Perfumery F. Millot asked him to design perfume bottles and boxes for beauty products (see Thiébaut, "*Le style Guimard*," fig. 2). In addition, he received an order from the prestigious Sèvres Porcelain Manufactory for a glazed-stoneware vase (see cat. no. 74) and cachepot and, two years later, for a large planter (see cat. no. 73). Alas, the account books of the manufacturer show that the success of these creations was limited. Guimard took his cachepot design, which he called the "Chalmont Vase," to the Fives-Lille factory. Simplified and executed in ceramic slip, it seems to have been more popular.

One reason for Guimard's popular acclaim was his project for the entrances to the Paris subway system. Although he had not entered the competition for these structures, which had disappointing results, he was thrown into the project nevertheless. But beginning in 1903, Art Nouveau began to lose momentum. At this time, Guimard also had his first conflicts, financial and artistic, with the Métropolitain Railway Company, marking the beginning of a long period of relative inactivity. His fortuitous opportunity forced him to rationalize his ideas and develop ingenious technical solutions. With only a few months to work on the project, he decided to explore the potential of modular elements that could

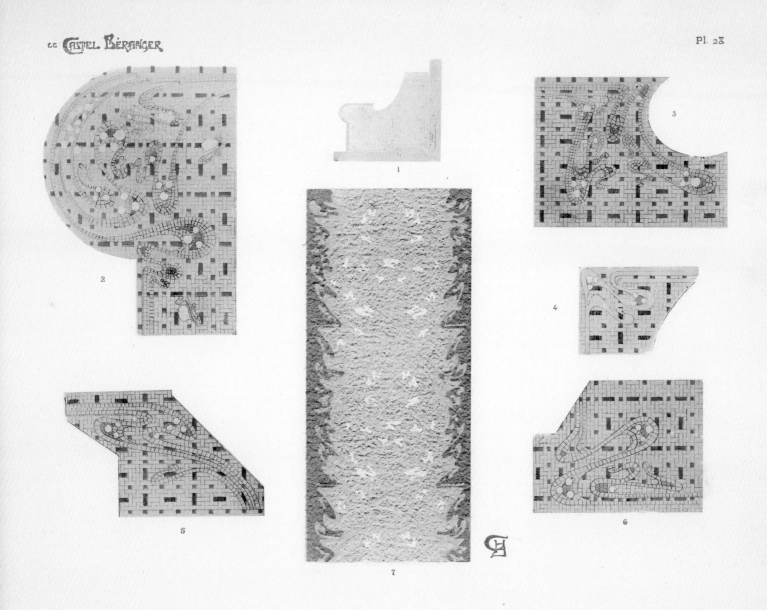

be assembled in multiple ways and to rely on molded materials, such as cast iron, glass, and lava stone, for the individual structures. Guimard envisioned tall gateways equipped with lighting, visible from afar and at all hours, as well as railings with decorative panels integrated into the cityscape without ever obstructing it. The scheme proved that these utilitarian works, which would normally be assigned to engineers or industrial firms, could be conceived by an artist. The modernity of Guimard's construction system paralleled the modernity of subway transportation; pliable and airy, his contributions featured decoration that was unfamiliar yet measured and signage with original calligraphy.

The era was not ready to fully welcome Guimard's restless imagination, more audacious and unsettling than that of his colleagues (with whom he refused to be associated). In addition to creating his work for the Métro, during the years 1904 through 1907 Guimard conceived an ensemble of decorative elements in cast iron, more than three hundred items, to be used in residential design. The pieces were principally balconies, in several sizes, but also doors, door handles, and house numbers. Also included in this astonishing catalogue were legs for benches and tables, mantelpieces, and even garden ornaments or tombs. The plaster or wood models were probably created in the workshops Guimard had established on avenue Perrichont; the production of the designs was destined for the Saint-Dizier Foundries. The construction of the furniture of his so-called classical period, including the magnificent ensembles for the Hôtels Nozal, Guimard, and Mezzara, remained at the workshops. In a way that is rather surprising, but that reveals the architect's desire to adapt his imagination to a still-conservative clientele, these designs feature perfectly symmetrical compositions that use modular motifs, repeated, reversed, or inverted, and conducive to a visual unity, to animate the sinuous treelike structures.

Guimard began to use his building products in the Jassedé building at 142, avenue de Versailles and continued to use them until the end of his career. Indeed, they eventually accounted for most of the exterior decoration of his buildings, especially as sculptural decoration began to disappear. They also influenced the furniture that Guimard designed from 1904 onward, which was simpler, more classical, and devoid of useless protrusions.

The idea that the cast-iron decorative objects could respond to almost any need points to Guimard's goal of adding artistry to the buildings of his contemporaries, even utterly mundane structures. Although the Saint-Dizier Foundries were committed to the product line, publishing a catalogue complete with details of dimension and price, the "*Style Guimard* Artistic Cast Iron" is seen primarily in the cemeteries around Saint-Dizier. Use of the items on only a small number of scattered apartment buildings likely indicates that this ambitious and costly project did not find the proper promotional tools.

The limited success of the product line did not prevent the architect from planning collaborations with other manufacturers. In November 1908, Guimard prepared a contract with P. Aubert for the production of jacquard carpeting; soon after, he teamed up with Langlois for the creation of a series of light fixtures under the brand name Lustre Lumière. Numerous sketches and gouache renderings related to the light fixtures testify to the great care Guimard brought to their design (fig. 2). As with his Métro entrances, Guimard developed a modular system that could be used to create chandeliers and sconces of varying sizes and forms. Delicate glass pendants, for which a patent was applied in June 1910, surrounded the lighting pieces.[1] A presentation of Guimard's lighting took place at the Salon des artistes décorateurs in 1914.

The last documented agreement was prepared in 1913 with Olivier et Desbordes for the production of twelve exemplars each of various pieces of furniture. But the beginning of World War I interfered with the execution of the contract. Guimard's arrangements had points in common: he would keep the artistic rights to all of his creations; the pieces would be clearly marked "*le style Guimard*"; and in each case, a special catalogue would be published. Guimard's contract with Olivier et Desbordes indicates, rather sadly, that the architect did not succeed at commercializing the furniture created in his workshops. He seems to have used his *hôtel particulier* at 122, avenue Mozart as an expansive showroom: the inventory drawn up during Hector and Adeline Guimard's time in the United States reveals a truly irrational overabundance of furnishings, including fourteen tables and more than forty chairs.[2]

Several groups of archival material relating to these collaborations with manufacturers are now in the collection of the Musée des arts décoratifs in Paris. A label describing part of this ensemble of more than two hundred items reads: "Photographs and Drawings – Works of Hector Guimard – Architecture – Bronze, Lighting – Mirrors – Furniture – Tombs – Vases, Fireplaces – Gift of Mme Guimard, July 1948." A few images, related to buildings that preceded or followed the period during which Guimard signed the contracts, seem to have been added to some of the groups, making them a little hard to understand. Nevertheless, the majority of the documents were produced to provide

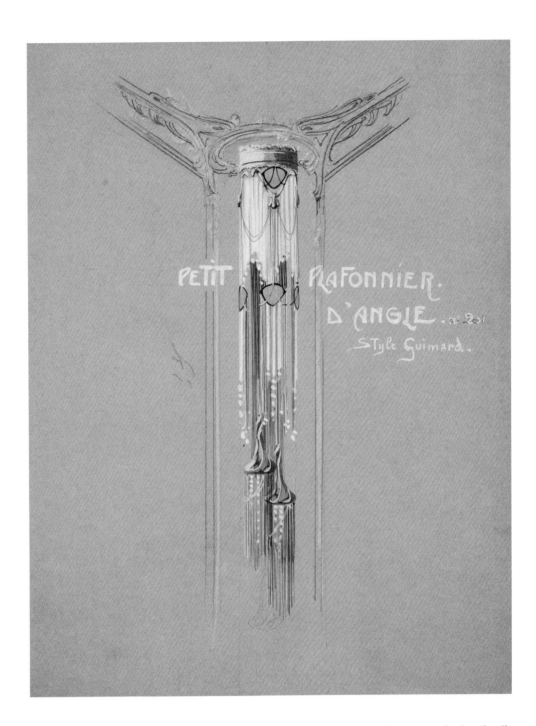

FIG. 2. Guimard, rendering of a Lustre Lumière chandelier, Corner Ceiling Light, c. 1909. Gouache on paper. Musée des arts décoratifs archives, Paris.

designs for independent manufacturers. Many of the photographs are meticulously silhouetted, most likely to hide the background; others present carefully measured objects; most bear titles in which the name Guimard is mentioned.

Some of the more coherent groups are devoted to vases (fig. 3), small marble columns for living rooms, frames for mirrors, mantelpieces, pieces of hardware—sometimes in the form of plaster models—cane handles, charming designs for silverware (fig. 4), fabrics, rugs, and lamps. One surprising group consists of a series of tombs, some as small models, others at full scale and installed outside (fig. 5), perhaps in an exhibition of funerary art. The collection is accompanied by photographs of Guimard buildings that present his artistic cast iron in situ as well as older interiors, such as those of Castel Henriette, Hôtel Nozal, or the bedroom in the Maison Coilliot house in Lille. Some of the photographed furniture is well known and held by museums or private collections; other

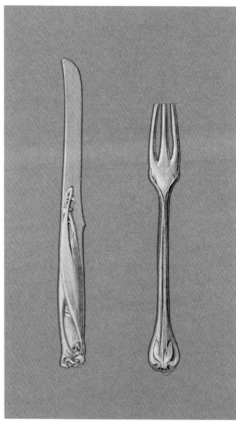

FIG. 3. Guimard, rendering of a Marble and Bronze Decorative Vase, c. 1909. Gouache on paper. Musée des arts décoratifs archives, Paris.

FIG. 4. Guimard, rendering of a knife and fork, c. 1909. Gouache on paper. Musée des arts décoratifs archives, Paris.

pieces are little known, with photographs taken during temporary exhibitions or in the avenue Perrichont workshops. Among these are an unusual and amusing crib and a bed of unknown model (figs. 6–7). The documents in the Musée des arts décoratifs suggest that Guimard may have collaborated with other industrial firms, although the only traces that remain are numbers linked to references in commercial catalogues. After World War I, Guimard ended all attempts at new creations in the decorative arts, no longer having a workshop in which to realize them. When he needed three chairs for the office of the French village town hall (Mairie du village français), built for the Exposition internationale des arts décoratifs in 1925, he ordered simplified copies of the Hôtel Nozal chair from the Eagle firm.

In the early 1900s, Guimard tried to adapt the methods used to publicize his decorative arts creations to his architecture as well. But due to the modest size of his firm, his capacity to take on large projects was limited; for that reason, he developed groups of buildings that offered at best only subtle variations of a single model. His first large-scale undertaking was several buildings linked to the Parc Beauséjour, a vast housing development in the *département* of Essonne. The 1905 project was planned around Castel d'Orgeval, built by Guimard in 1904 for the developers of the park, Achille and Léon Laurent. At the Salon d'automne of that year, Guimard presented a curious little brochure in which he described fourteen small fantasy houses. They had picturesque names, among them Clair de Lune, one of the two workers' houses Guimard built in the park in 1906. Similarly, a house in Eaubonne, in the *département* of Val d'Oise, built a short time later, seems also to have been part of a larger subdivision.

The Essonne and Eaubonne projects, both in the suburbs of Paris, did not have the importance of those in the capital. After Hector Guimard married Adeline Oppenheim in

OPPOSITE: FIG. 5. Guimard, tomb, probably photographed at an exhibition of funerary art, c. 1909. Musée des arts décoratifs archives, Paris.

GEORGES VIGNE

1909, the architect could take advantage of both the vast tract of land owned by his friend Léon Nozal in Auteuil and substantial financial support from his father-in-law. Guimard relaunched a project from 1906, and the real estate development firm he created for the occasion, the Société générale de constructions modernes, put several housing developments in the 16th arrondissement; these would occupy Guimard for about fifteen years. Of the thirteen apartment buildings planned, only six were constructed; the one on rue Agar was the most ambitious.

The four years of World War I reduced Guimard and his contemporaries to almost total inactivity. But the end of the conflict gave him hopes of a profitable opportunity to build standardized houses for the devastated regions in northern and eastern France. Between December 1920 and January 1921, Guimard put together twelve patent applications for ingenious systems of prefabricated houses. With the help of some colleagues, he conceived sixteen types of houses.[3] He himself experimented with prefabrication in a small private house in square Jasmin. Construction took just a few days, and Guimard was careful to have the entire process photographed (see Bergdoll, "Signature vs. Standardization," figs. 2–3). The French village town hall for the 1925 Exposition internationale des arts décoratifs was built with the same methods and the same rapidity. Unfortunately, Guimard's ingenious inventions do not seem to have generated any interest. Disappointed, he returned to his usual projects, including a failed housing development based on his upscale building at 18, rue Henri-Heine—for which he received a

FIG. 6. Guimard, crib, probably photographed in Guimard's workshops, 1903–14. Musée des arts décoratifs archives, Paris.

FIG. 7. Guimard, bed, photographed in Guimard's workshops, 1903–14. Musée des arts décoratifs archives, Paris.

Facade Competition prize in 1928—and a few others. Exterior ornament on these buildings relied for the most part on the texture and projections of the masonry construction.

Throughout his career, Guimard sought to go beyond the role of the architect, attempting to assume control over all aspects of a dwelling, from the entry door handle to the tableware. But he was able to attain the ideal of perfect continuity between exterior and interior in only three projects—Villa "La Bluette" in Hermanville, Castel Henriette in Sèvres, and Hôtel Guimard in Paris. Even at Castel Béranger, a rental apartment building, he was not able to supply beds, tables, or chairs. And elsewhere, for financial reasons or because furniture already existed, Guimard could create the complete decoration of, at most, a single room.

One of the distinctive characteristics of Guimard's practice was his taste for self-promotion, which increased over the course of his career. At the time of the Housing Exhibition in 1903, he produced a series of postcards to publicize his buildings. He regularly presented decorative ensembles at the salons or at international exhibitions. And he insisted on the publication of catalogues devoted to his creations.

In the early 1900s, Guimard had to make do with the rudimentary and inadequate advertising methods of his day. Some of his difficulties may have arisen from the breadth of his interests in various techniques and his personal belief in the value of his aesthetic language. It is worthwhile in this regard to compare Guimard to some of his contemporaries: Charles Plumet was able to make himself known as a fine *"ensemblier"*; Jules Lavirotte—the other great master of turn-of-the-century architecture—was not much involved in interior decoration and thus less able to promote his own work; Léon Benouville, who died too young, made only episodic incursions into the field of mainstream furniture. Perhaps the best comparison is to Guimard's friend Henri Sauvage. Sauvage realized some beautiful furniture and several interiors that were appreciated in their time, but his foray into the world of decorative arts was unfortunately brief and limited. Guimard would have enjoyed significantly more effective means of promotion if he had been active a hundred years later.

NOTES

1   République française, Office national de la propriété industrielle, Hector Guimard, "Franges-pendeloques diffusantes pour luminaires, lustres, etc." Patent no. FR416914, applied for June 9, 1910, published November 2, 1910. https://worldwide.espacenet.com/publicationDetails /originalDocument?CC=FR&NR=416914A&KC=A&FT=D&ND=4&date=19101102&DB=EPODOC &locale=en_EP, accessed November 18, 2019. Guimard also applied for a British patent for the same invention in the following month.

2   Bedel Inventory, 1937. Adeline Oppenheim Guimard papers, Manuscripts and Archives Division, New York Public Library.

3   République française, Office national de la propriété industrielle, Hector Guimard, patent nos. FR529104–FR529107, applied for December 28, 1920, published November 23, 1921; patent nos. FR529469–FR529470, applied for January 7, 1921, published November 29, 1921; patent nos. FR529896–FR529900, applied for January 18, 1921, published December 8, 1921; patent no. FR530424, applied for January 31, 1921, published December 22, 1921. https://worldwide.espacenet.com /searchResults?submitted=true&locale=en_EP&DB=EPODOC&ST=advanced&TI=&AB=&PN=&AP =&PR=&PD=&PA=&IN=guimard%2C+hector&CPC=&IC=, accessed November 18, 2019.

Manufacture Nationale de Porcelaine de Sèvres

Atelier d'Emaillage

Design for Production

An essential aspect of Art Nouveau in general, and Guimard's work in particular, was the acceptance of technology and the machine as a means of creating a modern style. Although Guimard's architectural commissions were created for specific clients, with the aim of achieving a unity of architecture and furnishings down to the smallest detail, he also designed for industrial production. Following the success of Castel Béranger, Guimard received design commissions from various manufacturers. In 1900, the directors of the École des Beaux-Arts engaged him to create two prototypes for vases to be produced by the Sèvres workshops for the Exposition universelle, held the same year. Included in the exhibition at the Salon des artistes décorateurs in Paris, also in 1900, was a showcase Guimard designed to demonstrate how stores should display his products. He also designed perfume bottles for the Exposition universelle—small, abstract sculptures in glass—for the F. Millot company. Lighting was yet another manufactured product Guimard experimented with: his Lustre Lumière electric lamps and fixtures were made of cast bronze with curtains of glass pendants that shimmered in the light. His embrace of industrial processes and his interest in designs that could be mass-produced identified Guimard as a modern, twentieth-century architect.

Guimard's interest in technology extended to material explorations in his buildings. He was particularly attracted to the molding and production possibilities of cast iron, which allowed him to replicate designs—either linear or sculptural—rapidly and in quantity. Cast-iron designs for the Saint-Dizier Foundries were included in the manufacturer's trade catalogue of 1908 and illustrate the range of his designs in this material. Particularly interesting are the cast-iron street numbers in Guimard's unique typeface. Guimard installed the cast-iron elements on many of his own buildings; other architects of the period used the products as well, though not so widely as the designer may have hoped.

Sèvres Porcelain Manufactory postcard, showing artisans working on a Chalmont Vase. Dominique Magdelaine, Paris.

Sèvres Porcelain Manufactory

The Sèvres Porcelain Manufactory, the French national fabricator near Versailles, has been producing porcelain since 1756. At the turn of the century, Sèvres began to include Art Nouveau designs in its line and also introduced iridescent crystal glazes influenced by Japanese porcelain. Sèvres commissioned two new models from Guimard in preparation for the 1900 Exposition universelle in Paris. The first design was the Chalmont Vase, a cachepot based on a ceramic design the architect had created for Castel Béranger. The second work was the Cerny Vase. Its crystalline glaze, in subtle, earthy tones of brown, rust, and green; its undulating form; and the perforated elements at its rim were inspired by nature. Guimard used this design in several interiors, including Hôtel Guimard. In 1901, Guimard undertook another commission for Sèvres, this time for the Saint Louis World's Fair of 1904: the Binelles Vase. Named after rue des Binelles in the town of Sèvres, this vessel is the largest and most impressive of the three. Other French artists, in particular Taxile Doat, a designer at Sèvres from 1877 to 1905, drew on Guimard's forms and decorations. In 1909, Doat immigrated to the United States and began to work at the Art Academy and Porcelain Works when it was first established in a suburb of Saint Louis, Missouri, where he produced designs similar to Guimard's Sèvres porcelain.

D. A. H.

73
Binelles Vase
1903
Stoneware
51¼ × 15⅜ × 15⅝ in. (130.2 × 39.1 × 39.7 cm)
Produced by Sèvres Porcelain Manufactory, Sèvres
THE METROPOLITAN MUSEUM OF ART, ROBERT A. ELLISON JR.
COLLECTION, PURCHASE, 2011 BENEFIT FUND, 2013.502

74
Cerny Vase from Hôtel Guimard
Designed 1900, executed 1908
Stoneware
10⅝ × 5¼ × 5¼ in.
(27 × 13.4 × 13.4 cm)
Produced by Sèvres Porcelain
Manufactory, Sèvres
COOPER HEWITT, SMITHSONIAN
DESIGN MUSEUM, NEW YORK,
GIFT OF MME HECTOR GUIMARD,
1948-114-2

75 (opposite left)
Lustre Lumière: Nouvel appareil électrique,
bréveté en France et à l'étranger
Catalogue
c. 1900
Letterpress
Length: 9 in. (23 cm)
Published by Langlois et Cie, Paris
THOMAS J. WATSON LIBRARY, THE METROPOLITAN MUSEUM OF ART,
GIFT OF MRS. HECTOR GUIMARD, 1197449

76 (opposite right)
Plate Showing Lamps, nos. 518 and 501, from *Lustre Lumière:*
Nouvel appareil électrique, bréveté en France et à l'étranger
Catalogue
c. 1900
Lithograph
Length: 9 in. (23 cm)
Published by Langlois et Cie, Paris
THOMAS J. WATSON LIBRARY, THE METROPOLITAN MUSEUM OF ART,
GIFT OF MRS. HECTOR GUIMARD, 1197449

DESIGN FOR PRODUCTION

Lustre Lumière

Guimard's designs for the lighting manufacturer Langlois et Cie at 20, rue Malher in Paris were collected under the name Lustre Lumière. Guimard applied for a design patent in France on June 9, 1910, and in Great Britain on July 7 of the same year, for his invention of icicle-like suspended glass pendants for use in lamps—"*frangespendeloques diffusantes*" and "diffusing fringes," respectively. He exhibited examples of these modern fixtures at the 1914 Salon des artistes décorateurs, publishing an accompanying trade catalogue. In 1949, Madame Guimard gave a copy of the twenty-six-page catalogue, which illustrates in hand-tinted photographs the luminous ensembles of bronze, copper, or iron with glass, to the Metropolitan Museum of Art. The cover of the catalogue features a stylized graphic representation, drawn by Guimard, of the hanging pendants that allows two open spaces for text: "Lustre Lumière" and "Nouvel Appareil Électrique." The shaped armatures and glass pendants of the lighting fixtures represented *le style Guimard,* as noted by some of the catalogue captions. A number of lamps are classified according to historic era, such as "Style Louis XVI" or "Style Renaissance." Guimard used the lighting in interiors he designed, including in the salon, dining room, his wife's bedroom, and the stair hall of Hôtel Guimard.

D. A. H.

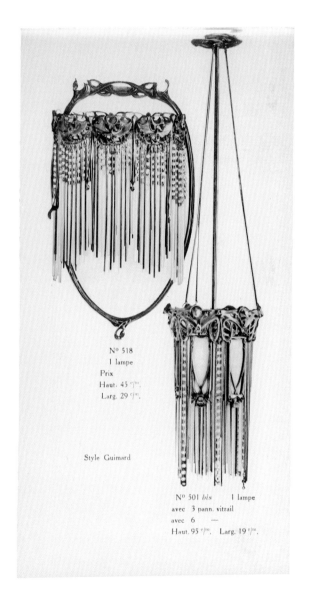

77 (*opposite*)
Lustre Lumière Hanging Lamp
c. 1912
Gilt bronze, glass
19¼ × 13 × 13 in.
(48.9 × 33 × 33 cm)
Produced by Langlois
et Cie, Paris
THE COLLECTION OF RICHARD H.
DRIEHAUS, CHICAGO, 30937

78
Lustre Lumière Table Lamp
1900–1910
Gilt bronze, glass
19¾ × 7¾ × 10½ in.
(50.2 × 19.7 × 26.7 cm)
Produced by Langlois
et Cie, Paris
THE COLLECTION OF RICHARD H.
DRIEHAUS, CHICAGO, 31162

F. Millot

For the 1900 Exposition universelle in Paris, the prominent perfumery F. Millot (established 1839) commissioned Guimard to design the entirety of their stand, taking full advantage of the architect's keen interest in furniture, interiors, product design, and graphic design/typography. Guimard was responsible for both larger environmental components, including the wall treatment (wood paneling and printed silk hangings) and display shelves, and smaller discrete elements, such as cosmetics complete with their boxes and logos. F. Millot introduced three new lines for the fair, among them Kantirix ("the flower of Mexico"),

for which Guimard designed the bottles, powder boxes, labels, and packaging. The sensual dynamism of the molded glass bottles, echoing the asymmetry characterizing many of Guimard's buildings, announced the modernity of the fragrances, for which the company was awarded a gold medal. Never one to pass up an opportunity for self-promotion, Guimard affirmed his authorship by incorporating the monogram "HG" into not only the product design but the related pieces for the various beauty products.

Y. Y.

79
Kantirix Perfume Bottle
1899
Partially gilt glass
7¾ × 3½ × 2½ in.
(19.7 × 9 × 5 cm)
Produced by F. Millot, Paris
CHRISTIE MAYER LEFKOWITH
COLLECTION, NEW YORK

80 (*opposite*)
Kantirix Lotion Bottle
1899
Partially gilt glass
15¾ × 4¹³⁄₁₆ × 2¾ in.
(40 × 12.2 × 7 cm)
Produced by F. Millot, Paris
CHRISTIE MAYER LEFKOWITH
COLLECTION, NEW YORK

DESIGN FOR PRODUCTION

81
Prototype Plaque for Kantirix Perfume Bottle Box
1899
Embossed and gilded cardboard
5 × 5¾ in. (12.7 × 14.6 cm)
Produced for F. Millot, Paris
CHRISTIE MAYER LEFKOWITH COLLECTION, NEW YORK

82 (*opposite*)
Prototype Plaque for Kantirix Perfume Bottle Box
1899
Embossed cardboard
8 × 6⅛ in. (20.2 × 15.5 cm)
Produced for F. Millot, Paris
CHRISTIE MAYER LEFKOWITH COLLECTION, NEW YORK

Saint-Dizier Foundries

Guimard worked with several foundries in Saint-Dizier (in the district of Haute-Marne in northeast France), including the Val d'Osne Foundry for the Paris Métro, to produce practical yet beautiful mass-manufactured objects. He collaborated with the Saint-Dizier Foundries on a series of standardized and modular architectural, garden, and burial elements in cast iron. Easy to manufacture, transport, assemble, and even combine in innumerable configurations, these designs were published in the 1908 catalogue *Fontes artistiques pour constructions, fumisterie, articles de jardins, et sépultures: Style Guimard*. Aware that the publication of such catalogues

was critical to disseminating knowledge of his creations, Guimard labeled each model in a manner that underscored the totality (and encyclopedic aspirations) of *le style Guimard*.

While constituting one of Guimard's key experiments with prefabrication—the objects ranged from jardinieres and fireplace mantels to house numbers and balcony grille elements—this industrial venture was, sadly, and like many of his endeavors, not financially successful. With the exception of architects in Saint-Dizier, Guimard was his own best customer.

Y. Y.

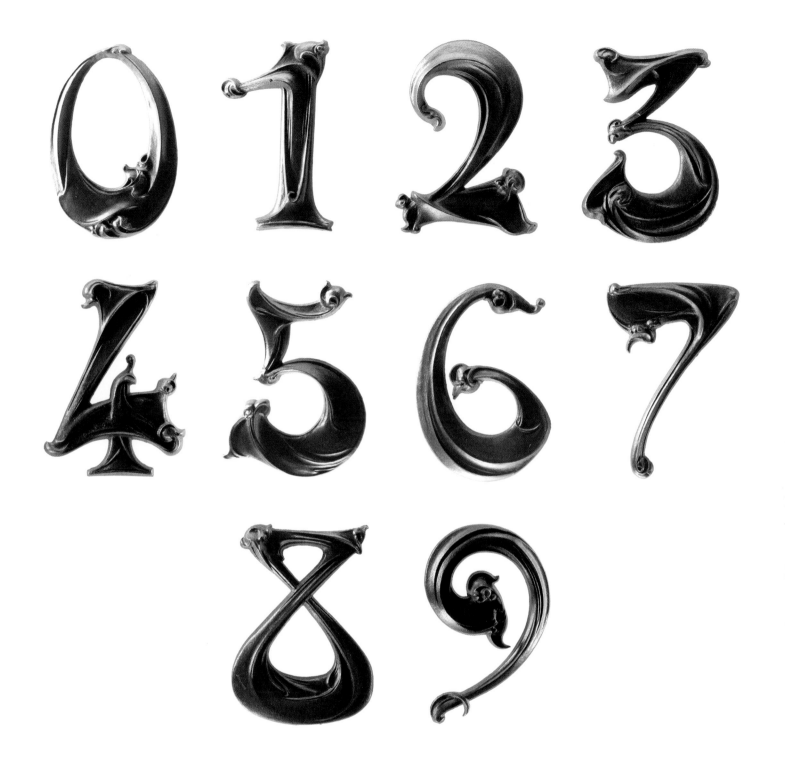

83 (*opposite*)
Fontes artistiques pour constructions, fumisterie,
articles de jardins, et sépultures: Style Guimard Catalogue
1908
Letterpress
11 × 14¹⁵⁄₁₆ in. (28 × 38 cm)
Published by Saint-Dizier Foundries, Saint-Dizier

84
House Numerals, Zero through Nine
c. 1900–1908
Cast iron
5½ × 4 in. (14 × 10.2 cm) each
Produced by Saint-Dizier Foundries, Saint-Dizier

85
Bracket for Bench, Model GO
c. 1912
Painted cast iron
34 × 22 × 3 in. (86.3 × 55.8 × 7.6 cm)
Produced by Saint-Dizier Foundries, Saint-Dizier
THE COLLECTION OF RICHARD H. DRIEHAUS, CHICAGO, 10214

86
Garden Bench, Model GN
c. 1912
Painted cast iron, wood
36 × 52 × 29½ in. (91.4 × 132.1 × 74.9 cm)
Produced by Saint-Dizier Foundries, Saint-Dizier
THE COLLECTION OF RICHARD H. DRIEHAUS, CHICAGO, 10002

87
Front Elevation of Paris Apartment Building Clad with
Cast Iron Components Designed by Guimard
1925
Photostat on paper
20⅞ × 13⁷⁄₁₆ in. (53 × 34.2 cm)
COOPER HEWITT, SMITHSONIAN DESIGN MUSEUM, NEW YORK,
GIFT OF MME HECTOR GUIMARD, 1950-66-55

IMMEUBLE DE RAPPORT CONSTRUIT A PARIS
AVEC LES FONTES DE St DIZIER

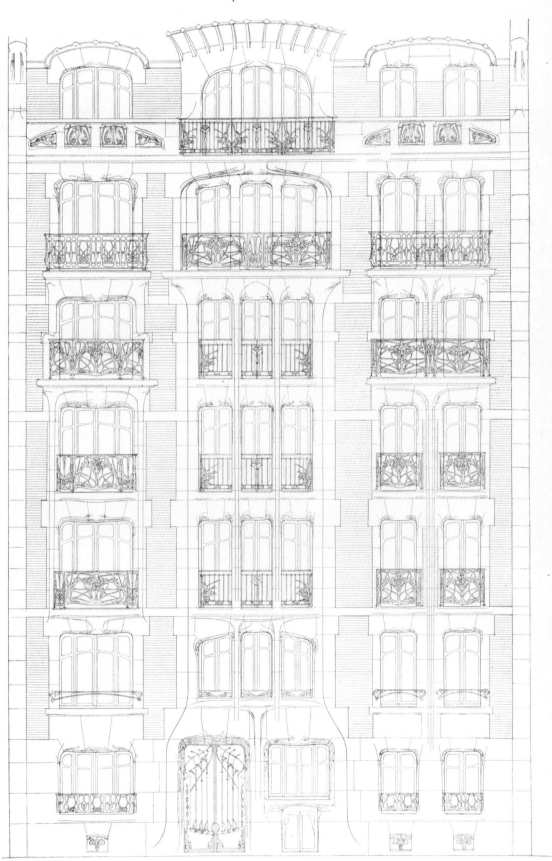

Papier, Gravure et Impression L. GEISLER.

88
Grille, Section of Tomb Enclosure, Model GB
Before 1908
Cast iron
17 × 8 × 1 in. (43.2 × 20.3 × 2.5 cm)
Produced by Saint-Dizier Foundries, Saint-Dizier
THE COLLECTION OF RICHARD H. DRIEHAUS, CHICAGO, 20331

89 (*opposite*)
Grille, Section of Tomb Enclosure, Model GA
Before 1908
Cast iron
28¼ × 7½ × 1 in. (71.7 × 19 × 2.5 cm)
Produced by Saint-Dizier Foundries, Saint-Dizier
THE COLLECTION OF RICHARD H. DRIEHAUS, CHICAGO, 20332

90
Balcony Railing for a Casement Window, Model GI
c. 1908
Cast iron
16¹⁵⁄₁₆ × 46⅞ × 1¼ in. (43 × 119.1 × 3.2 cm)
Produced by Saint-Dizier Foundries, Saint-Dizier
THE COLLECTION OF RICHARD H. DRIEHAUS, CHICAGO, 20334

91
Railing for a Casement Window, Model GE
c. 1905–7
Cast iron
4⅝ × 48 × 1¼ in. (11.7 × 121.9 × 3.2 cm)
Produced by Saint-Dizier Foundries, Saint-Dizier
COOPER HEWITT, SMITHSONIAN DESIGN MUSEUM, NEW YORK,
GIFT OF HARRY C. SIGMAN, 2013-21-7

92
Mantelpiece, Model GB
c. 1908
Silvered cast iron
35¾ × 39⅛ × 6 in. (90.8 × 99.8 × 15.2 cm)
Produced by Saint-Dizier Foundries, Saint-Dizier
THE COLLECTION OF RICHARD H. DRIEHAUS, CHICAGO, 60038

93
Jardinière, Model GD
c. 1908
Cast iron
20½ × 28 × 19 in. (52 × 71 × 48 cm)
Produced by Saint-Dizier Foundries, Saint-Dizier
THE COLLECTION OF RICHARD H. DRIEHAUS, CHICAGO, 80505

94
Jardinière, Model GF
c. 1908
Cast iron
7¾ × 40¾ × 11 in. (19.7 × 103.5 × 27.9 cm)
Produced by Saint-Dizier Foundries, Saint-Dizier
THE COLLECTION OF RICHARD H. DRIEHAUS, CHICAGO, 80302

Signature vs. Standardization
Guimard and Prefabrication
Barry Bergdoll

Signature and standardization were the poles between which Hector Guimard's entire career played out. As both architect and graphic designer, he sought at once to craft an immediately recognizable personal style and to invent a system of architecture that might be assembled without his on-site presence. Guimard was probably the first architect to realize the potential that inexpensive photographic postcards offered for spreading his work far from the place of its production; a set of twenty-four he issued in 1903 tellingly included both views of his buildings in their settings and cropped close-ups directing attention to his signature material palette, much of it industrially produced (see cat. nos. 47–55 and pages 70, 176, and 180). In particular, the detail views focused on the artistic metalwork that carried the sinewy line of his autograph, even as it was a line of products that could be sold by the Saint-Dizier Foundries, a commercial ironworks. Parts of buildings, such as Guimard's iron window grilles and balcony fronts, or, in the case of the Paris Métropolitain, entire structures, achieved individuality in expression through replicable factory parts. The postcards were, significantly, issued for the Exposition internationale de l'habitation (Housing Exhibition), held in Paris in 1903. The design of dwellings would predominate in Guimard's career, unlike the public buildings that made most reputations in nineteenth- and early twentieth-century France. In this, Guimard was one of the first French modern architects to achieve fame largely through his work in the private sector, first during the real estate boom of the opening years of the century in Paris and then during the housing crisis exacerbated by the destructions of World War I. It was in that context that a temporary alliance was forged between Guimard's zest for signature and his quest for standardization.

By the 1920s, the Art Nouveau master was at the same time famous and forgotten. *Le style Métro* had made Guimard a household name, yet one that was permanently associated with turn-of-the-century Paris. When Guimard exhibited a French village town hall (Mairie du village français) at the Paris 1925 Exposition internationale des arts décoratifs, he was deemed old-fashioned by those who even noticed his building amid the dazzling structures of the newly fashionable Art Deco. Some commentators were surprised to discover that the architect was still active, so completely was *le style Guimard* associated with another epoch.[1]

Guimard had not been sitting still: his style had changed significantly since he designed the Métro entrances in advance of the Paris Exposition universelle of 1900. If he was still defending Art Nouveau in the pages of *La construction moderne* in 1913, as that style passed from fashion, he was also actively dedicating himself to a social engagement in architecture, an ethos that was to rise to the forefront of his concerns after World War I. In December 1913, he wrote to his friend the journalist Fernand Hauser that he had just finished several designs for industrial production aimed at "le Beau à la portée de tous"—beauty affordable to everyone—"this is a goal that appeals to me and I would

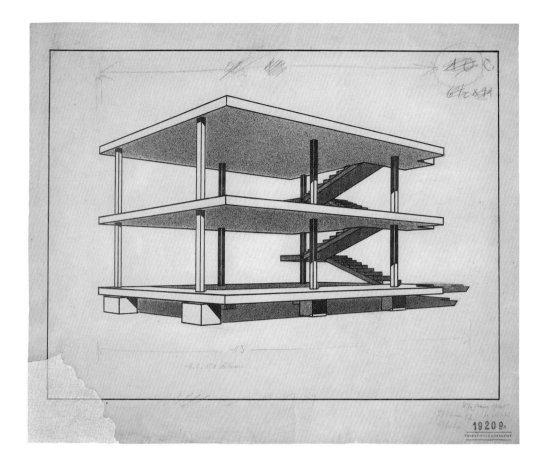

like to know if my efforts are in vain."[2] During the war, the Guimards retreated, as did many French Jews (his wife, Adeline, was Jewish), from Paris to a hotel in Pau, in unoccupied France. There, Guimard devoted himself to penning pamphlets on reforming the system of rents in France and on appeals for an international organization—a kind of proto League of Nations—to administer peace after the resolution of the war. At the same time, he was moved, as were so many others, to respond—with research into prefabricated housing—to reports of widespread destruction in Flanders in the war's first months. He was not alone in trying to imagine how houses could be produced as rapidly in the aftermath of the war as armaments had been shipped to the front during the first campaigns of what observers thought would be a short and efficient conflict. If considerable housing research had been undertaken in Paris in the years before the war, now the scale was daunting and the urgency felt as much in the countryside as in the capital. By the time war ended in 1918, more than half a million houses had been lost. Systems of prefabrication were a panacea studied by many in the early 1920s.

As is well known, the young Charles-Édouard Jeanneret, later to rebrand himself Le Corbusier, responded to the crisis as early as late 1914 with drawings for a reinforced-concrete frame that could be quickly produced in series with standardized reusable shuttering delivered to a site, where the units could be outfitted with non-load-bearing walls to enclose space and create dwelling (fig. 1). He baptized it Maison Dom-ino, a play on the idea of the game of dominos but also, some have speculated, an amalgam of *domus* (the ancient Roman house) and *industry* (the motor of modernity). Le Corbusier worked on the concept with the engineer Max Dubois, even launching a company to control fabrication, and hoped it might be granted a patent. Although less celebrated by historians today, Guimard likewise took up the challenge of prefabrication, addressed by architects episodically and primarily focused on the working class in the late nineteenth and early twentieth century. His aim was to expand the research into a universal system applicable to all classes of dwelling and for all landscapes, the latter because the war-time destruction was as much of countryside villages as of towns and cities.

Historians have pointed out the extent to which World War I was one of the first conflicts to be guided by new forms of industrialization. But the mechanized world—perhaps ushered in by the first assembly-line production of vehicles in 1913 by Henry Ford—would also be turned to peaceful ends. Some industrialists, architects, and housing reformers even wondered if houses might be better fabricated in factories and shipped where needed. Yet the industrialization of housing, although much in the air—and soon to be a major preoccupation not only of Guimard and Le Corbusier but of architectural avant-gardes from the Weimar, Germany, to the young Soviet Union—ran counter to both the established construction industry, which was based on on-site materials and labor, and the financing system that underpinned building. The company that Le Corbusier set up, the Société d'entreprises industrielles et d'études, was bankrupt by 1920, though in 1924 he would renew his experiments with worker's housing, largely organized for serial production, in Pessac, under the patronage of the Bordeaux industrialist Henri Frugès.

Panelized systems had been proposed in France even before World War I, although they have been little studied by historians. Around 1908, the architect Édouard Jules Claude Bérard built a series of seventeen houses of cast-cement panels, some still standing, in Migennes, in the *département* of Yonne.[3] Meanwhile, as Isabelle Gournay has noted, experiments in the application of factory-produced panel systems in the United States had received considerable attention in France. In 1920, Jacques Gréber published his observations on American building culture as *L'architecture aux États-Unis* (The architecture of the United States), calling out for specific praise the panelized, reinforced-cement system the architect Grosvenor Atterbury had pioneered as early as 1909 in Forest Hill Gardens in Queens, New York.[4]

Guimard, married since 1909 to the American painter Adeline Oppenheim, may have had personal reasons to follow such American developments, although the immediate challenges were those in France that would lead, eventually, to the adoption of the Loucheur Law in 1928, after years of debate in the French legislature. This legislation became the foundation for state financing of working-class housing. Immediately after the war, Guimard began producing drawings of a simple prefabricated system in wood for housing in the rural regions of France. Designed in a picturesque countryside idiom, the housing was to be produced by the Société anonyme cooperative l'idéale, a cooperatist movement with origins in the prewar years. Guimard was as interested in forms of house production that would reform the financial underpinnings of dwellings as he was in the production of more economic buildings, and the factory production of the wood elements largely followed the logic of prewar efforts in prefabrication. After 1919, an ambitious proposal was approved to transform the terrain of Paris's ring of fortifications, slowly undergoing demolition since the end of the Franco-Prussian War in 1871, into a ring of social housing around the city, promising an imminent escalation of building contracts. But when work finally got underway in 1924, the construction methods remained chiefly traditional. In the interim, Guimard pushed ahead with his research, combining his long-standing interest in the rights of workers—he had joined the Ligue des droits de l'homme (French Human Rights League) soon after its founding in 1898—and his engagement with modest-scale real estate development in Paris's western quarters. Rather than turning the construction site into an assembly line, bringing Henry Ford's manufacturing

BARRY BERGDOLL

invention to the straight streets of a newly laid-out housing estate on virgin territory, he posed the opposite question: would inventing a repertoire of building blocks that could be produced at various sizes and assembled at any scale, from a single building to a whole city, and deployed on any terrain, whether open land or existing city fabric or a village partially destroyed by war, make possible production by nonspecialized manual labor? In economic terms: was it possible to envision a hybrid system that would move even more construction materials off-site to factory production of a kit of parts and at the same time streamline on-site labor? This was the essence of the company Guimard established in 1921 and christened "Standard-Construction." Thus, he was poised for a decade in which the population of the Paris region would increase by more than one million,[5] although the moment he launched his experiment was also a moment of significant challenges, since the French franc was attempting to recover its prewar value and the entire real estate economy was uncertain.

Standard-Construction was a short-lived experiment. It is known today primarily through the photographs and drawings that the ailing Guimard brought with him to New York in 1938, on the eve of World War II (figs. 2–4). After his death in 1942, Adeline Guimard began the arduous process of placing these documents, as well as the many models that the couple stored in the basement of the Musée des antiquités nationales in Saint-Germain-en-Laye before sailing to the United States, in public collections. It is telling that in the 1950s—the height of post–World War II interest in prefabricated housing in the United States[6]—Adeline placed the documentation of Guimard's system, which he had patented, in the repositories of two architecture schools: Columbia University's Avery Architecture Library and the Cooper Union's Museum for the Arts of Decoration (now Cooper Hewitt, Smithsonian Design Museum).[7]

It would seem that Guimard intended a publication of some sort from early on, to judge by the uniform layout of the sheets recording the components of the system. These sheets not only made it possible to use the system for any design but also laid out

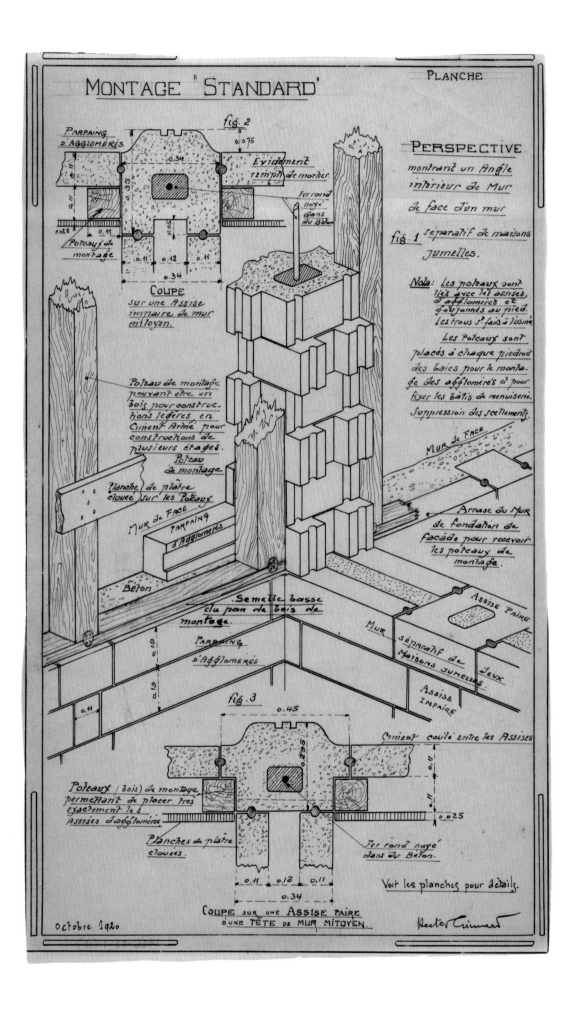

MONTAGE "STANDARD"

PLANCHE

fig. 2

PARPAING D'AGGLOMÉRÉS

0.075

0.34

0.35

Évidement rempli de mortier.

Fer rond noyé dans du Béton.

0.025 0.11

0.11 0.12 0.11

0.34

Poteaux de montage

COUPE
sur une Assise impaire de mur mitoyen.

PERSPECTIVE

montrant un Angle intérieur de Mur

de face d'un mur

fig. 1 séparatif de maisons jumelles.

Nota: Les poteaux sont liés avec les assises d'agglomérés et goujonnés au pied. Les trous s'font à l'usine.

Les Poteaux sont placés à chaque piédroit des baies pour le monta.ge des agglomérés et pour fixer les bâtis de menuiserie.

Suppression des scellements.

Poteau de montage pouvant être en bois pour constructions légères, en Ciment Armé pour constructions de plusieurs étages. Poteau de montage.

Planche de plâtre clouée sur les Poteaux.

MUR DE FACE

PARPAING D'AGGLOMÉRÉS

Béton

Semelle basse du pan de bois de montage.

0.19

PARPAING D'AGGLOMÉRÉS

0.19

0.11

MUR DE FACE

Arrase du Mur de fondation de façade pour recevoir les poteaux de montage.

Assise Paire

Mur séparatif de Maisons Jumelles. Jeux

Assise Impaire

fig. 3

0.45

0.295

Ciment coulé entre les Assises

0.11

0.11

0.025

Poteaux (bois) de montage permettant de placer très exactement les Assises d'agglomérés.

Planches de plâtre clouées.

Fer rond noyé dans du Béton.

0.11 0.12 0.11

0.34

COUPE SUR UNE ASSISE PAIRE
D'UNE TÊTE DE MUR MITOYEN.

Voir les planches pour détails.

Octobre 1920

Hector Guimard

Guimard's use of it to demonstrate the various types, scales, and settings of the kinds of housing it might create. Guimard also carefully assembled photographic documentation of the entire prefabrication process, from the production of the building blocks in small-scale workshops—for indeed the photographs of the house parts being made show a small artisanal, rather than a factory, setting—to the construction of the single realized prototype. This test case was a small party-wall house, Hôtel du square Jasmin, tucked away in a newly opened dead-end mews at the heart of a real estate development the architect was just launching (figs. 5–7). Adeline Guimard had bought the land in 1921 on what was known as the Grenoble method, where every future owner invests the future value of their future dwelling, which the controlling architect could customize, at the outset of the undertaking. The Guimards themselves, however, would move in 1930, in the midst of the fallout from the 1929 stock market crash, into an apartment building, also of Guimard's design but conventional in its construction, at 18, rue Henri-Heine, the largest building completed of the planned development.

Here then was an unusual combination of real estate development by *îlot*—an area bounded by existing streets—with off-site, workshop-scaled production of the building elements. Guimard's photographs, mounted on boards, carry handwritten explanatory captions on a printed label with the notation "Système et éléments dont la propriété est réservée au Standard-Construction, concessionnaire des 10 brevets Guimard" (system and elements whose ownership is restricted to Standard-Construction, franchise holder of Guimard's ten patents). While Le Corbusier had sought a single patent for Maison Dom-ino, Guimard's system was composed not only of elements that could be combined in a variety of ways but also a series of inventions. The label must have been printed while the system was being developed: in the end, Guimard applied for no fewer than eleven patents, all during an intensive four-week period between late December 1920 and late January 1921.

The resulting system was open-ended, and Guimard would work on possible permutations and elaborations for the rest of 1921, imagining that if it were to achieve success, he would retain intellectual ownership of the components or subsystems. While his patent applications were still under review, he began construction of the demonstration house—destined to remain a unique example—at number 3, square Jasmin. For this enterprise, he had created another company, the Société générale de constructions modernes. Quite possibly, Guimard hoped that the demonstration house would place him in the running for the large-scale housing construction under discussion by the Paris municipality for the development of the city's former defensive fortifications. By 1923, he was ramping up the operation, joining forces with several colleagues supported by Henri Sauvage, veteran of experimental housing solutions, to form the Groupe des architectes modernes. But the group was also to be a fleeting experiment, dissolved in the summer of 1925 after they had supplied designs for temporary housing for the Exposition internationale des arts décoratifs.

Few passersby today would stop in their tracks in front of the modest-seeming facade of Guimard's three-story house in square Jasmin. Somewhat modified to mild protests in 2004,[8] it seems a demure complement to the more sculptural apartment houses Guimard designed on avenue Mozart and less compositively inventive than the buildings that flank it. But the series of patent applications behind the house's conception indicates just how committed Guimard was to thinking through the implications of a radical reorganization of the construction process, from sequencing to the nature of labor on the building site. Nine of the patents Guimard—or an assistant—filed were in the

FIG. 4. Guimard, drawing, *Design for a Mass-Operational House,* October 1920. Pen and black ink, graphite on tracing paper. Cooper Hewitt, Smithsonian Design Museum, New York.

FIG. 5. Photograph of 3, square Jasmin (under construction) designed by Hector Guimard, 1922. Cooper Hewitt, Smithsonian Design Museum, New York.

FIG. 6. Guimard, sketch, *Hôtel particulier Villa Jasmin,* 1921. Ink and pencil on paper. Avery Architectural and Fine Arts Library, Columbia University, New York.

BARRY BERGDOLL

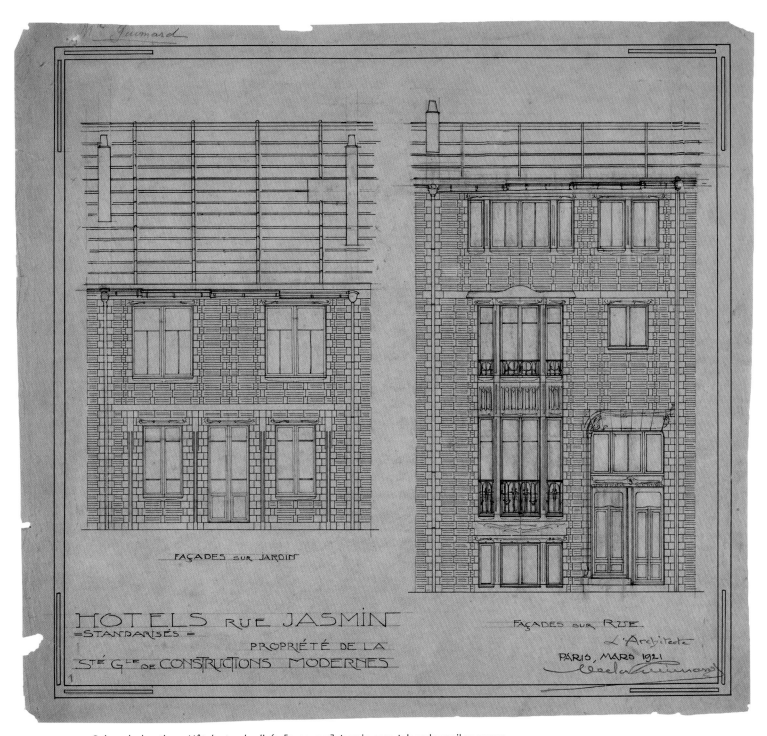

FIG. 7. Guimard, elevations, *Hôtels standardisés,* [3, square] *Jasmin,* 1921. Ink and pencil on paper.
Avery Architectural and Fine Arts Library, Columbia University, New York.

category of "Construction for Public and Private Building," subcategory "Architectural Works, Interior Outfitting, Fireproofing"; a tenth was in the category of locksmith work. The system was, indeed, to be a turnkey operation. The first four patents, filed on December 28, 1920, spell out the major innovations: allowing a house to be built with minimal need for adjusting measurements on-site and with little mortar used during the raising of the walls. Site work was both streamlined and rendered more precise by the combination of two devices: minimizing the mortar on-site and production of a precise system of wooden guiding scaffolds off-site. The scaffolds follow a system of reference points and can be redeployed from house to house. These inventions rendered on-site alterations unnecessary and also allowed the principal parts of the building to be built continuously and without recourse to thick masonry party walls. "Using this system, a general structure of construction allows for the assembly without interruption of all parts of the building: floors, skeleton, roof, stairs, interior room partitions, interior fitting out, window framing, doors, etc.," explains the first patent (no. 529.104, lines 16–20). The same system can be implemented whether the basic structure is wood, reinforced concrete, or steel, all of which would use the premeasured construction scaffold. The next patent (no. 529.105) is for a system of flooring on a level surface that is "economical, rapid, and insulated from humidity." The application states, "This patent is one of a series that have to do with procedures for construction using only standardized elements fabricated entirely in the factory, interchangeable and allowing assembly, without adjustment or correction on the construction site, by nonspecialized workers who will not need to use surveying equipment to carry out the work" (lines 41–49).

Ten days later, Guimard filed two more patents; one (no. 529.470) was for a roofing system composed of prefabricated panels. He insisted this approach did not require specialized workers to achieve a watertight result. Then two weeks later the architect was back at the patent office to file five more patents for the system. These documents further detail the combination of labor-saving devices achieved by separating fabrication of materials in specialized building workshops off-site and relying on on-site workers simply to apply the system by following the rules inherent in the system's components. Today this would be referred to as a deskilling of construction workers, but Guimard was seeking to streamline the process, even as he wanted to guarantee precision. The patents submitted on January 18, 1921, primarily concern the major innovation of the architectural system: various blocks of cast composite stone with interlocking ridges that allow the individual pieces to be laid up without mortar (fig. 8). The principal blocks are hollow in the center, allowing insertion of an iron rod and then infill of poured concrete to give them composite strength. A simple coating of liquid mortar would seal the joints after construction was finished, a labor-saving replacement for the complex work of laying mortar and sculpting the mortar joints.

Guimard had essentially created an updated and more artisanal version of the Cottancin system of concrete poured into hollowed bricks. This technique had been employed to spectacular effect in Anatole de Baudot's Church of Saint-Jean-de-Montmartre but was largely forgotten with the near universal application of the more technologically advanced Hennebique system.[9] Hennebique's patented system, unlike Guimard's, required specially skilled workers.

While the fifteen shapes of blocks detailed in the patent applications—approved in September 1921—would, in theory, allow another designer to use the system with a different result, Guimard had, in fact, designed the principal connections in such a way that the DNA of the system was his. The very skin of the building bore traces of his hand, even

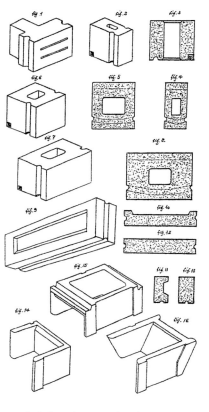

FIG. 8. Guimard, patent drawing for "system of rubble walls" application, January 18, 1921.

FIG. 9. Guimard's signature on the facade of Hôtel du square Jasmin.

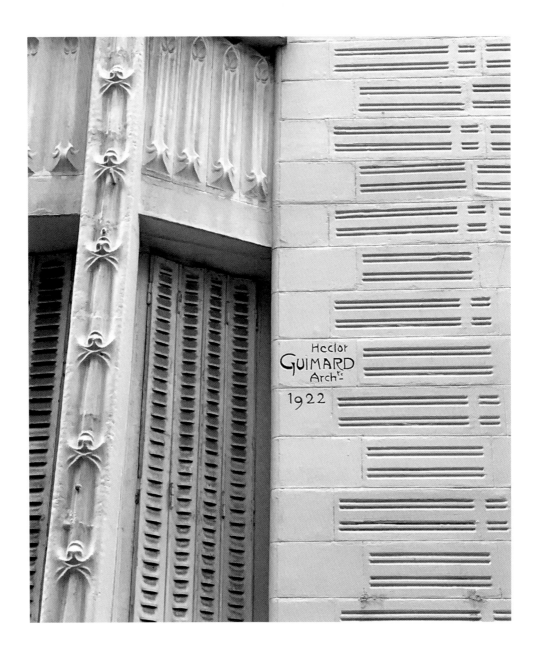

if replicated in each cast, since a simplified version of the Art Nouveau lines characteristic of his more luxurious, elegant, and expensive residences and apartment houses ornamented the face of the blocks used to create the facade. This ornamentation introduced texture, and thus shadow, by means of horizontal grooves cast into the blocks. For the street facade of the house in square Jasmin, the only example ever built, the grooves were cast into thin panels that clad the construction blocks. The quoining of smooth blocks around the bay window, where the cast cladding elements are enhanced with emphatically Art Nouveau–style ornament, includes two blocks that were clearly custom made. One is cast with the "signature," "Hector Guimard, Arch^{te}," the other with the date "1922" (fig. 9). While 3, square Jasmin was a test case, between February 1921 and August 1922 Guimard worked on at least sixteen different types of houses (preserved in drawings at Cooper Hewitt and Avery Library). But as Philippe Thiébaut first pointed out, some of the drawings that extend the system to specific designs for Maisons ouvrières standard (Standard Worker's Houses) and for rural applications of the system—none realized—in fact, bear signatures of other architects who appear to have been working, at least briefly,

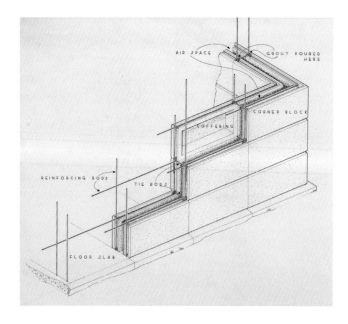

FIG. 10. Frank Lloyd Wright, axonometric diagram, Usonian Automatic System Project, 1954. Ink on tracing paper. The Frank Lloyd Wright Foundation Archives (The Museum of Modern Art | Avery Architectural and Fine Arts Library, Columbia University, New York).

with Guimard. One of the drawings carries the inscription "Projets de Maisons ouvrières de Malabry" (Projects for worker's houses in Malabry); Malabry, a suburb to the south of Paris, was later famous for one of the earliest French adaptations of the English garden city suburb. That drawing bears as well the names of architects who were either associated with Guimard at the stage of conception or would later adapt his system, including the architect Joseph Bassompierre, a pioneer in social housing.[10]

Guimard's work has intriguing parallels with Frank Lloyd Wright's textile block system, which was first deployed in the 1923 Millard House in Pasadena, California, as well as with Wright's French contemporary, the younger Le Corbusier. In both Wright's and Guimard's systems the key invention is the shapes of the blocks—cast stone for Guimard, humble concrete designed in ornamental patterns for Wright—which achieve structural stability in similar fashion: by means of the on-site creation of hardened cores of concrete poured around steel rods—these rods are like "strings" onto which the constructive "pearls" are threaded (fig. 10). One important distinction, however, is that Wright imagined his blocks as elements to achieve complex spatial compositions and even, through their perforations, as a means of creating natural lighting. He used his system to achieve entirely new spatial effects and domestic atmospheres. Guimard, on the other hand, was content to create houses that are surprisingly conventional in appearance and spatial arrangements; the unconventional method of construction is apparent only upon close inspection. While the architectural expression of Guimard's system made fewer claims for the attention of architectural historians than did Wright's textile blocks, it held greater promise for wide acceptance by clients and users. Both architects, however, sought to marry technological innovation—embodied in patent applications—with the ethos of a system deployable by a range of construction workers; in Wright's conception, even the house owner might produce the blocks on-site. But unlike Wright, for whom the textile block was the sine qua non, Guimard, through his patents, sought to extend the benefits of precision construction by nonspecialized workers to a whole range of materials, among them concrete and wood. For a series of rural houses (Maison rurale standardisée construite en usine), he imagined construction in wood, developing a system of simple elements more akin to pre–World War I kit and panel houses, only some of which are referenced in his patent applications.

If architectural history has preserved the heroic memory of Le Corbusier's Maison Dom-ino rather than Guimard's Standard-Construction, it is ironic to note that just a few hundred feet south of the often-overlooked 3, square Jasmin stands Le Corbusier's 1923–24 Maison La Roche, site-built rather than prefabricated and today a major destination for architectural pilgrims. Guimard, like so many architects who sought to apply their signatures to a patentable system of replicable construction instead of devoting themselves to the composition of singular buildings, maintained his faith that one day the system might overcome the financial and production obstacles that so often lead to premature obsolescence of an idea intended to enjoy a long life. Over the course of a decade, Guimard had created a spectrum of solutions that could, he hoped, ultimately convert his signature—and patented—creation, his authorship, to a system adaptable to all contexts, social classes, and regions of France.

Did he ever imagine that these projects might have an afterlife in the United States? By 1942, when Guimard died in obscurity in New York, Walter Gropius and Konrad Wachsmann, both of whom had migrated from Nazi Germany to the United States, were organizing the General Panel Corporation for the production of the "Package House," an idea that had known brief success in Weimar Germany. And by the 1950s, when Adeline Guimard donated his drawings and photographs to American repositories, there were literally hundreds of companies trying to launch themselves into factory-produced housing in the United States in order to solve the housing shortage exacerbated by the "baby boom" in the wake of World War II.[11] Guimard's intensive research was lost from view in the flurry of new designs worldwide, from the work of Jean Prouvé in France to the myriad architectural and commercial experiments in prefabricated houses intended to meet the needs of GIs returning from the war. If Guimard was disappointed in concrete results, his research is key to understanding his lifelong commitment to finding a synthesis of artistic and manufacturing invention.

NOTES

1   Antoine Goissaud, *La construction moderne* 41 (November 8, 1925): 63–66.

2   Hector Guimard to Fernand Hauser, December 11, 1913, signed letter cited in an auction catalogue of Hôtel Drouot, July 3, 1992, Documentation Musée d'Orsay.

3   See "Les Maisons Berard: Un mode de construction original, artistique e economique," Office de Tourisme du Migennois, https://www.tourisme-migennois.fr/les-maisons-berard, accessed November 23, 2019.

4   Jacques Gréber, *L'architecture aux États-Unis* (Paris: Payot et Cie, 1920); cited in Isabelle Gournay, "France Discovers America, 1917–1939: French Writings on American Architecture" (PhD diss., Yale University, 1989), 117–21.

5   Rémy Butler and Patrice Noisette, *Le logement social en France 1851–1981: De la cité ouvrière au grand ensemble* (Paris: La découverte/Maspero, 1983), 61.

6   See, for instance, Burnham Kelley, *The Prefabrication of Houses: A Study by the Albert Farwell Bemis Foundation of the Prefabrication Industry in the United States* (New York: John Wiley and Sons/Technology Press of the Massachusetts Institute of Technology, 1951).

7   Adeline also placed copy photographs in the photography files of the Department of Architecture and Design, Museum of Modern Art.

8   "L'Art nouveau, détruit," editorial, *Le Monde*, February 24, 2004, clipping in the Guimard file, Documentation, Musée d'Orsay.

9   On the Cottancin and Hennebique systems, see Peter Collins, *Concrete: The Vision of a New Architecture* (London: Faber and Faber, 1959).

10 Philippe Thiébaut et al., *Guimard,* exh. cat. (Paris: Gallimard/Réunion des musées nationaux, 1992), 422.

11 See, most recently, Barry Bergdoll and Peter Christensen, *Home Delivery: Fabricating the Modern Dwelling* (New York: Museum of Modern Art, 2008).

Porte Dauphine

METROPOLITAIN

N° 19

Hector Guimard, Archte, Paris.

Guimard for the People

Guimard was perhaps the only architect in France who brought Art Nouveau, often associated with luxury, to a mass audience. The Paris Métro, his most famous commission, demonstrated his concern for the workers who used the system; he regarded it as a way for all people to move freely throughout the city and to connect across the boundaries of social class. Intended to serve all of Paris and all Parisians, the lines were planned for both poor and wealthy areas. Guimard used standardized, prefabricated cast-iron pieces, which could be quickly assembled, for the railings, lampposts, and sign supports. The various components demonstrate how he exploited iron's malleability to translate his curving, nature-based designs for mass production. Guimard's efficient construction techniques ensured that many of the new stations were open in time for the Exposition universelle in 1900.

The Métro was not Guimard's only endeavor to design for the greater social good and make art accessible to the masses. Through his new art forms, Guimard sought to address the problems of poverty and lack of affordable housing. Key ventures include his attempts to create mass-produced housing, especially in the 1920s when an acute housing shortage followed World War I. He established the company Standard-Construction to fabricate his system of "building blocks"—building elements that were easy to transport and assemble. The method did not catch on as Guimard hoped: only one building, a residence on square Jasmin, was constructed using the process.

Guimard's common-good projects were no doubt tied to his political convictions and activities. A Socialist, he was a founding member of the pacifist Association for the Study and Propaganda of the International Pax-State and applied his interests in industrial design and mass production to reshaping society, especially housing. Guimard's ideas on standardization, represented in designs for workers' housing, rural house types, and multifamily residences, emphasize his preoccupations of the 1920s—once again an architect ahead of his time.

Postcard no. 19 from *Le style Guimard* series, showing covered-stairway Métro entry, c. 1903. Olivier Pons, Paris.

Paris Métro, 1900

The Paris Métro subway system brought Hector Guimard wide acclaim and made his name synonymous with French Art Nouveau. Of the original 141 Métro entrances, 86 remain in Paris as protected historical monuments, though only two of the famed glass canopies are intact. Guimard's design elements represented a new aesthetic of "abstract naturalism," just as the system itself represented new freedom of movement within the city. The organic lines of the tall stalk-like lampposts holding amber glass light fixtures speak to a present-day audience as much as they did to early Métro riders.

Guimard produced three main entrance types—open stairways, covered stairways, and pavilions with waiting rooms and ticket offices—all of which shared an aesthetic and distinctive organic motifs. The decorative cast-iron elements were standardized and replicable, and industrial production made quick fabrication possible. Indeed, the speed, process, and economy of mass production were key components of the entrances' modernity. Every piece was modular, so variations could be created by omitting or adding pieces, though the appearance remained consistent. Also, part of the Métro system was Guimard's distinctive calligraphy design for the signage, which presented contrasting thick and thin lines as if handwritten.

The Métro was restricted to the city limits of Paris; entrances were planned for all sections of the city—rich and poor—and so helped equalize opportunities for the French public. It also provided easier access to the vast green spaces of the Bois de Boulogne and Bois de Vincennes. Finally, the Métro was a principal instrument in expanding tourism in Paris; its long-delayed creation became a reality in time to carry international crowds to the grounds of the Exposition universelle.

D. A. H.

View of Métro Entrance, *Entrées du Métropolitan de Paris modèle adopté pour les lignes*, showing open-stairway entry, c. 1900. New York Public Library, Manuscripts and Archives Division.

95 (*opposite*)
Métro Entrance Medallion
c. 1900
Painted cast iron
29 × 24 × 3¼ in.
(73.7 × 61 × 8.3 cm)
Produced by Val d'Osne
Foundry, Saint-Dizier
THE COLLECTION OF RICHARD H. DRIEHAUS, CHICAGO, 20102

96
Métro Entrance Panel
c. 1900
Painted cast iron
19 3/8 × 30 × 4 1/2 in.
(49.2 × 76.2 × 11.4 cm)
Produced by Val d'Osne
Foundry, Saint-Dizier
THE COLLECTION OF RICHARD H.
DRIEHAUS, CHICAGO, 20103

Postcard no. 18 from *Le style Guimard* series, showing Métro entry pavilion, c. 1903.
Frédéric Descouturelle, Montreuil-sous-Bois, France.

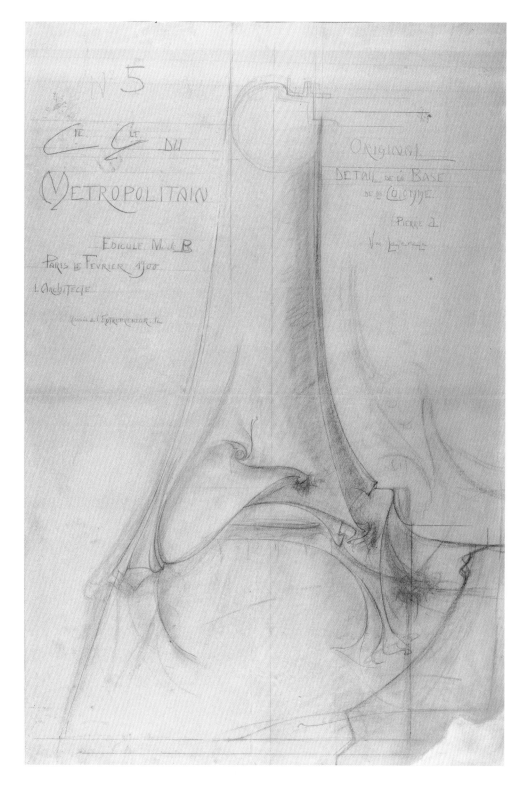

97
Design of a Column Base for
a Métro Entrance, Paris
1900
Pencil and charcoal on
heavy paper
38 5/8 × 27 1/8 in. (98 × 69 cm)
MUSÉE D'ORSAY, PARIS, GP 521

98 (*opposite*)
Working Drawing for the Gare
de Lyon Métro Station, Paris
November 19, 1900
Pencil and charcoal on
tracing paper
44 7/8 × 31 7/8 in. (114 × 81 cm)
MUSÉE D'ORSAY, PARIS, GP 862

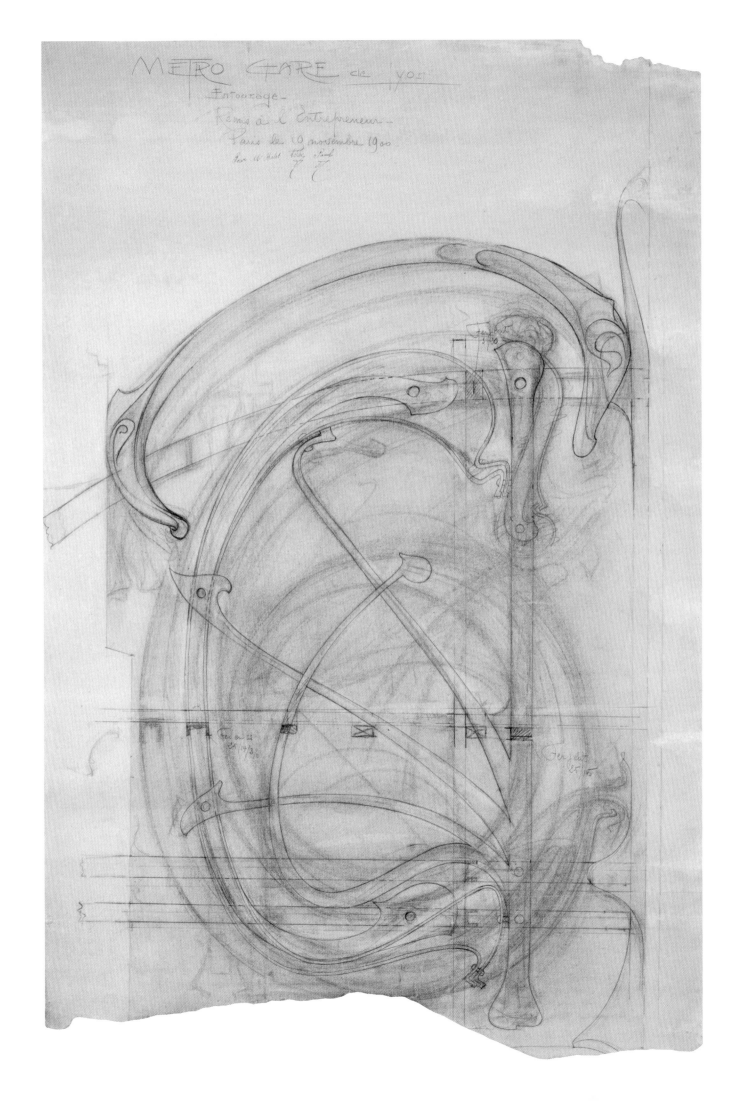

METRO GARE de Lyon

Entourage.

Remis à l'Entrepreneur.

Paris le 10 novembre 1900

Saint-Gobain, Chauny & Cirey

During the 2000 restoration of one of the two surviving glass-covered Métro entrances designed by Guimard—this one at Porte Dauphine—two shards of cast glass from the original canopy supplied by Saint-Gobain, Chauny et Cirey were discovered in the near vicinity. Each measuring 6 millimeters thick, these shards have allowed scholars to piece together the puzzle concerning the entrances designed to have glass overhangs in the shape of dragonfly wings, the largest having been Étoile and Bastille (both now demolished). In fact, one of the two fragments—gold-tinted with an abstract pattern of small dots and stylized tendrils—corresponds to number 18, Oriental, in a trade catalogue of cast-glass samples assembled by the manufacturer in 1913.

Archival evidence suggests that Guimard, in collaboration with master glassmaker Charles Champigneulle (1853–1905), who was contracted by the Métropolitain Railway Company on April 27, 1900, to install awnings, roofs, and canopies, designed Oriental specifically for the Métro project. Though Guimard sourced glass from Saint-Gobain for many of his endeavors—they are listed as one of his collaborators on the printed invitation to the opening of his Pavillon le style Guimard (Pavilion for a Summer Gathering in a Park) at the 1903 Housing Exhibition—this is the first indication of Guimard's foray into cast-glass design.

Y. Y.

Postcard showing glass roof over Métro entrance. Dominique Magdelaine, Paris.

99
Hector Guimard and Charles Champigneulle
Fragment of Window Glass from the Porte Dauphine
Métro Station Entrance
c. 1900
Glass
2 1/8 × 4 1/2 × 1/4 in. (5.5 × 11.3 × .6 cm)
Produced by Saint-Gobain, Chauny et Cirey, Courbevoie
FRÉDÉRIC DESCOUTURELLE,
MONTREUIL-SOUS-BOIS, FRANCE

100
Hector Guimard and Charles Champigneulle
Fragment of Roof Glass from the Porte Dauphine
Métro Station Entrance
c. 1900
Glass
1 5/8 × 3 1/8 × 1/4 in. (4 × 8 × .6 cm)
Produced by Saint-Gobain, Chauny et Cirey, Courbevoie
FRÉDÉRIC DESCOUTURELLE,
MONTREUIL-SOUS-BOIS, FRANCE

Verre Imprimé Nº 18

Verre Imprimé Nº 19

101
*Album des verres coulés: Manufactures des glaces et produits
de Saint-Gobain, Chauny et Cirey* Catalogue
1924
Offset lithography and letterpress
5⅞ × 9⅞₆ in. (15 × 24 cm)
Produced for Saint-Gobain, Chauny et Cirey, Courbevoie
THOMAS J. WATSON LIBRARY, THE METROPOLITAN MUSEUM OF ART,
TP 854.F8 M36 1924

102
Sketch, Métro, Paris
c. 1900
Colored pencil on tracing paper
9⁹⁄₁₆ × 15 in. (24.3 × 38.1 cm)
MUSÉE D'ORSAY, PARIS, GP 141

103
Concept Drawing, Étoile Metro Station, Paris
c. 1900
Lead and black ink on tracing paper
17¼ × 14¼ in. (43.8 × 36.1 cm)
MUSÉE D'ORSAY, PARIS, GP 819

GP 8 19

HERPOPVL

Ercuile Mac Mahon - Wagram

Affordable Housing: Société anonyme cooperative l'idéale, 1900

104
Rear Elevation, Pavilion Project
No. 2 for the Société anonyme
cooperative l'idéale
c. 1900
Pen and black ink, graphite
on tracing paper
15³⁄₁₆ × 10⅞ in.
(38.6 × 27.6 cm)
COOPER HEWITT, SMITHSONIAN
DESIGN MUSEUM, NEW YORK,
GIFT OF MME HECTOR GUIMARD,
1950-66-74

105 (*opposite*)
Floor Plan of the Ground Floor,
Pavilion Project No. 2 for
the Société anonyme
cooperative l'idéale
c. 1900
Pen and black ink, graphite
on tracing paper
15¼ × 10⅞ in.
(38.7 × 27.6 cm)
COOPER HEWITT, SMITHSONIAN
DESIGN MUSEUM, NEW YORK,
GIFT OF MME HECTOR GUIMARD,
1950-66-76

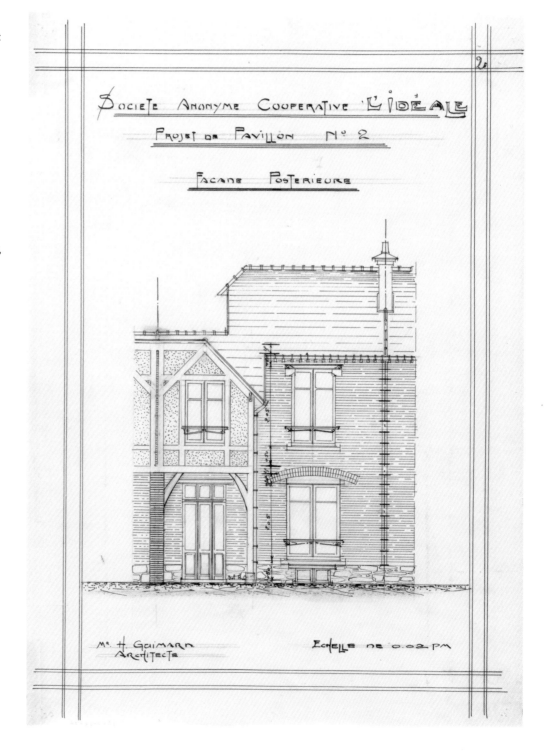

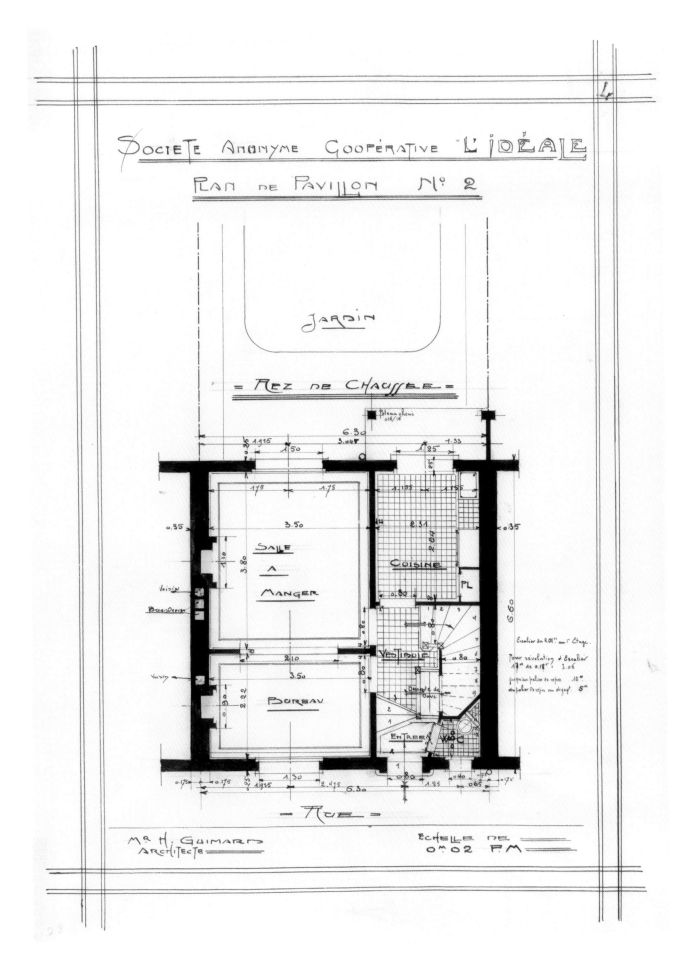

SOCIÉTÉ ANONYME COOPÉRATIVE "L'IDÉALE"

PLAN DE PAVILLON N° 2

JARDIN

= REZ DE CHAUSSÉE =

Poteau chêne 0.16/16

6.30

3.045

1.50

1.25   1.33

1.75   1.75   1.125   1.125

0.35   3.50   2.31   0.35

SALLE   3.80   2.84   CUISINE   6.60

À   PL

MANGER   0.80

Voisin

Buanderie

2.10   VESTIBULE   0.80

3.50   Descente de Cave

Voisin   2.22

BUREAU   ENTRÉE   WC

0.75   0.75   1.125   1.30   2.475   0.80   1.35   0.40 0.65 0.75

6.30

Escalier du R.Ch. au 1er Étage.

Pour révolution d'Escalier 17m de 0.18 = 3.06

jusqu'au palier de repos 12m

du palier de repos au dégagt 5m

= RUE =

Mr H. GUIMARD
ARCHITECTE

ÉCHELLE DE
0m02 P.M

Standard-Construction: Guimard's Response to the Post–World War I Housing Crisis

Guimard's designs for a series of rural houses, which were never realized, reflect a long-standing interest in standardized construction, especially in light of the post–World War I housing crisis. Three rural house types, designed specifically for the "devastated regions" of the countryside, could be built quickly and inexpensively from simple, standardized wooden elements. The structures were to be prefabricated in a factory (including flooring, stairs, doors, casement windows, shutters, carpentry fittings, furnace, kitchen sink, water closet, septic tank, and piping), transported to the building site, and rapidly assembled by a team of laborers. This process was similar to the streamlined one Guimard had employed twenty years earlier for the Paris Métro entrances.

The three house types are simple in conception, facilitating rapid construction. Each is two stories high with a pitched roof, central fireplace, and basement. The ground floors are identical, organized into two open spaces, one for a dining room with a built-in galley kitchen and the other for a bedroom or studio with an alcove that could serve as an additional bedroom. The second-floor bedroom and attic layouts are more varied. Windows and front and rear doors are positioned to maximize natural light and efficient use of space.

A. C.

106 (*opposite*)
Elevation Views, Cross Section, and Floor Plans, Standardized Rural House, Type A
October 1920
Diazo print on beige wove paper
12½ × 8⅞ in. (31.8 × 22.5 cm)
COOPER HEWITT, SMITHSONIAN DESIGN MUSEUM, NEW YORK, GIFT OF MME HECTOR GUIMARD, 1956-78-1-63

107 (*page 194*)
Elevation Views, Cross Section, and Floor Plans, Standardized Rural House, Type B
1920
Diazo print on beige wove paper
12¹/₁₆ × 8⁷/₁₆ in.
(30.7 × 21.5 cm)
COOPER HEWITT, SMITHSONIAN DESIGN MUSEUM, NEW YORK, GIFT OF MME HECTOR GUIMARD, 1956-78-1-64

108 (*page 195*)
Elevation Views, Cross Section, and Floor Plans, Standardized Rural House, Type C
1920
Diazo print on beige wove paper
12¹/₁₆ × 8⁷/₁₆ in.
(30.7 × 21.5 cm)
COOPER HEWITT, SMITHSONIAN DESIGN MUSEUM, NEW YORK, GIFT OF MME HECTOR GUIMARD, 1956-78-1-65

MAISON RURALE

STANDARDISÉE CONSTRUITE EN USINE
POUR
RÉGIONS DÉVASTÉES
TYPE A

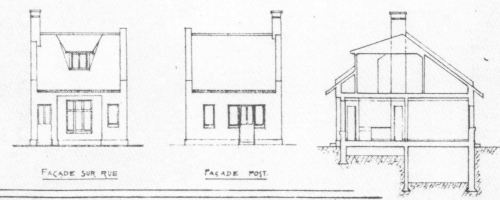

FAÇADE SUR RUE   FAÇADE POST.   COUPE

LÉGENDE — SURFACE DE LA CONSTRUCTION : 62 m².
FAÇADE D'AXE EN AXE DES MURS MITOYENS : 6 METRES
L'USINE FOURNIRA LES ÉLÉMENTS SUIVANTS, PRÊTS A ÊTRE POSÉS
PLANCHERS, CHARPENTES, ESCALIERS, PARQUETS, PORTES, CROISÉES, VOLETS,
HABILLEMENTS EN MENUISERIE, FOURNEAU, EVIER, W.C. ET FOSSE SEPTIQUE,
CANALISATIONS D'EAU, GAZ ET ELECTRICITÉ

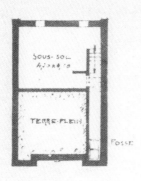

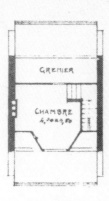

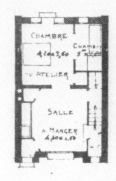

PLAN DU SOUS-SOL   PLAN DE L'ETAGE   PLAN DU REZ DE CHAUSSÉE

ÉCHELLE 0.005 P.M.   NOTA L'ÉTUDE DE L'USINE EST LIMITÉE AU BOIS

MAISON RURALE

STANDARDISÉE CONSTRUITE EN USINE

POUR

RÉGIONS DÉVASTÉES

TYPE B

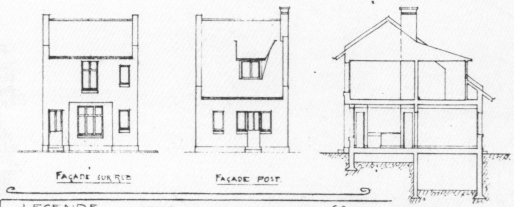

FAÇADE SUR RUE FAÇADE POST. COUPE

LÉGENDE._ SURFACE DE LA CONSTRUCTION 62 M²
FAÇADE D'AXE EN AXE DES MURS MITOYENS : 6 METRES
L'USINE FOURNIRA LES ÉLÉMENTS SUIVANTS, PRÊTS A ÊTRE POSÉS :
PLANCHERS, CHARENTES, ESCALIERS, PARQUETS, PORTES, CROISÉES, VOLETS,
HABILLEMENTS EN MENUISERIE, FOURNEAU, ÉVIER, W.C. ET FOSSE SEPTIQUE,
CANALISATIONS D'EAU, GAZ ET ÉLECTRICITÉ._

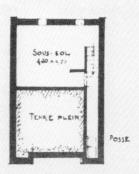

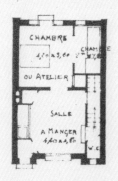

RUE

PLAN DU SOUS SOL PLAN DE L'ÉTAGE PLAN DU REZ DE CHAUSSÉE

ÉCHELLE   0,005 P.M.   NOTA. L'ÉTUDE DE L'USINE EST LIMITÉE AU BOIS ._

MAISON RURALE

STANDARDISÉE CONSTRUITE EN USINE

POUR

RÉGIONS DÉVASTÉES

TYPE C

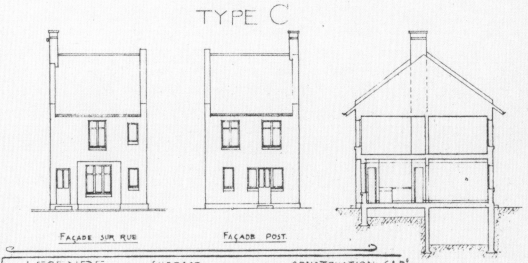

FAÇADE SUR RUE   FAÇADE POST.   COUPE

LÉGENDE — SURFACE DE LA CONSTRUCTION: 62 m²
FAÇADE D'AXE EN AXE DES MURS MITOYENS: 6 m.

L'USINE FOURNIRA LES ÉLÉMENTS SUIVANTS PRÊTS A ÊTRE POSÉS:
PLANCHERS, CHARPENTES, ESCALIERS, PARQUETS, PORTES, CROISÉES, VOLETS,
HABILLEMENTS EN MENUISERIE, FOURNEAU, EVIER, W.C. ET FOSSE SEPTIQUE,
CANALISATIONS D'EAU, GAZ ET ÉLECTRICITÉ —

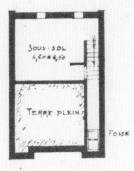

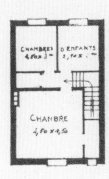

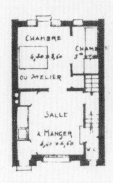

RUE

PLAN DU SOUS-SOL   PLAN DE L'ÉTAGE   PLAN DU REZ-DE-CHAUSSÉE

ECHELLE   0,005 P.M.   NOTA — L'ÉTUDE DE L'USINE EST LIMITÉE AU BOIS

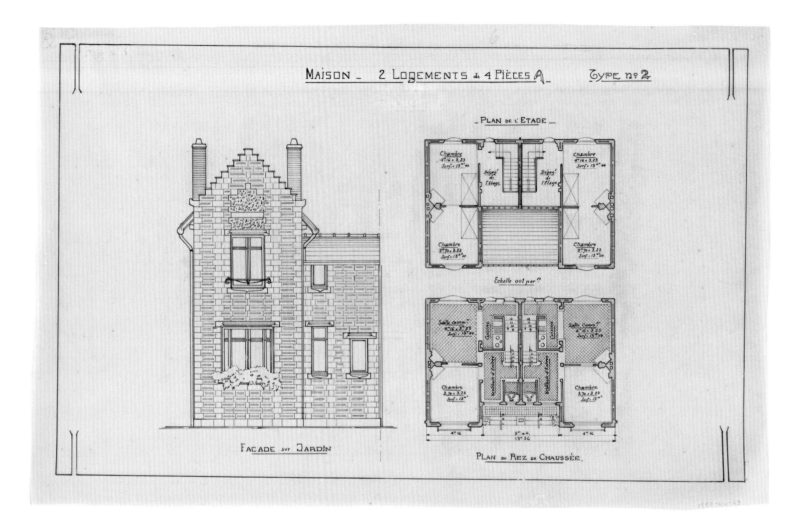

MAISON _ 2 LOGEMENTS de 4 PIÈCES A_   Type nº 2

PLAN de l'ÉTAGE

Échelle 0.01 par 1

FACADE sur JARDIN

PLAN du REZ de CHAUSSÉE.

Among the many solutions Guimard proposed to address the housing crisis following World War I were designs for standardized houses. In the early 1920s, he devised numerous dwellings, including two-family houses, workers' houses, and rural houses, that could be prefabricated and then easily transported to and assembled on site. A series of eight two-family residences, each with a unique arrangement of architectural elements and interior spaces, took advantage of the prefabrication techniques and components he developed for his company Standard-Construction. Despite the modernity of Guimard's system, details such as the gabled roofs and rusticated masonry evoked familiar French forms and materials.

Type number 4, a one-story building, has two entrances on opposite sides protected from the elements by a sloping roof. Each half of the house contains a narrow vestibule, two bedrooms, and a communal room and kitchen. The facade is rather staid, with regular fenestration and a standardized brick pattern that is interrupted only by strips of coursed masonry. A two-story residence with a dominating stepped gable roof, type number 5 is more nuanced in its composition and its use of materials. The entry porches, located on the front facade, are supported by wooden beams. The first floor is similar to type number 4; the floor above accommodates two bedrooms. Second-floor windows and textured stone at the top center animate the main facade.

A. C.

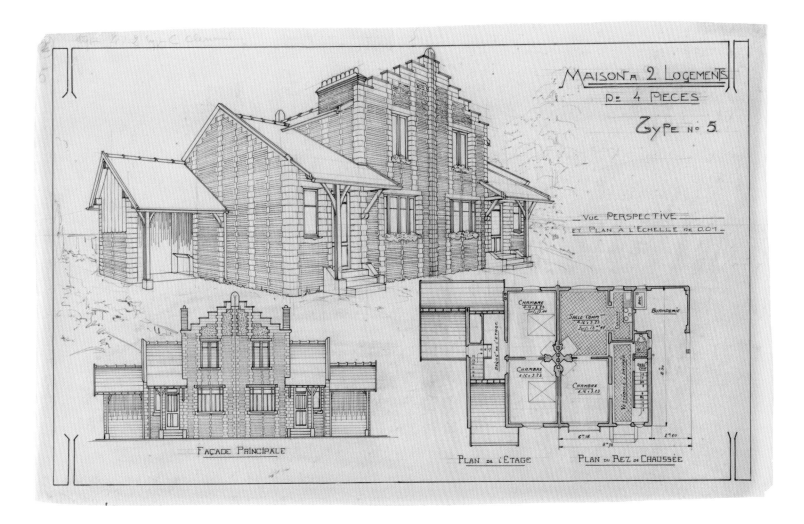

109 (*opposite*)
Elevation and Floor Plans, Two-Family Mass-Operational House,
Type Number 2
c. 1921
Pen and black ink, graphite on tracing paper
12¼ × 19½ in. (31.1 × 49.4 cm)
COOPER HEWITT, SMITHSONIAN DESIGN MUSEUM, NEW YORK,
GIFT OF MME HECTOR GUIMARD, 1950-66-63

110
Elevations and Floor Plan, Two-Family Mass-Operational House,
Type Number 5
c. 1921
Pen and ink, graphite on tracing paper
11¹³⁄₁₆ × 19 in. (30 × 48.3 cm)
COOPER HEWITT, SMITHSONIAN DESIGN MUSEUM, NEW YORK,
GIFT OF MME HECTOR GUIMARD, 1950-66-66

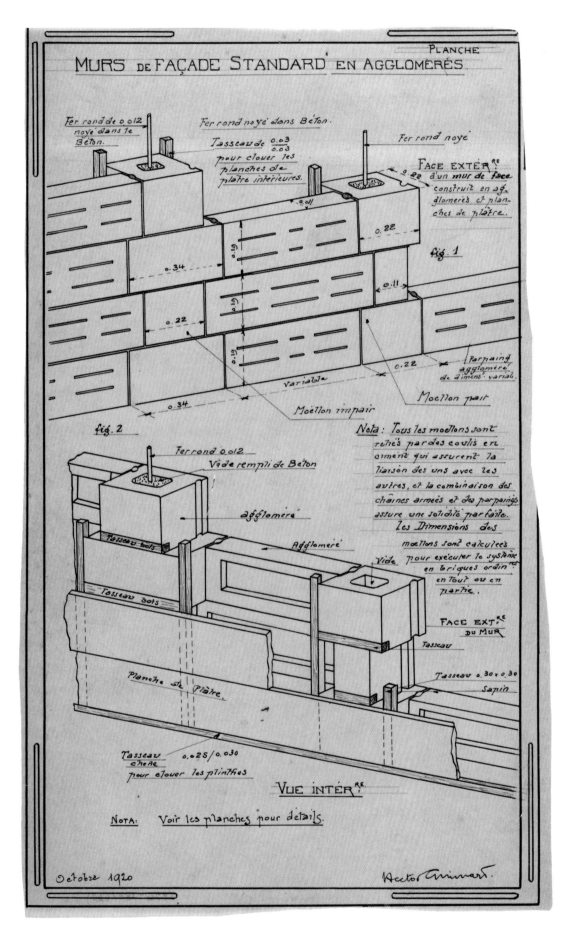

Photograph of the construction of a mass-operational house designed by Hector Guimard (number 29), 1921. Cooper Hewitt, Smithsonian Design Museum, New York, gift of Mme Hector Guimard, 1951-160-2-29.

111
Plate Illustrating the Construction of Reinforced "Standard" Facade Walls, Standard-Construction
October 1920
Pen and black ink, graphite on tracing paper
12 5/16 × 7 13/16 in.
(31.3 × 19.8 cm)
COOPER HEWITT, SMITHSONIAN DESIGN MUSEUM, NEW YORK, GIFT OF MME HECTOR GUIMARD, 1956-78-1-22

112

Plate Illustrating the
Construction of Reinforced
Common Walls,
Standard-Construction
October 1920
Pen and black ink, graphite
on tracing paper
12⁵⁄₁₆ × 7⁵⁄₈ in.
(31.3 × 19.4 cm)
COOPER HEWITT, SMITHSONIAN
DESIGN MUSEUM, NEW YORK,
GIFT OF MME HECTOR GUIMARD,
1956-78-1-25

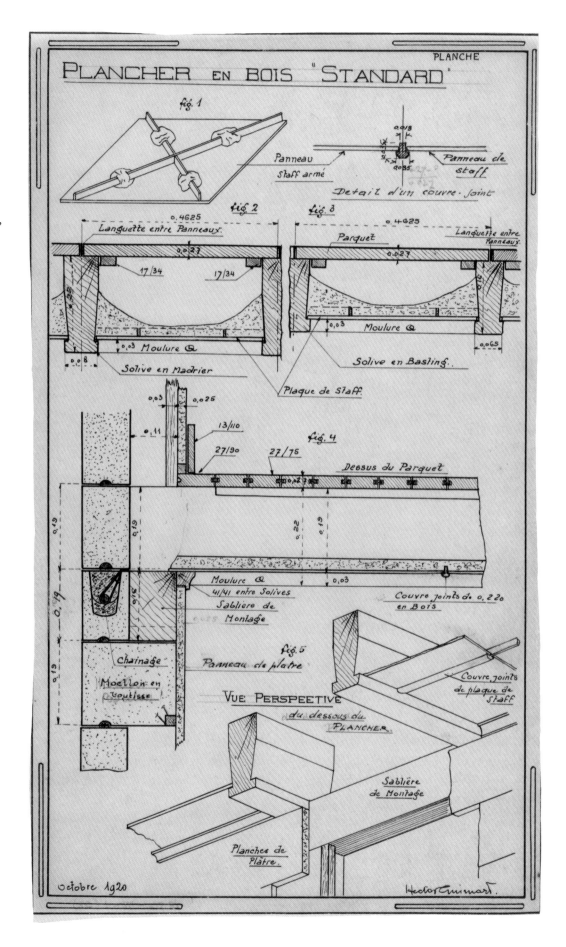

Adeline Oppenheim Guimard
Creating the Architect's Legacy
Sarah D. Coffin

Hector Guimard, who had a reputation as a self-promoter, met his match when the architect married Adeline Oppenheim in 1909; he was forty-three and she was thirty-seven. Trained and practicing as an artist, the American-born Adeline soon played a critical role in advancing her husband's work. While little personal documentation exists, such as letters between the couple, Adeline left a significant public trail of correspondences with museums that chronicles her efforts to enhance her husband's reputation and safeguard his legacy.

Mme Guimard, as she became, can be credited for generous and strategic donations intended to expose Americans to her husband's work (and, to a certain extent, her own work). Materials belonging to the Guimards—architectural drawings, blueprints, and photographs, as well as furniture, ceramics, textiles, and metalwork—are today in the collections of American museums, notably Cooper Hewitt, Smithsonian Design Museum;[1] the Museum of Modern Art; the Metropolitan Museum of Art; the Philadelphia Museum of Art; and Columbia University's Avery Architectural and Fine Arts Library. In keeping with her husband's wishes, she promoted Hector Guimard's legacy in France as well, even though her Jewish origins were the primary cause of the couple's hasty departure for New York in 1938. Mme Guimard's gifts have had a significant impact on securing Hector Guimard's reputation and ensuring that his designs are available to scholars and for important exhibitions.

Adeline Oppenheim was born into a wealthy family in New York in 1872 (figs. 1–2). She took several trips to Europe with her family starting in 1877.[2] Her father, Edward, who immigrated to the United States from Brussels in 1857, started a banking and brokerage business shortly thereafter. He became a naturalized citizen in 1873; at the same time, no doubt because he came from a family of international bankers with connections to the Rothschilds, he maintained his links to Europe.[3] Addie, as she was known in the family, studied at the Art Students League of New York and moved to Paris in 1898 to continue her artistic career. Her first exhibited painting in Paris, *Mauresque*, was shown at the Salon de la Société nationale des Beaux-Arts in 1899. Another example of Adeline's early artistic style, one that exemplifies the differences between her personal expression and her husband's, is a porcelain plate she painted, probably around 1890–1900 (fig. 3).[4] None of Adeline's teachers could be considered modern—neither Art Nouveau nor Impressionist. Rather, her early works, influenced by Old Master and Romantic paintings, were realistic, perhaps based on her studies with painter-decorator Henri-Léopold Lévy; Albert Maignan, another painter-decorator; and painter Joseph Bail. Female forms in Adeline's body of work, like those of her teachers, are characterized by a curvilinear vigor; Art Nouveau design also included S-curves as a recurring motif, such as in Hector Guimard's Binelles Vase, a standing ceramic vase of 1903 that looks like a draped female figure (see cat. no. 73).

FIG. 3. Plate, Austria, probably Vienna, painted by Adeline Oppenheim Guimard, late nineteenth century. Painted and glazed porcelain. Cooper Hewitt, Smithsonian Design Museum, New York.

Adeline Oppenheim had multiple addresses during her first years in Paris, but in 1905 she settled in an apartment of two rooms with a studio at 194, boulevard Malesherbes in the 17th arrondissement.[5] It is not known how she met Hector Guimard, though it may have been through Edgar David, a jeweler and antiques dealer at 20, rue de la Paix. He knew both Adeline and Hector and appeared as one of three witnesses to their marriage.[6] The wedding took place on February 17, 1909, after a short engagement, at the Church of Saint-François-de-Sales in the 17th arrondissement.[7] As part of the preparations for the intimate ceremony, Adeline told the officiant, the Abbé Bellanger: "It will be necessary for us to make of our whole life a work of art."[8] The Abbé quoted this statement in his homily and continued: "You are going to engage in a new future, with the thought of realizing in an intimate collaboration with the husband of your choice, as yet uncontemplated forms of Beauty. As for you, Monsieur, you are the Art Nouveau."[9]

Adeline's life and work before her marriage did not suggest a specific aesthetic connection with Hector. But their intentions and wishes—Adeline's stated wish to live for art and Hector's early identification of himself as "architecte d'art"—signaled a shared passion for artistry as well as a joint commitment. He explored media he had not tested before, such as jewelry and textiles (including Adeline's wedding dress), and she presided

FIG. 4. Adeline Guimard's bedroom in Hôtel Guimard, c. 1913. Cooper Hewitt, Smithsonian Design Museum, New York.

over the stylistically harmonious house he designed on avenue Mozart, Hôtel Guimard. The partnership was evident also in a series of monograms on napkins, leather upholstery, gilt wallet corners, and their wedding invitation (see page 37). Adeline's family wealth played a role in the relationship. The Guimards' marriage contract listed dowry funds of 250,000 francs (about $1.1 million today), a sum used to purchase the lot for and build their house.[10] Adeline's father and his associates soon invested in Hector's building firm, the Société générale de constructions modernes. Founded on July 1, 1910, the Société used Hôtel Guimard as its headquarters.[11]

Adeline Guimard's efforts to promote her husband's work started at the time of their marriage, although these endeavors are not as well documented as those after his death. In 1913, the couple hosted a dinner to present Hôtel Guimard and its interiors—site-specific designs, including furniture; objects Guimard had designed previously, such as frames from 1907; and Adeline's personal touches, including her own paintings and drawings—to friends, colleagues, and journalists.[12] That Adeline subscribed to the public

SARAH D. COFFIN

FIG. 5. Adeline Oppenheim's
Paris studio on rue Washington,
1903. Archives of American Art,
Washington, D.C.

and professional characteristics of the residence is evident from the fact that even her
bedroom (the master bedroom) was available to be seen: it was included in a group of
professional photographs taken of the interiors of the house, the most extensive set of
photographs that survives.

A view of the bedroom highlights Adeline's large painting of a female nude, her back
turned toward the viewer (fig. 4).[13] The room presents a stark contrast to a 1903 photograph of Adeline's studio on rue Washington, which shows a jumble of Renaissance-style
furniture intermingled with her paintings (fig. 5). The master bedroom also exhibited
Hector's frames for the nude, a Japanese print, and photographs of other paintings.
Presumably Adeline chose the artworks she wanted framed, though it is possible that she
selected works, especially personal photos, for some of the smaller existing frames.[14] The
stair hall featured another painting of hers, of a woman and titled *Pearl Stringer,* in an
integral wood frame designed by Guimard; this work was shown at the Salon de la Société
nationale des Beaux-Arts in 1905 (fig. 6).[15]

OPPOSITE: FIG. 6. Guimard, stair hall, Hôtel Guimard, photo c. 1913, showing Adeline Oppenheim Guimard's 1905 painting *Pearl Stringer*. Museum of Modern Art Archives, New York.

FIG. 7. Adeline Oppenheim Guimard, drawing, *Portrait of a Lady with Red Hair*, c. 1912. Graphite and crayon on illustration board, set in a partially gilt pearwood frame designed by Hector Guimard, c. 1905–13. Cooper Hewitt, Smithsonian Design Museum, New York.

FIG. 8. Guimard, tray, 1909. Gilt copper, made in Paris. Philadelphia Museum of Art.

The photograph of the parlor also exhibits various objects not designed by Guimard, perhaps objects that Adeline had brought into the marriage (see page 29). Inclusion of these pieces demonstrated that a client's existing bibelots and paintings could harmonize with and within a *style Guimard* setting. In the photograph are a wall-mounted drawing by Adeline in a frame designed by Guimard, a photograph in another frame by Guimard on the mantel, a gilt bronze vase, and a large gilt copper visiting-card tray (figs. 7–8). A gilt bronze version of this tray was exhibited at the Salon des artistes décorateurs in 1911 and acquired by the Musée des arts décoratifs in Paris from Guimard that same year. This appears to be the first instance of a Guimard work being acquired by a museum. Mme Guimard later gave the Guimards' own tray to the Philadelphia Museum of Art. It is per-haps an indication of the importance of the tray's design to Mme Guimard that she kept her example until the last round of giving in her lifetime.

During and after World War I, Hector and Adeline displayed an increasing commit-ment to social activism. Among the gifts to Cooper Union was a copy of the manifesto *Rapport général soumis à la Conférence de la paix sur le projet État Pax* (General report submitted to the Peace Conference on the project Peace State), indicating the Guimards' belief in this peace movement.[16] Hector explored design for the masses, and Adeline painted portraits to raise money for soldiers and the Red Cross. She also donated por-traits and held charity exhibitions, such as one at Galeries Lewis et Simmons in Paris in 1922. In typical Guimard promotional approach, she festooned rue de la Paix with posters advertising the exhibition. While Hector attempted to adjust his style and focus on lower-cost housing in the dampened postwar economy, his commissions declined dramatically, leading him to create apartment blocks for investment. A 1926 apartment building at 18, rue Henri-Heine, for instance, was supposed to be the first of a larger complex of build-ings, most of which went unbuilt. The stock market crash of 1929 almost certainly reduced Adeline's wealth. Except for a few projects in the early 1930s, little evidence exists of activity in the Guimard household after the couple moved to the building on rue Henri-Heine in 1930.

It is thus likely that decreasing fortunes were one factor in Hector and Adeline's decision to offer their rue Henri-Heine apartment for sale before embarking for New

York in some haste in 1938. Along with considerations of Hector's health and the pre–World War II buildup of tensions, Adeline's Jewish background and possibly Hector's Socialist views made living in Paris potentially dangerous. They maintained ownership of Hôtel Guimard in the years leading up to the war, apparently with the idea that they could return to it or transform it into a Guimard museum. But this hope seems to have been abandoned by 1939, when Hector wrote a letter from New York to his old friend and protégé, architect Auguste Bluysen.[17]

Adeline's statements on entry to the United States and other actions suggest her resolve to ensure that they, especially Hector, were not turned away as refugees: in 1937, she requested and was granted back her American citizenship, and on entry forms she described herself as "Hebrew," even though she had converted to Catholicism in preparation for her marriage and had become a French citizen when the event occurred.[18] It is not clear to what extent the decisions about what to take to New York were due to the increasingly poor health of Hector, which caused him to be hospitalized in July 1937, or to Adeline's role as a partner in business and life. While Hector apparently indicated his preferences, it was Adeline who ultimately decided what would be packed, both the few items that accompanied them and those that were placed into trunks intended for shipment but not actually shipped until after Adeline returned to Paris in 1948. The very absence of instructions from Hector suggests a tacit acceptance of their partnership, his trust in her to exercise his wishes, and her authority to decide.

After Hector Guimard died in 1942, Adeline Guimard's primary aim was to donate her husband's work to American museums. Not surprisingly, her original list of selections included pieces Hector designed for her at the time of their marriage: her wedding dress and a collar, executed by the haute couture house Maison Drecoll, for a satin coat worn on her wedding day (see cat. nos. 21–22).[19] Other items Adeline chose to go to New York were handkerchiefs, panels of embroidered curtains, and tablecloths Hector had designed for their house and objects he had designed for his own use, such as his prized office desk (see cat. nos. 24–25, 29). Adeline was also mindful of preserving Hector's designs, in the form of drawings and blueprints, for a variety of dwelling types, including some for lower-income occupants. Perhaps she thought they might be better appreciated in a United States still suffering from the Depression, or might express a concern for modern social issues, one that was not conveyed by the luxury objects made for Hôtel Guimard and for her personally.

With the exception of Alfred H. Barr Jr. at the Museum of Modern Art, whose advice and referrals she found invaluable, Adeline does not seem to have known or known of any museum professionals in either New York or France. Barr, an early advocate who had met and corresponded with the Guimards before the war, wanted Guimard's work in MoMA's collections not only for the passion evident in his innovative Art Nouveau design but for his modern approach, notably his use of new materials and methods. Barr's letters to Adeline indicate he faced considerable resistance from the museum board's collections committee.[20] Barr involved Philip Johnson, director of the Department of Architecture, in the acquisitions process; Johnson coaxed personal items as gifts and also referred Mme Guimard to Avery Library at Columbia University as an appropriate repository for architectural drawings and photographs of furniture and interiors.[21] In addition, Barr suggested that Adeline contact Mary Gibson, curator at the Cooper Union Museum for the Arts of Decoration, and subsequently Gibson's successor, Calvin Hathaway, both of whom immediately grasped the significance of such a gift.[22] Adeline's gifts to the Cooper Union and Avery made Hector's architectural designs available to students.

SARAH D. COFFIN

The order of the donations and the institutions' selections illuminate the rationale that may have been guiding Mme Guimard's offerings. In particular, the requests of Barr and Hathaway may have enabled Adeline to decide on donations to their institutions. By giving related materials to more than one institution, Adeline may have aimed to ensure their wider study. Examples of the shared-objects strategy include the Hôtel Guimard curtain textiles given to both the Metropolitan Museum of Art and Cooper Union, or the architectural drawings for workers' dwellings donated to both Avery Library and Cooper Union. In addition, Mme Guimard's attachment to certain pieces may have played a role. The Philadelphia Museum of Art received some prize pieces that could easily have been given earlier to other institutions.

When Adeline returned to Paris in 1948 for a relatively short time, she had already decided on some of her American museum gifts. A 1945 letter from Mary Gibson at Cooper Union thanked Mme Guimard for the "beauty you so graciously showed me on Friday. I hope to have a few moments to do something constructive in reference to your work, about which I am most enthusiastic. Also, I am very happy to know that the Museum will have examples of your husband's work."[23] By 1948, however, Adeline had a pressing need to empty Hôtel Guimard in preparation for disposing of it and also ensuring proper distribution of the possessions that had been stored. It was to be her last visit to France.

Since Adeline was not able to turn Hôtel Guimard into a museum, it was necessary that she disperse the rooms, complete with furnishings, she had intended to maintain in place. However, she did not want to ship full rooms to the United States without an assured museum home, which was not forthcoming.[24] Then she tried to find French museums to accept the rooms. Auguste Bluysen was the primary person in France with whom Adeline was in touch prior to this trip, and a substantial and lengthy correspondence between them illuminates his role.[25] In addition to safeguarding their possessions in Paris, he also tried to find museum contacts for her, recommending "Monsieur Guérin," curator of the Musée des arts décoratifs, and Robert Ray and Georges Selles of the Louvre;[26] the latter two do not appear to have responded, if indeed she wrote to them.

Despite Bluysen's direction to Monsieur Guérin, Adeline contacted René Jullian, curator of the Musée des Beaux-Arts de Lyon, which was in her husband's hometown. She gave the Lyon museum the bedroom suite from Hôtel Guimard along with her nude painting.[27] Her Lyon contacts led her to the Musée de l'École de Nancy, early home of French Art Nouveau style, where she donated furniture, and to Yvon Bizardel, director of Fine Arts Collections of the City of Paris. After Bizardel accepted the dining room from Hôtel Guimard, now at the Petit Palais, for the city collections, he sent a letter to Paul Ratouis de Limay, the chief curator of the library and archives of the Musée des arts décoratifs in Paris, connecting him to Mme Guimard and recommending her gifts.[28] The gifts to the museum comprised a tall case clock, a model of a worker's house, and sketches from Guimard's trips to England and Belgium; also included was a substantial amount of archival material: drawings and photographs for wall coverings, carpets, and other interior fittings.

A study of Mme Guimard's gifts to various museums reveals her intention to create a legacy of her own artwork in the course of placing that of her husband, perhaps considering her work as part of their joint artistry. But she was less successful in this endeavor, despite her lifelong commitment to painting and drawing. She remained a competent but not noteworthy artist, and she did not find an audience for her work outside of gallery exhibitions, even though she received respectful reviews of her charity exhibition in Paris in 1922 and her show of colored crayon portraits at Arthur Newton Galleries in New York in 1943. Although MoMA ultimately turned down her works,[29] Cooper Union accepted some of her drawings along with pieces incorporating work by both Guimards. These included two oval wood frames designed by Hector with drawings by Adeline; the frames, which hung in Hôtel Guimard, were probably designed expressly for these works.

Throughout her life, Adeline Guimard seems to have spent time primarily with a small coterie of family and friends and also in the pursuit of her art. She lived to see a renewal of interest in Art Nouveau opulence as a new group of scholars and collectors started to publish and display this design style. In a final act of generosity to her husband's country—and to a place that had inspired her artistry—Mme Guimard made a bequest to the École des Beaux-Arts for a prize named after Hector Guimard. Every four years, the French student in the final year who produces the most innovative scheme for a building or monument receives a cash award. Even this was not Adeline's last donation. During her life, she did not give away the jewelry that Hector had designed for her, including her engagement ring and a maquette for an alternative ring (see cat. nos. 13–14); she left it to her nephew, Laurent Oppenheim Jr. After her death, Laurent added the pieces to her gift to the Museum of Modern Art. These posthumous offerings, along with Mme Guimard's great number of substantial and significant donations to French and American museums and other institutions, have proven to be decisive not only in preserving Hector Guimard's legacy as an architect and designer but in deepening the understanding of an entire era.[30]

NOTES

1   At the time of Adeline Guimard's donations, Cooper Hewitt, Smithsonian Design Museum was known as the Cooper Union Museum for the Arts of Decoration.

2   For this and other key information on Adeline Oppenheim Guimard's family and family relationships, see Bruno Montemat, "Adeline Oppenheim Guimard (1872–1965), artiste et mécène," *Généalo-J: Revue française de généalogie juive* 131 (Fall 2017): 4–19. I am grateful to the staff at the Musée des arts décoratifs, Paris, for their assistance with this essay: Evelyne Possémé, Audrey Gay-Mazuel, Bénédicte Gady, and Laure Haberschill. I also thank Georges Vigne, Isabelle Gournay, David Hanks, and Kate Clark for their assistance in my research.

3   Montemat, "Adeline Oppenheim Guimard," 7.

4   The plate, Cooper Union accession number 1956-34-2-a,b, depicts a scene of Christ and Saint John with two cherubs. It is signed "A. Oppenheim" in the lower right of the image, indicating that it was painted prior to her marriage. She inscribed the source, a Rubens painting in the Kunsthistorisches Museum in Vienna, on the back of the plate. A decorative border by the porcelain factory, presumably the Imperial Porcelain Manufactory in Vienna, suggests that she may have bought the plate while in that city. Mme Guimard included this prized plate in her gifts to Cooper Union. The Cooper Union receipt does not include the factory or the precise date, even though Adeline was alive at the time of the donation.

5   Montemat, "Adeline Oppenheim Guimard," 8.

6   Montemat, "Adeline Oppenheim Guimard," 5.

7   Georges Vigne, *Hector Guimard: Architect, Designer, 1867–1942* (New York: Delano Greenidge Editions, 2003), 251.

8   Montemat, "Adeline Oppenheim Guimard," 1.

9   A. R. Bellanger, Church of Saint-François-de-Sales, typed transcript of homily, February 17, 1909, Adeline Oppenheim Guimard papers, Manuscripts and Archives Division, New York Public Library.

10 The marriage contract between Hector Guimard and Adeline Oppenheim, February 12, 1909, private collection, is cited in Montemat, "Adeline Oppenheim Guimard," 5n11.

SARAH D. COFFIN

11   Montemat, "Adeline Oppenheim Guimard," 9.

12   Vigne, *Hector Guimard*, 254.

13   After Adeline's death, her cousin and close friend Clare Beckwith, who visited the avenue Mozart house often, described the painting, by then in the Musée des Beaux-Arts de Lyon, as "life size nude." Information as given by "Miss Beckwith 11 April 1956," Cooper Union registrarial donor files, written on page accompanying photo.

14   Adeline Guimard gave to her sister, Corneile Jeanne Oppenheim (Nellie), a bronze frame by Hector that contained a photographic "ivoryette" portrait of Adeline taken in 1891 in New York (see fig. 1). Adeline and Corneile's cousin, Clare Beckwith, gave the frame to Cooper Union.

15   A receipt from Cooper Union to Mme Guimard, May 29, 1956, records the salon information. It is possible that the placement of this painting in the stair hall, where both trade and personal visitors could see it, is a subtle statement from Adeline about the source of funding for Hôtel Guimard and its contents. Montemat, "Adeline Oppenheim Guimard," 15, states that two of the nine investors in the Société générale de constructions modernes were dealers in fine pearls who were friends of Adeline's family. Adeline's father was the largest investor.

16   A receipt from Cooper Union to "Mme. Hector Guimard at the Hotel Alrae," June 6, 1949, includes the catalogue along with textiles, prints, plans, and photographs of the interior of "their house 122 rue Mozart."

17   Hector Guimard to Auguste Bluysen, April 27, 1939, Adeline Oppenheim Guimard papers.

18   Adeline's petition for naturalization is cited in Montemat, "Adeline Oppenheim Guimard," 12. The document itself, no. 298555, October 1, 1937, is in the National Archives and Records.

19   The receipt from Cooper Union, June 6, 1949, describes it thus: "Collar from the white satin coat worn by Mme. Guimard on her wedding day. Designed by Hector Guimard and executed by Drescoll [*sic*]." The receipt is referring to the haute couture house Maison Drecoll, owned by neighbors of the Guimards.

20   Alfred H. Barr Jr. to Adeline Guimard, June 1, 1949, Adeline Oppenheim Guimard papers.

21   In a letter of March 30, 1949, Adeline Oppenheim Guimard papers, Philip Johnson thanks Mme Guimard for donating to the museum the maquette of the engagement ring, a rosewood tray, and a hat pin; expresses his desire for a framed grouping of a handkerchief and a brooch; and suggests contacting Avery Library at Columbia University.

22   Alfred H. Barr Jr. to Adeline Guimard, May 1, 1945, Adeline Oppenheim Guimard papers. See also Calvin Hathaway to Adeline Guimard, October 23, 1948, Adeline Oppenheim Guimard papers.

23   Mary S. M. Gibson to Adeline Guimard, June 6, 1945, Adeline Oppenheim Guimard papers.

24   In a letter to Adeline Guimard of May 12, 1948, Adeline Oppenheim Guimard papers, Fiske Kimball, director, Philadelphia Museum of Art, declined the offer of a room, due to lack of space, but indicated that he would be grateful for other gifts.

25   Auguste Bluysen to Adeline Guimard, July 1, 1948; July 8, 1948; and May 3, 1951, Adeline Oppenheim Guimard papers.

26   Auguste Bluysen to Adeline Guimard, July 8, 1948.

27   René Jullian to Adeline Guimard, June 17, 1948, Adeline Oppenheim Guimard papers. Jullian became a friend through correspondence, soliciting Adeline's advice on installation matters, including her unfulfilled desire to see the Guimard carpet from the room remade for the display.

28   Yvon Bizardel to Paul Ratouis de Limay, June 24, 1948, Adeline Oppenheim Guimard papers. This correspondence refers to a visit from Mme Guimard, a "generous American, widow of Guimard," and gives her address and telephone number in Paris, Bibliothèque de la Musée des arts décoratifs.

29   In his letter of May 1, 1945, Alfred H. Barr Jr. tells Mme Guimard that he phoned Miss Gibson, who was "very much interested—indeed more spontaneously and actively interested—than Mr. Hamlin or Mr. Jayne." He also writes that the Cooper Union, "though founded as a school, has a museum of decorative arts without equal in this country." He also expressed the hope "that both the Metropolitan and Avery Library at Columbia will also be interested."

30   Vigne, *Hector Guimard*, 379.

Selected Bibliography

In 1975, the comprehensive *Hector Guimard Bibliographie* by Ralph Culpepper was published by the Paris Société des amis de la Bibliothèque Forney. This bibliography was updated by Georges Vigne in his 2003 book *Hector Guimard: Architect, Designer, 1867–1942* and has been further adapted and edited for this publication.

Bans, Georges. "Les gares du Métropolitain de Paris." *L'art décoratif*, October 1900.

Bigand-Marion, Agathe, Laurent Bouttaz, and Frédéric Descouturelle. "Le portfolio du Castel Béranger." *Le Cercle Guimard,* June 4, 2016; see https://www.lecercleguimard.fr/fr /nos-recherches/dossiers/lalbum-du-castel-beranger, accessed November 22, 2019.

Blondel, Alain, and Yves Plantin. "Guimard architecte de meubles." *L'estampille*, May 1970.

———. "Le monde plastique de Guimard." *Plaisir de France*, March 1971.

Brunhammer, Yvonne, Victor Beyer, Alain Weill, Jacques-Grégoire Watelet, Maurice Culot, François Loyer, Alain Blondel, and Yves Plantin. *Art Nouveau: Belgium/France*. Houston: Institute for the Arts, Rice University, 1976.

Brunhammer, Yvonne, and Gillian Naylor. *Architectural Monographs 2: Hector Guimard*. London: Academy Editions, 1978.

Le Cercle Guimard. https://www.lecercleguimard.fr/fr, accessed November 22, 2019.

Champier, Victor. "Le Castel Béranger et M. Hector Guimard." *Revue des arts décoratifs*, 1899.

Clendenin, Malcolm. "Hector Guimard, Political Movements, and the Paris Métro: Natural Sympathies, Governing Harmony, and Social Change." PhD diss., University of Pennsylvania, 2008. ProQuest (UMI Microform 3345921).

Cornu, Paul. "L'Exposition des artistes décorateurs." *Art et décoration*, 2nd semester 1907.

Couturaud, Pierre. "L'inauguration de la rue Agar." *La construction moderne* 28 (November 10, 1912).

Descouturelle, Frédéric, and André Mignard. "Hector Guimard: Le Verre." *Le Cercle Guimard,* November 1, 2009; see https:// www.lecercleguimard.fr/fr/nos-recherches/dossiers/hector -guimard-et-le-verre/, accessed November 22, 2019.

Descouturelle, Frédéric, André Mignard, and Michel Rodriguez. *Guimard: L'Art nouveau du Métro*. Paris: Éditions la vie du rail, 2012.

"Exposition de M. H. Guimard." *L'art décoratif*, April 1899.

"Exposition du Castel-Béranger." *La construction moderne* 12 (May 6, 1899).

Fabre, Abel. "Du gothique au moderne." *Le mois littéraire et pittoresque* 33 (September 1901).

Ferrand, Stanislas. "A travers l'Exposition: Pavillon style Guimard." *Le bâtiment: Journal des travaux publics et particuliers,* August 9, 1903.

Forthuny, Pascal. "La construction à Paris: Immeuble, 11, rue François-Millet, architecte M. Hector Guimard." *L'architecture moderne* 5 (October–November 1911).

Gelbert, A. "Notes d'art: Une conférence de M. H. Guimard." *La construction moderne* 22 (December 29, 1906).

Génuys, Charles. "Exposition universelle de 1900: Les essais d'art moderne dans la décoration intérieure." Parts 1 and 2. *Revue des arts décoratifs*, 1900.

Gil Blas. Illustrated supplement on the Housing Exhibition, October 12, 1903.

Graham, F. Lanier. *Hector Guimard*. Exh. cat. New York: Museum of Modern Art, 1970.

Guimard: Colloque international, Musée d'Orsay, 12 et 13 Juin 1992. Paris: Réunion des musées nationaux, 1994.

Guimard, Hector. "An Architect's Opinion of 'l'Art Nouveau.'" *Architectural Record* 12, no. 2 (June 1902).

———. "Les immeubles de la rue Agar et l'art moderne." *La construction moderne* 28 (February 16, 1913).

———. "La renaissance de l'art dans l'architecture moderne." *Le moniteur des arts* 91 (July 7, 1899).

"Hector Guimard, Paris." *Documents d'architecture moderne* 4, no. 9 (September 1905).

Jourdain, Frantz. "Les meubles modernes." *Revue d'art* 1 (November 4, 1899).

Lambert, Théodore. *Meubles de style moderne: Exposition universelle de 1900, sections française et étrangères*. Paris: Charles Schmid, 1900.

Mery, Maurice. "Les petits salons: L'exposition de M. Guimard." *Le moniteur des arts* 78 (April 7, 1899).

"M. Guimard." *L'architecture moderne* 2 (February 1909).

Molinier, Emile. "Le Castel Béranger." *Art et décoration*, March 1899.

Montemat, Bruno. "Adeline Oppenheim Guimard (1872–1965), artiste et mécène." *Généalo-J: Revue française de généalogie juive* 131 (Fall 2017): 4–19.

Peignot, Jérôme. "Guimard, son graphisme est du grand art." *Connaissance des arts* 217 (March 1970).

Poinsot, Maffeo-Charles. "Un exemple pour les jeunes: Hector Guimard." *Les pages modernes* 64 (May 1913).

Pons, Olivier, Nicolas Horiot, and Frédéric Descouturelle. *L'Hôtel Mezzara d'Hector Guimard*. Paris: Éditions du Cercle Guimard, 2018.

Rheims, Maurice, and Georges Vigne. *Hector Guimard*. New York: Harry N. Abrams, 1988.

Schmutzler, Robert. *Art Nouveau*. New York: Harry N. Abrams, 1962.

Thiébaut, Philippe. *Guimard: L'Art nouveau*. Paris: Gallimard/Réunion des musées nationaux, 1992.

———. *1900*. Paris: Réunion des musées nationaux, 2000.

Thiébaut, Philippe, Claude Frontisi, Georges Vigne, Marie-Laure Crosnier Leconte, and Marie-Madeleine Massé. *Guimard*. Exh. cat. Paris: Réunion des musées nationaux, 1992.

Vigne, Georges. *Hector Guimard: Architect, Designer, 1867–1942*. New York: Delano Greenidge Editions, 2003.

Contributors

BARRY BERGDOLL is the Meyer Schapiro Professor of Art History at Columbia University. He is also Curator of Architecture and Design at the Museum of Modern Art and served as Director of the department from 2007 to 2013. His exhibitions and accompanying catalogues include *Mies in Berlin* (2001) and *Bauhaus, 1919–1933: Workshops for Modernity* (2009).

ALISA CHILES is the Andrew W. Mellon Graduate Fellow in European Decorative Arts after 1700 at the Philadelphia Museum of Art and a PhD candidate in the history of art at the University of Pennsylvania. She specializes in modern architecture and decorative arts and has worked at the Metropolitan Museum of Art.

SARAH D. COFFIN was Curator and Head of Product Design at Cooper Hewitt, Smithsonian Design Museum from 2004 to 2018. Her exhibitions and accompanying catalogues include *The Jazz Age: American Style in the 1920s* (2017) and *Set in Style: The Jewelry of Van Cleef and Arpels* (2011).

ISABELLE GOURNAY (Emerita, University of Maryland) researches crosscurrents between France and North America; her current focus is Beaux-Arts architects. Her books include *The New Trocadéro* (1985) and the co-edited volumes *Paris on the Potomac: The French Influence on the Architecture and Art of Washington, D.C.* (2007) and *Iconic Planned Communities and the Challenge of Change* (2019).

DAVID A. HANKS is Curator of the Liliane and David M. Stewart Program for Modern Design. His previous publications for the Stewart Program include *The Century of Modern Design: Selections from the Liliane and David M. Stewart Collection* (2010) and *American Streamlined Design: The World of Tomorrow* (2005).

PHILIPPE THIÉBAUT was Chief Curator at the Musée d'Orsay from 1980 to 2013, specializing in Art Nouveau, and Scientific Advisor for Decorative Arts at the Institut national d'histoire de l'art in Paris. His previous projects include *1900* (2000) for the Musée d'Orsay and his exhibition and catalogue *Guimard* (1992) for the museum, the most important work on the architect to date.

GEORGES VIGNE is the former Director of the Musée Ingres in Montauban, France. He has written more than fifteen books, including *Ingres* (1981) and *Hector Guimard: Architect, Designer, 1867–1942* (2003). A specialist in nineteenth-century art, he has organized numerous exhibitions for the Musée d'Orsay.

YAO-FEN YOU is Senior Curator and Head of Product Design and Decorative Arts at Cooper Hewitt, Smithsonian Design Museum. She is the author of *Coffee, Tea, and Chocolate: Consuming the World* (2016).

Acknowledgments

An exhibition is always a collaborative effort, and we salute the many individuals and institutions in the United States and France who have made *Hector Guimard: Art Nouveau to Modernism* possible. The first acknowledgment must be to Richard H. Driehaus, founder of the Richard H. Driehaus Museum. He began acquiring the work of Guimard in 1992 as part of a comprehensive collection of French decorative arts of the nineteenth and early twentieth centuries. He has supported the exhibition not only with his passion for the designer but with critical loans from his collection.

At the Driehaus Museum, we would like to thank Anna Musci, Interim Executive Director, who guided the museum's participation in the catalogue and the exhibition with good humor and persever-ance. She also managed the collaboration with Cooper Hewitt and led fundraising efforts. Catherine Shotick, Curator of Collections and Exhibitions, attentively supervised all details of loans from the Collection of Richard H. Driehaus, including object photography. Catherine Nguyen, Registrar, was responsible for attending to the innumerable details in arranging loans to the Driehaus Museum and keeping track of the exhibition checklist. Amelia Anderson, Collections and Exhibitions Coordinator, procured essential photo-graphs and articles and directed the exhibition installation. Alex Revzan, Manager of Operations and Visitor Experience, oversaw the interpretation plan to ensure that museum visitors recognize the importance of Guimard's work. Liz Tillmanns, Director of Communications, looked after the public relations strategy and promotional efforts for the Driehaus Museum. Gregory Shutters, Associate Director of Retail and Branding, spearheaded product opportunities that keep Guimard's designs accessible and in circula-tion. Special thanks go to Joyce Lee, Director of Collections, and Ted Burger, Collections Manager and Registrar, of Driehaus Enterprises Management, Inc., who organized the conservation of objects from Driehaus's collection and made them available to the exhibition team. Museum consultant Rena Zurofsky had the initial idea of a project focusing on the work of Hector Guimard. James Caulfield took evocative and sensitive photographs of objects from Driehaus's collection. We are also grateful for the assistance of Maurice Culot and Fabien Choné in Paris; Consul General Guillaume Lacroix and Tanguy Accart in Chicago; and David Reithoffer and Brett August of the Paris Committee for the Chicago Sister Cities International program.

Cooper Hewitt, Smithsonian Design Museum staff enthusiasti-cally committed to the exhibition from the start. Former Director Caroline Baumann championed the exhibition from its inception. Sarah D. Coffin, former Curator and Head of Product Design and Decorative Arts (PDDA), was instrumental in initially shaping the themes and selecting the objects and remained part of the team after her retirement. Caitlin Condell, Associate Curator and Head of Drawings, Prints, and Graphic Design, was integral to the early formation of the exhibition and helped to advance its development in the initial stages. Former Director of Curatorial Cara McCarty has long advocated for an exhibition that would celebrate the museum's extensive Guimard holdings as well as show for the first time in the United States the magnificent Guimard drawings discovered in the 1990s. When Yao-Fen You joined the museum as Senior Curator and Head of PDDA in February 2019, she further shaped the exhibition and also selected drawings and contributed to the catalogue. Alisa Chiles undertook research on the architectural drawings during her tenure as a Smithsonian Fellow in PDDA. Foundations Relations Manager Deborah Fitzgerald and her colleagues in Advancement ably led development efforts, while Head of Registrar Wendy Rogers and her team skillfully handled the complex logistics related to the borrowing and shipment of loans. Members of the Conservation Department—Sarah Barack, Jessica Walthew, Kira Eng-Wilmot, and Perry Choe—extended much practical assistance in preparing Cooper Hewitt objects for photography, display, and traveling. Likewise, Matilda McQuaid, Deputy Director of Curatorial and Head of Textiles, championed the exhibition from the start and was eager to include Guimard-designed textiles. In the Exhibitions Department, Yvonne Gómez Durand and Molly Engelman diligently managed contracts and guided the exhibition design with characteristic finesse and humor, while Pamela Horn, Director of Cross-Platform Publishing and Strategic Partnerships, lent her wise counsel. Administrator Phoebe Moore provided crucial support and an abundance of good cheer that kept the loan requests and checklist moving forward at critical moments. Finally, Mir Finkelman, Cindy Trope, Greg Herringshaw, and Matt Flynn graciously contributed critical assistance in coordinating new photography of Cooper Hewitt objects for the exhibition catalogue, for which we are especially appreciative.

We owe special gratitude to the curators at the Musée d'Orsay who kindly shared their expertise and collections: Sylvie Patry, Chief Curator and Deputy Director for Curatorial Affairs and Collections; Elise Dubreuil, Curator of Decorative Arts; Isabelle Morin Loutrel, Chief Curator of Architecture and Head of Graphic Arts and Photography; Clémentine Lemire, Documentary Researcher in Architecture; and Fabrice Golec, Art Handler and Assistant Registrar for Graphics Arts and Photography. We extend heartfelt thanks to Clémentine and Fabrice, who facili-tated Yao-Fen's access to the trove of Guimard drawings. We are also immensely grateful to Laure Haberschill (Library) and Mathilde Pillien (Archives Department) at the Musée des arts décoratifs for allowing archival documents to travel to the United States for the first time. We also wish to thank Evelyne Possémé, Chief Curator; Audrey Gay-Mazuel, Heritage Curator, Nineteenth Century; and Bénédicte Gady, Heritage Curator, Department of Graphic Arts, for their support and advice since the beginning of the project.

We invariably received enthusiastic cooperation for loans from American museums. We are grateful to the Museum of Modern Art for loans from their important Guimard holdings at a time when the institution was undergoing a building expansion. We appreciate the support of Martino Stierli, Philip Johnson Chief Curator of Architecture and Design, and Juliet Kinchin, Curator of Architecture and Design. Paul Galloway, Collection Specialist, Architecture and Design, was an advocate for the exhibition and facilitated the loans, as did Pamela Popeson in the Design Study Center. In MoMA Archives,

Michelle Elligott, Senior Museum Archivist; Elisabeth Thomas, Assistant Archivist; and Jennifer Tobias, Librarian, were extremely helpful.

At the Menil Collection, we would like to thank Rebecca Rabinow, Director; Michelle White, Senior Curator; Anna Hollyer, Registrar; and Susan Slepka Anderson, Director of Collection Management. In 1971, Dominique de Menil purchased from the Galerie du Luxembourg a complete set of the Dizier cast-iron prototypes.

Loans from private collections included those from Christie Mayer Lefkowith and Ed Lefkowith, who lent the exquisite perfume bottles Guimard designed for F. Millot. Christie generously shared her expertise and information on these designs.

At Yale University Press, Katherine Boller, Mary Mayer, and Kate Zanzucchi led the team to make this publication possible, with the help of Raychel Rapazza, Editorial and Production Assistant. Andrea Monfried provided sensitive editing, expert guidance, and unfailing support. Natalie Shivers assisted with content editing and structuring of the introduction. Joan T. Rosasco translated the French texts. Isabelle Gournay provided vital assistance in clarifying the language, history, and culture of these texts. We also thank freelance copy-editor Alison Hagge; proofreader Julia Ridley Smith; and indexer Cathy Dorsey. The beautiful design of this catalogue, which honors Guimard's aesthetic so elegantly, is the work of Miko McGinty and Rita Jules.

A complete record of photographic sources is listed in the photo credits, but we wish to acknowledge, in particular, the extraordinary efforts of Jennifer Belt of Art Resource, Flore Campestrini of Musée des arts décoratifs, and Janice Hussain of Cooper Hewitt.

We are grateful to Wendy Evans Joseph, Monica Coghlan, and Cassandra Gerardo of Studio Joseph for their creative and inventive exhibition design, which captures the essence and flair of Guimard's work.

Le Cercle Guimard has made its research and resources available to us, and we are particularly indebted to Vice President Nicolas Horiot for his enthusiastic support of the exhibition. The organization has published a series of research articles by their members, experts in the field. Le Cercle reviewed the exhibition content and suggested loans from their members, including M. Horiot, Alain Blondel, Frédéric Descouturelle, and Olivier Pons, all of whom also provided valuable research. We appreciate as well responses to innumerable emails and help in locating photographs.

At the Metropolitan Museum of Art, we are grateful to the staff at the Thomas J. Watson Library, in particular Jared Ash, Associate Museum Librarian, Slavic and Special Collections; Yukari Hayashida, Senior Book Conservation Coordinator; and Sophia Alexander, Manager for Library Administration. In the department of Modern and Contemporary Art, we acknowledge Rebecca Tilghman, Collections Specialist, and Pari Stave, Senior Administrator. At the New York Public Library, Cara Dellatte, Reference Archivist, Rare Books and Manuscripts, was always helpful in providing access to the Adeline Oppenheim Guimard papers.

In my office, Kate Clark contributed to every aspect of the exhibition and catalogue. She assisted with research and comanaged preparation of the catalogue, including the procurement of photographs. Jan Spak provided advice and help on contracts and budgets.

We are deeply grateful for early commitments of support for this project. The exhibition at the Richard H. Driehaus Museum was made possible in part by the National Endowment for the Arts, Robert and Carolynn Burk, and the Richard H. Driehaus Annual Exhibition Fund. The exhibition at Cooper Hewitt, Smithsonian Design Museum was made possible in part by Marilyn F. Friedman. Additional support for the accompanying publication *Hector Guimard: Art Nouveau to Modernism* was provided in part by the Graham Foundation.

D. A. H.

Photo Credits

From "Hôtel particulier, quai d'Auteuil, á Paris, façade sur la Seine," *L'architecte*, May 1913, plate 29, photo by H. Leroy, architect CH Blanche: Gournay, "Revisiting Guimard's Auteuils," fig. 6.

Archives de Paris: Thiébaut, *"Le style Guimard,"* fig. 6.

Adeline Oppenheim Guimard papers, 1904–1943. Archives of American Art, Smithsonian Institution, photo by Harry C. Ellis: Coffin, "Adeline Oppenheim Guimard," fig. 5.

© Paris, Les arts décoratifs: cat. no. 10.

Hector Guimard architectural drawings and papers, 1903–1933, Avery Architectural and Fine Arts Library, Columbia University, gift of Adeline Oppenheim Guimard, 1949: Bergdoll, "Signature vs. Standardization," figs. 6, 7 (Inv. 1000.006.00036).

Photo by Barry Bergdoll: Bergdoll, "Signature vs. Standardization," fig. 9.

Bibliothèque nationale de France (BnF): Thiébaut, *"Le style Guimard,"* fig. 3.

Courtesy of Alain Blondel: "Introduction," fig. 10; cat. nos. 1, 34; p. 37 bottom.

Cooper Hewitt, Smithsonian Design Museum: "Introduction," fig. 9 (1956-79-1); Thiébaut, "The First Gesture," fig. 1 (1958-84-1); Bergdoll, "Signature vs. Standardization," figs. 2 (1951-160-2-14), 3 (1951-160-2-35), 4 (1956-78-1-10), 5 (1951-160-2-28); Coffin, "Adeline Oppenheim Guimard," figs. 1 (donor record), 2 (donor record), 3 (1956-34-2-a,b), 4 (1956-78-16), 7 (1956-80-1/ 1956-76-8); cat. nos. 2, 4–8, 18–25, 63–72, 74, 87, 104–12; pp. 20, 22 right, 26–27, 29 bottom, 34 bottom, 198 right. Photo by Matt Flynn: Coffin, "Adeline Oppenheim Guimard," fig. 7; cat. nos. 42–44, 56, 57, 79–82, 91. Photo by Ellen McDermott: Coffin, "Adeline Oppenheim Guimard," fig. 3.

Photo by Jean-Pierre Dalbéra: "Introduction," fig. 6.

© DeA Picture Library / Art Resource, NY, engraving by Bury, from Paris, monuments eleves par la ville, 1850–1880, by Felix Narjoux, Morel et Cie Editeurs, printed by Lemercier, 1883, Paris: Gournay, "Revisiting Guimard's Auteuils," fig. 5.

Courtesy of Frédéric Descouturelle: Gournay, "Revisiting Guimard's Auteuils," fig. 2; cat. nos. 99, 100; p. 180.

The Collection of Richard H. Driehaus, Chicago: "Introduction," fig. 7; Vigne, "Production, Promotion, Publicity," fig. 1; cat. nos. 35, 36, 58; p. 54.

© F.L.C./ADAGP, Paris/Artists Rights Society (ARS), New York 2019: Bergdoll, "Signature vs. Standardization," fig. 1.

Photo by Isabelle Gournay, 2019: Gournay, "Revisiting Guimard's Auteuils," fig. 7.

Courtesy of Nicolas Horiot: Thiébaut, *"Le style Guimard,"* fig. 1; cat. nos. 47–55, 59, 60; pp. 70, 102.

© Lyon MBA – Photo Martial Couderette: "Introduction," fig. 8.

© MAD, Paris: Vigne, "Production, Promotion, Publicity," figs. 2–7; p. 74.

Dominique Magdelaine, Paris: pp. 140, 184.

The Menil Collection, Houston, photo by Paul Hester: cat. no. 84.

Menil Library Special Collections, photo by Paul Hester: cat. no. 83.

© The Metropolitan Museum of Art, Art Resource, NY: cat. nos. 73, 75, 76, 101.

© Musée Carnavalet / Roger-Viollet Catalogue d'exposition: Gournay, "Revisiting Guimard's Auteuils," fig. 4.

Digital Image © The Museum of Modern Art: p. 16. Licensed by SCALA / Art Resource, NY: Coffin, "Adeline Oppenheim Guimard," fig. 6; cat. nos. 11–17, 29, 30, 38.

The New York Public Library, Manuscripts and Archives Division: "Introduction," fig. 1. Adeline Oppenheim Guimard papers (file 10): p. 178. Art and Architecture Collection: Gournay, "Revisiting Guimard's Auteuils," fig. 8.

Philadelphia Museum of Art: Coffin, "Adeline Oppenheim Guimard," fig. 8 (Gift of Mme Hector Guimard, 1949-43-1); cat. no. 9.

Courtesy of Olivier Pons: p. 176.

The Richard H. Driehaus Museum, Chicago. Gournay, "Revisiting Guimard's Auteuils," figs. 9–11. Photograph by James Caulfield: cat. nos. 3, 31, 32, 39–41, 45, 46, 77, 78, 85, 86, 88–90, 92–96.

© RMN-Grand Palais / Art Resource, NY: "Introduction," fig. 4 (GP 1271); Thiébaud, "The First Gesture," fig. 3 (ARO 1989-1); Thiébaud, *"Le style Guimard,"* figs. 4 (Collection Guimard, GP 128), 5 (Collection Guimard, GP 544); cat. no. 61. Photo by Franck Raux: "Introduction," fig. 2. Photo by Hervé Lewandowski: Thiébaut, "The First Gesture," figs. 2 (GP 1953), 7 (GP 518); cat. nos. 26, 27, 62, 97, 98. Photo by Thierry Le Mage: Thiébaut, "The First Gesture," fig. 4 (GP 1648). Photo by Stéphane Maréc: cat. no. 28. Photo by René-Gabriel Ojéda: Thiébaut, "The First Gesture," fig. 5 (GP 771); cat. no. 37. Photo by Tony Querrec: cat. no. 103. Photo by Patrice Schmidt: Thiébaut, "The First Gesture," fig. 6 (GP 1759); cat. nos. 33, 102.

Smithsonian Libraries, Washington, D.C.: Thiébaut, *"Le style Guimard,"* fig. 2.

Courtesy of Sotheby's: Gournay, "Revisiting Guimard's Auteuils," fig. 3.

Photo by Henry Townsend: "Introduction," fig. 5.

© Victoria and Albert Museum, London: "Introduction," fig. 3.

© 2019 Frank Lloyd Wright Foundation. All Rights Reserved. Licensed by Artist Rights Society (ARS), New York: Bergdoll, "Signature vs. Standardization," fig. 10.

Index